A Consumer's Guide to Food Regulation & Safety

by

James T. O'Reilly
University of Cincinnati

Oceana's Legal Almanac Series:
Law for the Layperson

Oceana®
NEW YORK

OXFORD

UNIVERSITY PRESS

Oxford University Press, Inc., publishes works that further Oxford University's objective of excellence in research, scholarship, and education.

Copyright © 2010 by Oxford University Press, Inc.
Published by Oxford University Press, Inc.
198 Madison Avenue, New York, New York 10016

Library of Congress Cataloging-in-Publication Data

O'Reilly, James T., 1947–
    A consumer's guide to food regulation & safety / James T. O'Reilly.
        p. cm.—(Oceana's legal almanac series : law for the layperson)
    Includes bibliographical references.
    ISBN 978-0-19-973021-6 (hardback : alk. paper)
1. Food law and legislation—United States. I. Title.
    KF3875.O74 2010
    344.7304'232—dc22   2009052065

Note to Readers:

This publication is designed to provide accurate and authoritative information in regard to the subject matter covered. It is based upon sources believed to be accurate and reliable and is intended to be current as of the time it was written. It is sold with the understanding that the publisher is not engaged in rendering legal, accounting, or other professional services. If legal advice or other expert assistance is required, the services of a competent professional person should be sought. Also, to confirm that the information has not been affected or changed by recent developments, traditional legal research techniques should be used, including checking primary sources where appropriate.

(Based on the Declaration of Principles jointly adopted by a Committee of the American Bar Association and a Committee of Publishers and Associations.)

This Book is Dedicated to

Donald D. Black.

Last of the Frontiersmen,

With Great Affection and Respect

For His Life of Courage, Integrity,

And Selfless Sharing with Others.

Table of Contents

PREFACE. xi

CHAPTER 1:
DEFINING KEY CONCEPTS IN FOOD
1. WHAT IS "SAFE"? 2
2. HOW ARE CONTAMINANTS CONTROLLED? 3
3. HOW ARE SAFETY STANDARDS CREATED? 3
4. HOW DO REGULATORS BECOME INVOLVED AT THE VARIOUS
   STEPS OF THE PROCESS? 4
5. HOW ARE SPECIAL CATEGORIES OF FOOD REGULATED? 5
6. WHAT STRATEGIES ARE UTILIZED? 6
7. SELLING FOOD 6
8. WHAT EFFECTS DO CONTAMINANT CHEMICALS HAVE IN FOODS?. 7
9. WHAT EFFECTS DO FOOD ALLERGIES HAVE ON POLICY? 7

CHAPTER 2:
GOVERNMENT OVERSIGHT OF FOOD SAFETY
1. GOVERNMENT'S ROLE IN FOOD SAFETY. 9
2. HOW FOOD IS INSPECTED, EVALUATED, MEASURED,
   AND MONITORED. 10
3. DIFFERENCES IN TYPES OF FOOD REGULATION 12
4. THE ROLES OF CONGRESS 13
   Examples and Illustrations. 13

CHAPTER 3:
GOVERNMENT OVERSIGHT OF FOOD LABELING
1. FOOD LABEL REGULATION BY FEDERAL AGENCIES. 15
2. DEFINITIONS MATTER 15
3. LABEL CONTENTS 16
4. HOW FOOD LABELING IS REGULATED. 18

5. THE SPECIAL CASE OF FOOD LABELING HEALTH CLAIMS 20
6. NUTRITION PANELS AND SERVING SIZES 20
7. SIZE, WEIGHT, AND ORIGINS OF FOODS 21
8. FRONT PANEL CLAIMS 22
9. SPECIAL DIETARY FOODS. 23
10. INFANT FORMULAS. 24
11. ORGANIC FOODS 24
12. BIOTECH AND GENETICALLY MODIFIED FOODS. 25
13. LABELING FOR ABSENCE OF BIOTECH PRODUCTS 26
14. LABEL UNIFORMITY AND STATE RULES UNDER THE 1990
    AMENDMENTS 26
    Examples and Illustrations. 27

CHAPTER 4:
REGULATION OF RAW AND ORGANIC FOOD SAFETY

1. INSPECTIONS 30
2. SEAFOOD 30
3. PESTICIDE RESIDUES ON VEGETABLES AND FRUIT 31
4. MEAT PRODUCTS 32
5. ORGANIC FOODS 33
   Examples & Illustrations 33

CHAPTER 5:
REGULATION OF FOOD PROCESSING AND INGREDIENTS

1. REGULATION OF INGREDIENTS AND ADDITIVES 37
2. REGULATION OF SAFE FOOD MANUFACTURING 38
   a. Raw Material Sourcing 39
   b. Preparation 40
   c. Fabrication 40
   d. Processing of the Food 41
   e. Post-Processing Handling Steps 41
   f. Packaging Foods. 42
   g. Distribution 43
   h. Rework. 43
   i. Paperwork or Digital Documentation Controls. 44
   Examples and Illustrations. 45

CHAPTER 6:
RESTAURANTS AND FOOD SERVICE DELIVERY

1. CONSUMER EFFECTS 47
2. FOOD SERVICE FACILITY SANITATION 47
3. LIABILITY STANDARDS 48

4. REGULATORY SCENARIO: HEALTH INSPECTION 50
5. PROBLEM INVESTIGATION 50
6. PENALTIES 50
7. CARRYOUT FOOD SERVICES 51
8. FOOD HANDLING 51
9. TYPES OF PROBLEMS ENCOUNTERED. 51
10. TRUCKING AND INTERNET FOOD DELIVERY SERVICES 52

CHAPTER 7:
FOOD IMPORTATION

1. HOW THE FDA WORKS AGAINST IMPORT PROBLEMS. 54
2. STATISTICS ON IMPORTED FOODS. 55
3. EFFECTS OF "JUST-IN-TIME" LOGISTICS. 56
4. IMPORT SCREENING ROLES OF THE FEDERAL AGENCIES 58
5. ADVANCE NOTIFICATION OF FOOD IMPORTS 58
6. WHEN SAMPLING IS LIKELY 59
7. WHEN IMPORT ALERTS ARE USED 59
8. ENTRY UNDER CUSTOMS BOND 60
9. DETENTION OF FOODS AT ENTRY PORTS 60
10. FDA POWER TO DETAIN AND DESTROY 61

CHAPTER 8:
ADVERSE EXPERIENCES WITH FOOD
AND THEIR CONSEQUENCES

1. WHAT ARE LIKELY ADVERSE EVENTS FROM FOODS? 63
2. HOW FOOD CONSUMERS CAN COMPLAIN EFFECTIVELY 64
3. FOOD COMPANY RESPONSES 66
4. HOW THE GOVERNMENT TYPICALLY RESPONDS. 67
5. HOW THE FDA RESPONDS TO FOOD PROBLEMS. 67
6. THE RECALL DECISION. 69
7. THE FDA'S REPORTABLE FOOD REGISTRY 69
8. THE MEDICAL CARE PROVIDER ROLE 70
9. CENTERS FOR DISEASE CONTROL ROLES 71
10. LAWYERS' ROLES 71
11. CONSUMER ORGANIZATION ISSUES 72
    Examples and Illustrations 73

CHAPTER 9:
DIETARY SUPPLEMENTS

1. FRAUD AND DIETARY SUPPLEMENTS 75
2. CONTENTS 77
3. EFFECTIVENESS 78

4. REMEDIES 79
Examples and Illustrations. 79

CHAPTER 10:
FOODS WITH PESTICIDE RESIDUES
1. CONTEXT IS IMPORTANT 81
2. EXPANDING PESTICIDE USES 83
3. EFFECTS FOR CONSUMERS 83
Examples and Illustrations. 84

CHAPTER 11:
BIOTECHNOLOGY AND FOOD
1. HOW BIOTECHNOLOGY IS LIKELY TO TRANSFORM FOOD 87
Examples and Illustrations. 89

CHAPTER 12:
CIVIL DAMAGE LAWSUITS FOR FOOD INJURY OR FRAUD
1. WHAT WILL THE JURY EXPECT? 91
Examples and Illustrations. 94

CHAPTER 13:
HOW DO FEDERAL AND STATE PROTECTIONS INTERSECT?
Examples and Illustrations. 97

CHAPTER 14:
FOOD ADVERTISING
Examples and Illustrations. 103

CHAPTER 15:
FOOD PACKAGING ISSUES
Examples and Illustrations 107

CHAPTER 16:
ENVIRONMENTAL ASPECTS OF FOOD PRACTICES
1. ENERGY 109
2. WASTEWATER 110
3. WATER UTILIZATION. 110
4. AIR EMISSIONS AND NUISANCES 110
5. RESIDUES OF PESTICIDE USE. 111

CHAPTER 17:
HOW THE "LOCAL FOOD" MOVEMENT RELATES TO FOOD SAFETY

CHAPTER 18:
PRICING, COMPETITION, AND MONOPOLY

CHAPTER 19:
THE FUTURE OF FOOD SAFETY

APPENDICES
1: FEDERAL TRADE COMMISSION WEBSITE CAUTION WEIGHING THE
EVIDENCE IN DIET ADS 121
2: PESTICIDE RESIDUES. 123
3: FEDERAL FOOD SAFETY RESOURCE WEBSITES 127
4: REPORTABLE FOOD 129
5: FEDERAL MEAT INSPECTION ACT (FMIA) 131
6: FAIR PACKAGING AND LABELING ACT. 169
7: NUTRITION LABELING AND EDUCATION ACT (NLEA) 179
8: FEDERAL FOOD, DRUG, AND COSMETIC ACT CHAPTERS I–IV. 199

RECOMMENDED READINGS 251

PREFACE

The Broadway remake of Dickens' Oliver Twist features a dozen scrawny orphans singing, "Food! Glorious Food!" We love food; we eat it, think about it, plan for it, choose it, and admire it. But sometimes the people who deliver the food hurt us by their mistakes or oversight (or, rarely, their intention). And sometimes the people who have the food want to separate us from our money by claiming things about the food that just aren't true. In either instance, this book may be a help.

Consider this a kind of "cookbook," not of the joys of cooking food but the challenges of presenting safe, wholesome food in a truthful manner to an interested audience. Use this book for basic answers to questions of why certain things happen, how they can be resisted or punished, and who can provide you with the relief that you seek.

Of course, if you've suffered an unfortunate outcome related to food, seek medical help and try to avoid that problem in the future. If there was a serious harm done, find an experienced and competent attorney who concentrates his practice in the subject of the harm. If you and others were cheated by a fraudulent sales pitch for a food, one of the specialized class action lawyers who handles consumer cases may take on your claims. Just as a special occasion merits a specially talented chef's meal, so litigation involving food injury or fraud warrants the use of an experienced specialist who knows how to effectively represent your interests.

Best wishes, and Bon Appetit!

James T. O'Reilly
University of Cincinnati

CHAPTER 1:
DEFINING KEY CONCEPTS IN FOOD

We begin with the basic terms that will be used throughout this book. "Food" is a solid, liquid, or other form of ingested material that is used for taste or nourishment. Basic definitions in common use in the food industry, like "safe food," are subjective terms that may not match the expectations of the consumer. To a consumer, a safe food would be pure with no contaminants. The industry definition allows low levels of contaminants and considers relative safety, taking into account the intended cooking and other methods of reducing risk, and judges safety as a relative factor within the comparative context of similar foods. Normally, the consumer expects food to be cheap and safe, tasty and not poisonous, attractive and not contaminated. At the consumer level, these expectations are usually met, and one often hears, "We have the safest food supply in the world."

The food producer—a farm or ranch operator "upstream" in the processing sequence for consumer food—is accustomed to seeing some very normal and predictable contaminants in every truckload of food, whether dirt on the potato or feces on the pigskin. That farmer or rancher or warehouse operator expects further cleaning and processing will occur in later stages, and that quality and safety will be enhanced. So food producers tend to be much more tolerant of contaminants than the average consumer of the finished food would be. By the time the food reaches the consumer's plate, it should be safe, and the systems should be in place to track its safety.

This book explores food "safety" broadly. We take the food consumer's viewpoint, and we recognize that some food producers will disagree. Overall, a greater consumer awareness of food safety regulation and its limitations helps everyone—from growers to diners. Safety is not automatic; and it is not without considerable costs built into the system.

On the food industry side, companies with the greatest marketplace strength receive the greatest consideration from Congress and regulatory agencies. The law's structures and incentives seem to accommodate and even reward the largest, most mechanized and most systematized growers and processors. A three hundred-acre carrot producer is less likely to have an impact on regulators than a wheat conglomerate with twenty-five grain elevators. Our nation's food supply and economic system is oriented to reward and incentivize the largest industrial food processors. The gap between the actual growers of food and those who eat the products of the land appears to be growing. The "Bibliography and Recommended Reading" later in this text lists a dozen books that adopt the viewpoint that there is a growing cultural shift that favors locally grown food. Unwritten, but equally true, is that cost subsidies and financial arrangements tend to disfavor the smaller, local grower. So readers should recognize from the outset that our concepts of food safety are no longer built upon comfortable familiarity with the grower or producer, but safety is measured on an industrial scale.

1. WHAT IS "SAFE"?

Safety can be defined as the absence of harm or injury. "Food safety" refers to the general desire of consumers and government agencies for an absence of avoidable human illness related to the ingestion or handling of food. For example, beef with high levels of maggots or lettuce with *Escherichia coli* (*E. coli*) are not deemed to be safe food. "Food security," a parallel but distinct term, means the protection of food from intentional tampering, poisoning, terrorism, or otherwise evil actions.

The safety of processing, manufacturing, and importing food is a centrally important issue throughout this book. Consumers don't want to eat bad food, and they don't want to worry about whether the food is safe and has been handled safely. Avoiding illness is important to the consumer and taxpayer. When companies fail to protect the food they sell to the public, the company and their managers may be punished in court and in the stock market; when regulators fail to avoid harms, they are replaced or de-funded.

Defining "safety" involves subjective perceptions. Safety is not the total absence of risk, but it is the quality of a product's condition that makes it reasonable to assume that no harm will be caused from ingesting the food. Congress has struggled with this balancing several times, and the "reasonable certainty of no harm" is the most recent compromise language. Parents want a reasonable certainty that the food they buy or cook will not cause harm to their children; and Congress seeks a similar goal in federal food safety legislation.

The increasing dissemination of scientific knowledge about viruses, bacterial particles, and tiny nano-sized contaminants has put a lot of scientific information into the public's hands, and some portion of that knowledge has aided the awareness of needs for protective activities. The FDA and state health inspectors use a series of tests to determine if a particular food is "safe" by counting the contaminants or doing lab testing of a sample of the food. Some bad material will usually be detectable, but how much is present? The "defect action level" concept is applied, meaning that a food can be contaminated to a small extent— e.g. twenty parts of flies in a pound of fresh butter—but cannot have more contaminants than FDA scientists believe would cause disease or other harms. If the contaminant quantity exceeds the "level," then the product is deemed to be "adulterated." It is the end condition of the food as eaten that matters; for example, properly cooked beef does not pass *E. coli* infections to humans.

2. HOW ARE CONTAMINANTS CONTROLLED?

Who is the nation's "food safety guru"? For meat, poultry, and eggs, the Food Safety Inspection Service of the U.S. Department of Agriculture (USDA) is the regulatory agency. For all other foods, the FDA and the state counterpart agencies that parallel the FDA are in charge of safety surveillance. The State Department of Agriculture or the State Department of Health train inspectors to visit food processing plants within the state on a regular basis to examine whether there is sufficient protection from harmful ingredients or illness-causing bacteria. They share data and findings with the FDA and often take parallel enforcement actions in holding back interstate and in-state shipments. The regulatory control of food safety is one part of the solution; corporate food processing companies need investor confidence and positive consumer loyalty, and that is another part of the incentives for safety. A minor but notable aspect of the safety incentive is the liability cost or bankruptcy that a company would face if its food caused injury, and if a jury agreed that damage awards should punish that firm's negligent conduct.

3. HOW ARE SAFETY STANDARDS CREATED?

Who decides what "safety" should look like? At the top of the "food chain" are congressional decisions on what should be regulated and in what ways. Congress can expressly require a specific set of ingredients and levels, as it once did for infant formula. This is the rare exception. Most of the laws Congress has adopted for food safety are delegations of power to administrative agency managers in the FDA and the USDA to use their discretionary power to protect the safety of foods.

Broader delegations and looser legislative language give more discretion to the agency managers and sets up the FDA or the USDA to make a decision about safety. A set of final, binding rules, established by processes that assure public awareness and comment, are the next level below the authority of legislation. These rules provide the agency's view of the most firm and enforceable standards of safety. Most participants in the food processing and distribution chain obey these binding rules, most of the time. Those who ignore the rules and are caught can be severely penalized.

The next level of standards (in terms of a hierarchy of enforcement ability) are "guidelines" or "policy statements" that indicate to food firms what the government agency expects, or explain how the government agency interprets the words Congress has used in statutes like the Meat Inspection Act or the Food Drug & Cosmetic Act. FDA guidance documents are not binding rules. While it is helpful to have some guidance to clarify uncertainties, FDA guidance documents are readily changeable, can be ignored if particular circumstances warrant, and often appear with disclaimers that limit the value of their protective intentions.

The lowest forms of directives are the letters written in particular cases in reply to questions from the industry. Is this action allowed? Will I be in trouble for doing this? Does your agency have a problem if I combine these two ingredients? Easy to obtain but hard to rely upon, these are the changeable statements of a busy bureaucracy that provide guidance in a particular case without having any longer-term weight in the world of regulation. Implicitly, they offer some assurance that the action can be taken or the measurement would be acceptable without criticism of that action by the regulators.

Not expressed to consumers, but publicly available in FDA internal manuals, are the "defect action levels," measurements at which quantitative points the FDA would start an enforcement action for adulteration, e.g. ten rodent hairs in powdered potato flakes. Food defects vary with types of foods and types of defects. These levels have been set and sometimes updated to reflect the findings that FDA staff makes during their actual hands-on inspections and lab tests of the food processing industry.

4. HOW DO REGULATORS BECOME INVOLVED AT THE VARIOUS STEPS OF THE PROCESS?

Government agencies act through regulation-writing, known as "rule-making"; inspection and penalty assessment, known as "adjudication"; and prosecuting the worst offenders in court, known as "enforcement."

From the consumer's viewpoint, the slowest of these is rulemaking, and the one with the most impact is enforcement. Most of the administrative work is in adjudication of particular cases, with inspectors visiting plants and agency hearing officers imposing financial penalties or suspending licenses for inadequate compliance with food safety laws.

Consumer complaints about food issues typically go into the adjudication process. For example, an inspector will follow up a "glass in product" call or a quality complaint about a packaged food. Part of adjudication is the decision about whether a complaint is a rare occurrence, an aberration in a company whose reputation is stellar, or whether it is reason to shut down the company as a persistent safety violator. Remedies for specific cases vary: some will be forced to recall, some will be assessed fines, some will lose licenses, and some will be fully exonerated after the investigation clears the food firm of responsibility (e.g. for a tampering or intentional individual poisoning episode).

5. HOW ARE SPECIAL CATEGORIES OF FOOD REGULATED?

There are also special categories of food, recognized in specific federal laws, including dietary supplements, organic foods, and food additive ingredients. Each category has a special regulatory status, which is related to the desire of Congress to preserve certain products from further limitations. Congress carved out a special, less stringent rule for these product categories. The FDA and USDA treat these products in light of these special exceptions and statutory exclusions.

The largest category of food that has the intentionally weakest regulation, because of an excellent lobbying effort in 1994, is the category of "dietary supplements." This category is shielded from most of the FDA's controls, which apply to other categories of food. Dietary supplement makers have been able to avoid all of the FDA approval steps, and the controls that remain have been neutralized so as to be no real protection at all. Chapter 10 discusses this category in detail.

Another category of food that deserves special recognition is the so-called "organic" food products, which are intended to be grown or processed without the use of chemicals or biological pesticides. These products can be labeled "organic" because they comply with rules set by the U.S. Department of Agriculture, adapted from international standards. The rules prescribe the limited use of fertilizers, pesticides, and other chemicals as the crops are growing. Some controversy surrounds the USDA acceptance of some practices as being "organic." The price of organic food tends to be higher than that of conventional food, to make up for the losses incurred by the organic farmer when his or her crop yield is reduced as a result of the limitations on fertilizers and pesticides. The perception of greater purity may be an illusion in some circumstances; but if consumers are willing to pay more for lower chemical exposure, then the marketplace will deliver what the consumer wishes, at a price.

Chemical products used in conjunction with food can be termed food ingredients, food additives, colors, or future "functional foods" undergoing development efforts. In the latter case, the company is attempting to demonstrate that their food product is different because of its unique attributes that enhance a consumer benefit. Chapter 5 discusses raw and organic ingredients and their legal issues.

6. WHAT STRATEGIES ARE UTILIZED?

American food law allows great flexibility to the food marketer, but that flexibility is tied to severe penalties if harm occurs to consumers from serious errors. "Sell at your own risk" approaches put the burden on food company executives to pay close attention to lists of safe ingredients and to avoid the ones on the lists that present problems. Preapproval is rarely used in food safety regulation, only the newest chemical additives are likely to receive detailed FDA scrutiny.

For meat products, a historic shift of approaches has occurred. The use in meat plants of a sophisticated planning and evaluation system called the Hazard Analysis of Critical Control Points (HACCP) increased in the last two decades to become the dominant theme in meat product safety, displacing generations of "hands-on" physical inspection of each carcass in each meat plant. By identifying where problems are most likely to arise, the focused effort of the HACCP safety program should reduce harm. Chapter 5 covers these issues.

7. SELLING FOOD

Food marketers tend to make excessive benefit assertions. Some creatively aggressive sales claims appear on the food labels; some marketers use advertising to assert their benefit claims. Back in 1938, Congress split jurisdiction over claims of food frauds between the Federal Trade Commission, the FDA, and the states. State attorneys general challenged a number of health benefit claims made for foods. In recent years, as a result of abuses in the system, Congress has designated the FDA to receive more appropriations for its enforcement roles, to make the FDA a more energized regulatory police agency against fraudulent claims in the food category. Chapter 3 addresses this area.

8. WHAT EFFECTS DO CONTAMINANT CHEMICALS HAVE IN FOODS?

The presence of insects and other predators on seeds, fruits, and vegetables has been a natural fact for millennia. Modern chemistry has the capacity to poison the predator and preserve the crop from destruction, sometimes by spraying a chemical and sometimes by breeding into the plant a natural protection through genetic engineering. The effect of the modern agricultural chemical "miracle" on foods has been cheaper, more readily available food that will last longer, mature later (after transcontinental air movement), or avoid problems that have led consumers to reject such food in the past. There is a trade-off for having more, better, and greener plant products—it is the human effects of pesticide residues. To the extent a new chemical pesticide has been tested and shown to have a potential human health consequence, its use can be limited by "tolerances," which are quantitative limits measured at harvest and after processing. Chapter 10 explores these in depth.

9. WHAT EFFECTS DO FOOD ALLERGIES HAVE ON POLICY?

Governments cannot change biology; some humans will have allergic responses to certain plant or animal aspects, such as a wheat gluten allergy. But governments can do more to require cautionary labels on products and to make people aware of the potential risks of ingesting food that has allergens present, whether in basic or in processed food. In the United States, after numerous state laws were enacted, a federal law on allergen warnings was adopted in 2004 and went into effect in 2006. Chapter 3 explores these issues.

As we enter the later chapters of this book, please keep these concepts in mind, as they are the shorthand versions of more complex topics. A guidance document on colors with contaminants is not infallible, but the context of its use against a food to punish the safety violator is built on the defined terms that we have discussed in this chapter.

CHAPTER 2:
GOVERNMENT OVERSIGHT OF FOOD SAFETY

1. GOVERNMENT'S ROLE IN FOOD SAFETY

Three principal governmental agencies have roles in protecting the food supply in the United States: the federal Food and Drug Administration (FDA), the Food Safety Inspection Service of the U.S. Department of Agriculture (USDA), and a group of several hundred state and local health and food safety agencies, most of them members of the Association of Food and Drug Officials of the United States (AFDO). The FDA has been involved with food since 1906, when its legal authority over interstate food was created as part of its onetime role as the Bureau of Chemistry of the USDA. The FDA has broad authority over all food generally. The USDA covers safety inspection of meat, poultry, and eggs and sets standards of economic regulation, such as size or quantity, for many other crops as a non-safety control on the crops' marketing.

Of these three channels for government involvement in food safety, the third, the AFDO member state and local entities, receives the least public attention and is in the headlines least, but performs the most important local and regional health coverage for food that reaches the consumer. This third group is closest to the point of food delivery to the consumer and receives many of the complaints from unhappy diners or consumers. The primary inspectors of most local food processing and storage facilities are thousands of employees from city, county, and state health inspection agencies. It has been estimated that 80 percent of food safety inspections are done by these local agencies, whose inspectors routinely look for sanitation problems, temperature problems with refrigerated or stored foods, and employee sanitation concerns, such as personal hygiene among food handlers. Closing filthy restaurant kitchens or ordering destruction of a truckload of defrosted meat in a broken trailer does not get headline news coverage, but this phase of real consumer protection is vitally important. Being close to the actual delivery point of food to the consumer, the AFDO member departments provide local residents with a greater assurance of safe operating conditions.

The second most active agency is the U.S. Food and Drug Administration and its Center for Food Science and Applied Nutrition. The FDA, which coordinates food disease scrutiny with the Centers for Disease Control and local health departments, is the premier food safety agency in the world. The FDA acts through its district offices to conduct thousands of food safety inspections in factories, storage warehouses, rail and truck shipments, and at incoming sea and air shipping points. FDA inspection does not assure that a product is safe; but it assures that the makers of a product are aware of their obligations and that they will take precautions to stay in compliance with national regulatory requirements. The food industry is more protective of consumer health because it knows the alternative is a punitive action by the FDA.

The third most significant enforcer is the U.S. Department of Agriculture, which has several sub-agencies that play safety roles. The USDA has historically felt a series of conflicting pressures for its various roles because it represents the makers and marketers of food products, while it also protects consumers by inspections and enforcement actions in some product categories. Consumer organizations sometimes praise the USDA for having closer scrutiny than the FDA can afford, within USDA's defined categories such as eggs and beef. But more often than not, consumer organizations criticize the tendency of the bureaucrats inside the USDA to protect the public confidence in products, despite the presence of real health problems. One frequent charge is that these regulators are "captives" of the lobbyists for farm groups who work with selected congressional subcommittees to restrain more vigorous regulatory controls. Another is that the USDA is an apologist for bad decisions made by the food conglomerates and tailors its rules to satisfy industry more than to satisfy the needs of the taxpaying public. Political appointees in the leadership of the USDA are more often accused of cheerleading big agriculture and inadequately controlling misconduct by the industrial giants.

2. HOW FOOD IS INSPECTED, EVALUATED, MEASURED, AND MONITORED

For millennia, humans have been growing vegetable, fruit, and animal products for use in food. Levels of bad quality have been met with responses such as rejection, remedial processing, warnings, and the like. Governments have been involved since the days when Hammurabi ordered protections for consumers of bread in ancient Mesopotamia. Punishments have evolved from flogging or amputation, down to civil forfeiture and disgorgement of profits by the convicted fraudulent seller. So today's high-tech equipment and software-driven assessment tools are just the latest of the ways in which food consumers have been protected by their governments.

Food *inspection* is the first hurdle for growers or processors. Samples of food are taken, storage warehouse conditions such as the existence of rat or bird contamination are examined, purity of the products is evaluated, and inspectors coordinate with laboratory specialists to decide what findings are likely to intercept a fraudulent or harmful container or shipment.

Funds to perform inspections have declined steadily in recent years. Your author leads his students in the FDA Law class to a midwestern FDA office each year for a "reality check" discussion with actual decision-makers there. In 2005, one regulator bemoaned the loss of experienced staff inspectors and the inability to fund positions for the scheduled food inspections as well as the unexpected national responses to failed or contaminated food products. "Last one out, turn out the lights" was the depressed mood in the earliest years of this century. The outlook seemed to improve in 2009 with the new Administration and its public mandate for change.

Food *evaluation* is the next step in the oversight process. Is this really a proper infant formula with protein, or has the chemical melamine been added to fool the baseline tests and shave dollars off the costs for the producer? Mass spectroscopy is a wonderful tool to catch thieves who rip off the food consumer, but the machine and its operator are so costly that there are only a handful that routinely are available for the support of safety investigators. Gross contamination of butter with dead flies can be seen in a lab with inexpensive microscopes and cameras; most of the elaborate food fraud cases have required far more sophisticated detection methods to catch the adulterating ingredient. Most important to the consumer is that the detective work be within lawful methods so that it can be allowed at a court trial; investigatory lab work requires methods that carefully evaluate a documented sample through to a correct report. All the television glamour that is suggested for crime laboratories has jaded the population of jury members to assume that bad conduct is readily detected and the perpetrators are captured. In truth, the evaluation stage for food problems requires a carefully calculated approach, lots of documentation, and protocols or methods that will survive cross-examination in court by lawyers for the alleged criminal companies.

Measuring quantities of food is another challenge for government, while consumers just assume that their kitchen tablespoon measure is sufficient. In this instance, claims about food ("now with 12% protein," "40% less fat") require measurements and accurate label explanations. So the government standardizes the weights and measures, requires calibration of factory measurement devices, and drafts protocols for product volumes, package descriptions, and the all-important RACC (Reference Amounts Customarily Consumed or "serving size") on which consumer food advertisements and labels must depend. How many tiny breath mints is one "serving"? If it is one mint, the regulation says that the product can claim zero calories by "rounding down" to zero from 0.4; if a serving size is three mints, the law would ban a "no-calories" claim as misleading. What may seem trivial has enriched several law firms in Washington, DC, as battles of breath mint counting have raged between one, two, or three mints, with lawyers on either side and survey measurement experts and pollsters happy to assist in the debate for a price.

Monitoring food is a fourth governmental function, as hundreds of truckloads of spoiled food are consigned to landfills each year. The monitor may work for the producer, the retailer, the wholesaler, or the interstate transporters, but each looks for signs that the product is no longer safe or wholesome. Monitors from the FDA and USDA watch the outflow of foods from facilities and evaluate which do not meet quality standards. Sub-quality food was once given away to food banks, but today's litigation risks have made food companies more willing to landfill their off-quality goods than to experience a safety-related lawsuit brought by free distribution recipients.

3. DIFFERENCES IN TYPES OF FOOD REGULATION

Food safety doesn't happen by accident. Planning for the avoidance of food problems is important. The leading system of quality assurance is HACCP, the Hazard Analysis of Critical Control Points, which pays attention to the several points in the food preparation cycle in which temperature or other protective measures are "critical" to assuring that the food will not deteriorate. By reviewing the precautionary measures taken at each of these critical points, the methods of avoiding problems can be diagnosed and the processing plant can improve the quality of its output.

HACCP's focus on specific parts of the manufacturing process, instead of entire lines of production, has displaced the former USDA system known as "continuous inspection." The long-time system of federal meat inspectors standing in the meat factory line has been replaced by the use of a technician, statistical failure analysis, and a sensor system which produces readouts of line temperatures and other quality control measures.

Another aspect of regulatory oversight is the system for product marking, coding, and labeling to assure compliance with standards. The products that comply with standards get spray-on or stamped package labeling with a symbol and with retention or "use by" dates.

Spot inspections of retail food for quality are the final step of food quality evaluation. Local food inspectors visit the delicatessen or ready-made food section of a store and test refrigeration, cleanliness, and the quality of the food. Food contamination immediately before consumers eat the food is best avoided with local inspectors.

Hotlines for consumer complaints and opportunities for competitor-initiated enforcement round out the systems.

4. THE ROLES OF CONGRESS

Political power comes to those who know how to use it aggressively. The farm lobby has long been in control of national food policy, with programs that subsidize some farms and authorize limited sales arrangements as a gatekeeper on market supplies of certain foods. The larger food conglomerates have found ways to use this to their advantage. Much farther down the list of effective lobbying influences is the "average food consumer." If all members of Congress talk about their sincere desire to help the consumer, as they do, most do not go on to acknowledge that the consumer is disadvantaged by many of the federal policies. Active consumer involvement in food decisions (safety, labeling, and cost) is only a small part of what influences budget appropriations and legislative changes.

Examples and Illustrations

A statewide product recall of "Brand Z Pepperoni Pizza" is announced by the manufacturer after retail chain Safeway complains of health concerns. The USDA has jurisdiction over the part of the plant where the pepperoni sausage is made, cut, and installed; the FDA has jurisdiction over the dough, tomato sauce, and other ingredients. State agriculture inspectors and city health inspectors also examine the plant and find that unsanitary conditions were the reason for the defects. The FDA decides not to take action since the company then cleaned up the plant in light of the local inspections.

CHAPTER 3:
GOVERNMENT OVERSIGHT OF FOOD LABELING

1. FOOD LABEL REGULATION BY FEDERAL AGENCIES

Who protects the ordinary trusting consumer from falsity in food labels? In the field of food labeling, several regulators have a role, but the Food and Drug Administration has the most extensive set of regulations dealing with food labeling for the widest range of food products. Since the founding in 1906 of the FDA's predecessor, the Bureau of Chemistry, the agency has traditionally had an extensive interest in food labels as a means to avoid deception and "misbranding" of foods. The FDA has utilized inspections, public meetings, responses to trade inquiries, and guidance documents to communicate its expectations for proper and lawful labeling of foods.

Although some food products are subject to the separate jurisdiction of the U.S. Department of Agriculture for their meat content, it is the FDA to which most food labeling issues are directed. Appendix 5 describes law relating to meat products, while Appendix 8 covers the wider range of the Food Drug & Cosmetic Act. When examining imported food shipments, inspecting U.S. plant sites, or handling consumer complaints, FDA field offices use the guidance documents prepared by FDA headquarters to instruct their inspectors regarding permissible product labels in the food marketplace. FDA headquarters monitors food industry practices, receives complaints from competing firms, and revises policies when needed.

2. DEFINITIONS MATTER

Definitions matter for regulatory purposes. A "label" is on the food container; "labeling" is a statement or picture that physically accompanies the food container, such as an in-store leaflet or a shelf tag.

"Advertising" is a statement that is made about the product by its sponsor, but which is physically separated from the food, e.g. on a billboard or an Internet advertisement. "Regulations" have the force and effect of law, and they must be obeyed. "Guidance documents" are the current best interpretation by government of food laws and regulations, but the documents themselves do not control what must be done by any person.

3. LABEL CONTENTS

The text of the food product package "label" is subject to very tight FDA requirements to assure that the product is uniformly handled and labeled for the benefit of the consumer. The FDA, for example, requires the front label to include a descriptive identification of the type of food and the weight or volume of the food, using standardized terms and measurements. The side or rear panel must include the ingredients of the packaged food and information about its nutritional value in a specific "nutrition facts" format. Terms of the Fair Packaging and Labeling Act are found in Appendix 6.

The FDA does not regulate brand names for food, or colors of packages, or artwork on packages (unless the name selected for the food would be deceptive to the average consumer), but all other information on the label is likely to be subject to the FDA's detailed oversight. This central uniformity helps the FDA in the event of a criticism or challenge, such as a contamination or fraud that affects consumers. In practice, the FDA has only a small handful of professionals monitoring food labeling nationwide; so the FDA learns about most labeling flaws from competitors and from state or local food inspectors who make inquiries about suspected violators.

The first category of label information that is of interest to consumers is the name of the product inside the package. If the product is composed completely of one substance, such as sliced apples, that would be the name used under the brand name, e.g. "Safeway Sliced Apples"; if it is a processed food with multiple ingredients, the product will have some reasonable description and, in some cases will have the name of a standardized food, such as enriched wheat flour, e.g. "Safeway Enriched Wheat Flour Mixed Berry Pancake Mix." The purpose of the description is to avoid confusing consumers who might expect one thing in a package, only to find another. In the 1920s, the U.S. Supreme Court upheld the FDA's authority to challenge apple cider vinegar, that was a cheapened extract of waste apples, as deceptive to consumers who expected better-quality vinegar from fresh apples. And so the courts have been willing to accept FDA attacks against food product labels that might mislead the ordinary consumer. If a brand name such as "Zero-Cal" would be deceptive, the FDA might require some additional disclosure that lessens the potential for misleading the hurried grocery purchaser. These qualifications and limits take several forms, like requiring "Cranberry Delight Brand Juice" to be marked, with large letters, "22% cranberry juice" on the package.

The weight or volume of the food product is subject to label disclosure regulations under the Fair Packaging and Labeling Act (FPLA), a law that is intended to facilitate consumer comparisons among packaged products such as food. The FPLA is described in Appendix 6. Is 15 ounces of pancake mix a better purchase decision than 13.7 ounces of multipurpose biscuit, waffle and pancake batter? Are consumers deceived by "giant quart" claims on a food package? The FDA has adopted very extensive regulations and guidelines dealing with the FPLA-required disclosures and the ways in which the measurement of content is to be declared on the labels of various foods.

Packaging is overseen by the FDA, is sometimes called to the FDA's attention by state health or agriculture officials, and is frequently the subject of competitors' complaints to the FDA. The FDA wants to ensure that the consumer is not deceived, for example, by a very large cardboard package with a very small powdered food product inside. The label describing the quantity of food is rigidly standardized to include the weight of the product first, followed by the metric weight of the food. The ways of expressing this information are very specifically controlled so that "giant-sized quart" claims have virtually disappeared.

A third aspect of the food package label is the ingredient statement. Ingredients are required to be listed in descending order of weight (with some exceptions), so that the consumer can discern whether the desired ingredient is the primary ingredient, in addition to fillers or other forms of additional ingredient materials. Percentage disclosure on the label of fruit juices was vigorously opposed by industry for decades, but is today a well-understood and accepted mandate for the education of food consumers. Ingredient descriptions are subject to specific FDA guidance documents to avoid exaggeration of claims. For example, a package with "All Georgia Peach Compote" on the front label of the can may be ambiguous or exaggerated, and the ingredient panel is required to list water, corn syrup, and other ingredients whose volume in the recipe exceeds the amount of peaches. "Peach Flavored Compote, Made with Georgia Peaches" may seem less exciting to creative marketers, but it is more accurate. The force of consumer protection law lags far behind the creativity of food marketers, but eventually will catch up and require violators to make the necessary changes.

The fourth, and most tightly regulated, aspect of food package labeling is the nutrition panel. Rigid requirements written by Congress and expanded on by the FDA control this mandatory part of every food label. This nutrition facts panel is to be included visibly on the side of the package, where it can be read and understood by any consumer. The nutrition facts panel is subject to FDA controls on the type face and sizes of type that can be used, e.g. 8 point type, descriptions of the vitamins and minerals present in the food, and description of calories, fat, and other materials. At Appendix 1 of this book, the consumer can see the FDA standard nutrition labeling panel. The core principle is the facilitation of comparison shopping by the food consumer, with uniformity and truthful explanations.

In addition to the vitamins and minerals disclosure for foods that claim to have health benefits, there must be disclaimers that accompany the nutrition statements for those ingredients that do not present an expected or anticipated benefit to the consumer (e.g. "not a significant source of calcium"). This set of regulatory controls on disclosure serves the purpose of dissuading food firms from creating perceptions of food benefit that are not truthful and accurate. Though the FDA rules are intricate and complex, it makes sense for consumers to be protected by holding food sellers to specific standards and particularized controls.

Also, allergen warnings are required on product labels if one or more of a specific list of ingredients are present in the food. Congress adopted a 2004 statutory change that has given the FDA new powers forcing the label of foods to disclose allergens and to provide warnings. Wheat, gluten, nuts, and other allergy-triggering substances must be described on the food label so the allergic person can avoid the product.

4. HOW FOOD LABELING IS REGULATED

Complaints by competitors are the primary source of labeling enforcement actions by the FDA. Labels that make one product stand out as superior may move consumers to switch brands, so competitive firms carefully monitor what changes may be underway with their opponents on the retail shelf. When a competing seller crosses the line in a manner that puts others at a disadvantage, those who are disadvantaged could accept the risk and follow, while others will initiate some form of enforcement challenge, The reason competitor complaints have such a strong impact is that the FDA assumes that to attract consumers, competing firms will show data, test results, or otherwise "make the case" against the offending. From the viewpoint of the busy regulator, the choice of which enforcement case to bring is simple—handed a well-prepared package of why one firm is in violation, the FDA enforcement team is more likely to pursue that firm, compared to its slow and steady internal development of a label enforcement charge against some other food marketer.

Consumer inquiries are a second category of concern that may lead to action on a food labeling dispute. Letters, e-mails, and telephone calls to the FDA about food problems may initiate a letter of inquiry to the affected food company. Large and sophisticated companies regularly track consumer complaints the FDA is receiving, in order to determine which ones merit change or merit the presentation of defensive information in the event of an FDA inquiry. Companies that care about consumer feedback keep a sharp eye on their incoming 800-line calls and Web site messages from consumers. By the time the FDA learns about a consumer question concerning the food label, the company has probably answered that same inquiry dozens of times and has a ready supply of facts to present when the FDA inspector arrives.

Inspector review of labels occurs when FDA or state inspectors come to a food processing or manufacturing firm and ask to review the company's documentation underlying its label claims. The inspector looks over the set of labels and may ask the plant management for access to the documentation that supports claims about calories, fat, etc. The FDA has the legal authority to obtain these records at the time of the inspection. Congress has also considered giving the FDA subpoena authority that would compel a company to deliver its records supporting food claims.

The USDA operates a different system for meat products. There is a central clearance of each meat product label by a designated preapproval team in Washington, DC. The FDA finds labels after the food reaches the market; the USDA prevents the use of a label on products that are subject to federal meat inspection until the label is stamped as approved by the USDA review team. USDA requirements are spelled out in rules and guidance, just as are the FDA norms; but meat companies also observe carefully what the actual reviewers accept or reject, so the meat marketers control what claims they will present to the USDA. It is deemed to be more prudent to avoid rejection by not making all the possible claims that another company in a non-meat category might be willing to assert on that product's label.

For the food consumer, which approach yields more truthfulness? The Department of Agriculture meat inspection system does. Overall, the preapproval of a label by the government is preferable to a system that depends on later scrutiny and later penalties, just as a speed control on a car would be a better constraint than the possibility of a traffic ticket.

The sparse funding of FDA enforcement in the years 2003–2007 crippled the ability of food inspectors to be actively vigilant about excessive claims. While we could debate which approach is "right" for the entire economy, consumers certainly benefit more from preapprovals.

5. THE SPECIAL CASE OF FOOD LABELING HEALTH CLAIMS

Selling food for its healthful qualities is quite normal; selling particular processed food because it may prevent illness is rarely successful in complying with government regulatory restraints. The power of public opinion and of regulatory agency weapons of enforcement combine to put controls on the health claims that food labels can assert. A June 26, 2009, headline in the newsletter, *Inside FDA Week*, showed this phenomenon: "FDA Looms Large as Bayer Surrenders One-A-Day Selenium Cancer Claims." While a food marketer, in this case a dietary supplement maker, can offer consumers great benefits from the food product in label claims and in advertisements, the reality is that most lack a sufficient factual basis, and most claims that the FDA attacks in public are likely to be withdrawn. Rarely does an FDA challenge to a food claim last so long that it evolves into an actual court decision; negotiators for the food company settle, because they readily recognize that consumers and the news media align with the FDA in the "court of public opinion." A food company could prevail in a months-long court case, then win on appeal after a year or two, but by that time consumers will have read and heard all the deficiencies in the company's claim, harming sales of the controversial food product.

6. NUTRITION PANELS AND SERVING SIZES

The 1990 legislation known as the Nutrition Labeling and Education Act (NLEA) was a flawed compromise, but it improved the several scattered provisions that had existed in prior FDA rules. Under the NLEA, a single standard boxed panel on the side of foods allows the consumer to compare two packaged foods and then decide if the calories, saturated fats, and cholesterol of the products being compared are desirable for that food purchaser. Industry recognizes that some consumers inevitably will switch away from a high saturated fat product to a "light" version, so FDA rules also constrain what the percentage reductions must be as a prerequisite to calling a food "light" or "reduced fat" or "low calorie."

Most consumers do not realize that the behind-the-scenes combat among food companies over the seemingly obscure topic of "serving size" has been vicious. A game is underway when the label is designed.

If the food maker takes advantage of "rounding down" from a number like 0.5 to a round number zero, the consumer feels great in getting a product whose labeling shows a zero number for one of the bad features (saturated fat, cholesterol, etc.). What the consumer does not often notice is the nutrition panel's third line, "serving size" and servings per package. Washington lawyers billed hundreds of thousands of dollars to their clients in the breath mint business during the "Tic Tac® wars." One maker of small mints wanted the serving size to be three mints; another wanted to make claims of "zero," which required the serving size to be only one mint. FDA rules have defined the amount for 139 categories of food, but FDA guidelines do not specifically cover every single food item.

The serving size is known in bureaucratic jargon as Reference Amount Customarily Consumed (RACC). Percentages and quantities are determined by dividing the entire package by the number of servings, so one single serving will have X calories, Y cholesterol, etc., determined by RACC quantities. The food maker has the option to put two parallel columns in the nutrition panel: one for the "raw" product and one as consumed, e.g., corn flakes alone and corn flakes with nonfat milk.

The FDA's food label rules are extensively set out in Part 101 of the FDA rules; a look at the index of topics in Appendix 2 to this text shows how micro-precise the FDA has tried to be in providing answers to the industry's many questions. Leaving issues unregulated could have been more flexible, but the FDA followed the 1990 legislative requirements carefully. The FDA recognized that it needed to fix the contents of the label in specific detail in order to aid consumer comparisons in food selection that become harder as labeling started to vary. This warranted a specificity of rules and guidance, which came as a policy choice; allowing a looser norm would foster creativity among competing firms, while label uniformity would simplify the average consumer's in-store purchasing decision. The FDA opted for the more rigid definitions.

7. SIZE, WEIGHT, AND ORIGINS OF FOODS

Comparing apples to oranges is not logical. Likewise, it is not logical for competitor A to sell a "giant 16-ounce caramel popcorn" while firm B sells "one pound of popcorn with caramel flavors added." Left unregulated, the bogus exaggerator will win and the truthful firm will be disadvantaged. The Fair Packaging and Labeling Act prescribes exactly how label statements will be printed, where on the carton, and in what detail.

The required weight information appears on the lower right side of the front of the box, with American labeling in pounds and ounces, followed in parentheses by metric quantities. Terms like "giant" would tend to mislead; words that allow fair comparisons are permitted. Artistic designers despair that rigid regulations make it much more difficult to produce an attractive, creative container for the food; FDA concedes there may be some loss of creative freedom, but the loss is more than made up for by attention to comparisons among the competing products. States and localities can continue to apply local requirements for accurate weights; if the packages are measured and are below the labeled content, a fine can be imposed by local enforcers.

Country of origin of the food must be described accurately. The FDA, USDA, and U.S. Customs have coordinated these disclosures so that consumers can tell where the constituents, e.g. fruit juices, were produced.

8. FRONT PANEL CLAIMS

In 2009, the FDA leadership became visibly less tolerant of food industry labeling decisions. Front panel checks, stamps, and claims about approved or beneficial aspects of foods proliferated, with an extreme reached when a high-sugar cereal claimed that it deserved a big positive "check" for containing fiber. Tolerance for aggressive marketing claims finally found a limit, as FDA warning letters went to the cereal companies, and a publicity backlash against them left the FDA to prominently call out their excessive marketing claims. The FDA may adopt rules in 2010–2012 that govern "front of package" (FOP) labeling on food products. This could involve new regulations, a uniform FOP nutrition label, and use of warning letters to target food manufacturers with deceptive labeling. The FDA announced in October 2009 a review of current symbols to determine whether they adhere to existing regulations. They also announced they would draft new regulations based on scientific and nutrition-based criteria, initiate a new consumer research program to assess whether certain symbols impart nutritional information more effectively to consumers, and begin an initiative to examine how uniform FOP labeling could improve consumer understanding of nutritional information.

The FDA told Congress in 2009 that the proposed regulations regarding front panel claims

> would more explicitly define the nutritional criteria that would have to be met by manufacturers making broad FOP or shelf label claims concerning the nutritional quality of a food, whether the claim is made in text or in symbols. FDA's intent is to provide

standardized, science-based criteria on which FOP nutrition labeling must be based.[1]

The FDA said that its rules prohibit false or misleading claims and restrict nutrient content claims to those defined in FDA regulations. The FDA said that if food labeling gives the consumer an impression of being healthy, but actually is not, then the label could be deemed misleading. And if the labeling neglects to disclose certain information, such as high levels of saturated fat, then the FDA could charge the company with a misbranding violation of section 201(n) of the law. For front panels, the FDA said, "proliferation of these symbols and icons and the various criteria they use necessitates our exercising that responsibility to look carefully at how the fronts of food packages are being used to impart such information."[2]

Because the preamble to a 2000 final FDA rule permits companies to make structure/function claims, such as the ability of calcium to build healthy bones, those claims would remain until or unless the rules changed. But the FDA forbids products from making disease immunity claims, and that is a subcategory in which aggressive marketing claims have become much more visible on cereals and other foods.

9. SPECIAL DIETARY FOODS

The elderly and institutionalized surgical patients are often given a liquid diet mixture of specialized nutrients. The FDA oversees the content of these products to assure that these most vulnerable patients can benefit from products aimed at their special needs. Some of these are prescription products for a specific medical problem, but most are regularly available at pharmacies, hospitals, or nursing homes without a prescription. When the FDA prioritizes which violations to pursue, these life-sustaining foods are at the top of the FDA's foods agenda for enforcement, inspections, and other protective measures. Detailed requirements for special dietary foods are found in FDA food rules. FDA regulations for special dietary foods, including vitamins and minerals, were adopted in 1973 but were rebuffed by lobbying efforts.

---

1   Letter from Margaret A. Hamburg, M.D., Commissioner of Food and Drugs to House of Representatives, House Appropriations Subcommittee on Agricultural Rural Development, Food and Drug Administration, and Related Agencies (Oct. 19, 2009), *available at* http://www.foodpolitics.com/wp-content/uploads/ DeLauro-Smart-Choices-10-19-09-FINAL.pdf.

2   Transcript for FDA's Media Briefing on Front-of-Pack Labeling (Oct. 20, 2009), *available at* http://www.fda.gov/downloads/NewsEvents/Newsroom/Media Transcripts/UCM187809.pdf.

The response against the FDA's special dietary foods regulations led Congress in 1976 to prohibit the FDA from controlling the potency of dietary supplements, although the agency maintained authority to regulate enriched foods like liquid protein products.

Fraudulent imitations of these products—imported or formulated locally with less nutritional value—have been treated by FDA as criminal counterfeits, and several of the importers have gone to prison for their crimes. Fraud that threatens the lives of elderly patients is likely to receive a very long prison term upon conviction.

10. INFANT FORMULAS

Congress rarely writes a recipe; but in the Infant Formula Act, legislators wrote a list of specific ingredients that should be in the basic formulas for specialized infant feeding. Young parents depend on these premixed sets of ingredients as sustenance for their children, or as a supplement to breast feeding. So Congress was shocked by news that omission of key ingredients in some brands to save money had caused harm to infants who had not received the necessary nutrients in some packaged infant formula brands. Congress later amended the law to delegate the recipe writing to FDA staff members who had the nutritional science expertise to keep up with evolving findings about child nutritional development. As with other special dietary foods, infant formulas are life-sustaining, so their quality and the accuracy of mixing them are essential to safety. The FDA closely monitors adverse reactions and inspects these facilities frequently.

11. ORGANIC FOODS

Ideally, all food would be wholesome, local, free of chemicals, and untainted by pesticide residues. Times and tastes have changed. Wintertime strawberries and tougher tomato skins are two illustrations of the changes. To increase supply and decrease losses, food growers and processors have moved away from that local ideal. Efforts to return closer to this ideal led to the movement in the 1960s for "organic" versions of common farm products, e.g. milk without additives and hormones and carrots with no pesticides. Eventually Congress gave the U.S. Department of Agriculture oversight of the definition of the term "organic" food. Commercially available quantities of "organic" foods were developed in the 1990s and have been widely marketed more recently as a result of consumer preference (as reflected in purchases of organic products at a pricing premium over conventional food). So long as consumers are willing to pay, the organic food growers expect to prosper. The recession of 2009 reduced the rapid growth of the organic food industry. Estimates were that after double-digit growth for years, sales of organic foods would drop 1.1 percent in 2009 to $5.07 billion. That percentage drop is still a huge one, of course. Farmers producing organic crops, who had become accustomed to 12 to 23 percent annual growth, saw fewer profit incentives to put in the extra costs and labor needed to stay organic.

After a 1990 law on "organic" labeling of foods, the FDA ceded most of its control over labeling the "organic" aspects of products to the U.S. Department of Agriculture. In turn, the USDA worked with advisors and trade groups to establish the rules for defining what is or is not "organic." Its rules in part 205 of Title 7, Code of Federal Regulations, are patterned after an international model, ISO Standard 65, and provide for each seller of organic food to be inspected and certified by a private certifying entity. The USDA then certifies the assessments performed by evaluative agencies. These federal rules and the international "organic" standard norms in turn specify a series of grower practices, which meet the federal definitions for absence of pesticide residues, etc. Loopholes and exceptions in the USDA rules have been criticized, but it appears there are reasonable bases for the rules.

12. BIOTECH AND GENETICALLY MODIFIED FOODS

Chapter 11 deals with biotechnological adaptation of food, but labeling is a part of the overall regulatory picture for biotech foods. The FDA does not require food labels to disclose the presence of genetically modified organisms (GMOs). The FDA, as a matter of policy, does not involve itself in the development by agricultural scientists of seeds for basic agricultural crops, until or unless actual food product safety is affected. The USDA Biotechnology Regulatory Service has the principal federal role for authorizing experiments with genetically modified seeds, plants, etc. The goal of the experimental developments is to design a better genetic quality of the seed so that crops resist natural predators, or so that crops will be able to grow despite the presence of weed-killing chemicals that otherwise would kill both the crop and the weed. Education about genetics, seed propagation, and plant strength has expanded dramatically over decades and has become much more visible in the last twenty years as public attention has been drawn to the modification of food crops.

This book focuses on the other details of food biotechnology in Chapter 11.

13. LABELING FOR ABSENCE OF BIOTECH PRODUCTS

Should consumers be informed about biotech ingredients in food? Much money has been spent on lobbyists and legal arguments to suppress the requirement for use of food label statements about the absence of biotech ingredients in foods. Food processors who use biotech products, like the recombinant bovine somatotropin (rbST) given to cows by injections to expand milk production, have vigorously resisted the demands by consumer groups, as well as state and local governments, for label disclosure of the presence of the biotech compounds in consumer foods. In May 1992, the FDA refused to mandate disclosure of the genetic engineering of foods. In the mid-1990s, Vermont dairy owners resisted a state law, advocated by consumers, which would have disclosed the presence of injected rbST in their cows' milk. Lawsuits went on until 1996, and the lobbying over congressional and state requirements resulted in an eventual compromise.

Labels can tell consumers that (1) the biotech ingredient is present, but must also tell consumers that (2) the FDA does not regard this product as different. In the words of the 1994 FDA Interim Guidance, milk labeled "From Cows That Have Not Been Treated With Recombinant Bovine Somatotropin" should also say that "No significant difference has been shown between milk derived from rbST-treated and non-rbST-treated cows."[3]

14. LABEL UNIFORMITY AND STATE RULES UNDER THE 1990 AMENDMENTS

Are you annoyed about misleading label issues for the packaged foods you buy? You can call your mayor or write to your governor, but they cannot do anything about your concerns regarding food labeling. The food industry won a significant victory in 1990, when Congress adopted a clause that bars state or local food labeling, but with narrow exceptions. States or local government rules or laws cannot force the label of a food to bear information other than the federally specified nutrition facts panel, weights disclosure, and other FDA-required label disclosures. The law allows an identical state law to be adopted, covering in-state foods that might arguably escape federal FDA controls. The 1990 law shows its political roots in exceptions for state maple syrup control (sponsored by the senator from Vermont) and for restaurant

---

3   *See* Voluntary Labeling of Milk and Milk Products From Cows That Have Not Been Treated with Recombinant Bovine Somatotropin, Interim Guidance, 59 Fed. Reg. 6279 (Feb. 10, 1994).

nutritional information, an area in which New York City had been a pioneering leader. Preemption of state powers by express congressional action is infrequent, but the food industry fought the states, and the industry's lobbying efforts succeeded.

Industry fears of states' label requirements had focused on the alarm about "label proliferation." Printing cylinders and shrink-wrap labeling offer great economies of scale for makers of national brand products. A change in a label from one state to another denies that marketer the savings in logistics that would come from a single label in fifty states. Retail chains endorsed the lobbying effort since their distribution of food often crosses state lines.

In California, cancer and birth defect warnings on products that contain state-listed chemicals are required under a 1987 law known as "Proposition 65." Industry wanted to preclude the state of California from enforcing that warning label law against national brands of food. Congressional debates led to a compromise that allows California to use its warning in the few cases where an ingredient in a food could cause cancer or birth defects; but other states are prevented from imposing similar requirements.

Examples and Illustrations

Scientists discovered that genetically modified hormones (GMO), implanted in cows, will generate a greater volume of milk consistently. Dairy A injects its cows and produces more milk; Dairy B declines to do so. Large retail chain sells lower-priced milk from Dairy A; consumer groups pressure chain to stop the use of the hormone; chain surveys shoppers; chain converts its suppliers to non-GMO use; and Dairy B can again sell its milk to the chain.

Persimmon Popcorn Inc. develops a fruit-flavored popcorn that has fewer calories, lower sweetener level, and a better taste than its original flavored version. Its new label says "Better for Diabetics," and a competitor complains to the Oregon Attorney General. The AG inquires and receives the company's data from a study of comparative sugars ingestion with different flavors of popcorn and diabetic physicians' opinions supporting the claim. The file is closed without action.

CHAPTER 4:
REGULATION OF RAW AND ORGANIC
FOOD SAFETY

Consumers know the difference between processed food and "raw" food, but they rarely know the differences in the safety systems that leave gaps in consumer protection. Processed foods are more likely to be inspected, tested, and subjected to quality control efforts; it is far less likely that the same measures would be taken for unprocessed, raw green vegetables and for fruits.

By raw food, we are referring to uncooked salads, tree fruits, seafood, etc. that have not been processed and are sold to be consumed directly— like apples, or after the the food the food is prepared by the consumer . Meat and fish are often sold by grocers in uncooked packages, to be cleaned and cooked by the end user. Farms, animal feed yards, and concentrated animal feeding operations like large chicken feeders, and increasingly "fish farm" aquaculture sites, can be significant sources of food safety problems. The rawness of the food puts consumers on notice that cleaning, boiling, etc. may be necessary. The legal system takes into account the expectation that raw foods will be cooked and/or cleaned before they are eaten.

By "organic" food, we refer to foods that are grown with agricultural practices using minimum quantities of chemicals and pesticides. The term has a rich popular cultural history in America, but Congress adopted a specific law in the 1990s to protect companies that were disadvantaged by false or misleading claims to the organic cleanliness or organic chemical-free status.

1. INSPECTIONS

Inspections by government agencies at food factories occur frequently, but regulatory visits to non-processed food sites, like an apple orchard, are relatively infrequent. While a factory that cooks and cans apple-sauce will be inspected periodically by state inspectors, and more rarely by FDA inspection teams, the apple grower who sells to individual or commercial buyers of apples will rarely encounter a health inspector who is interested or who is equipped to sample the pesticide residue levels on apples. Presumably, a state agriculture inspector has information about the EPA-permitted pesticides that can be used on apples. Presumably, a county health inspector could take samples of raw food from local sellers and submit them to a state food safety laboratory for safety testing. But these presumptions were assumed prior to recent budget problems in many state governments. The smaller apple producers are "below the radar" of the FDA, because their impact on interstate commerce is likely to be small, and their products do not regularly pose health risks that become urgent critical situations. So consumers in some states may falsely believe that inspections and safety testing is being done, when in fact it is not or it is being done less frequently than they would think.

That is not to say that apples are dangerous, of course, but merely to illustrate the effect that food product safety "supervision gaps" may have on consumer understanding or awareness of food safety. One of the historical ironies is that when major food legislation was debated in the 1930s, opponents from apple orchard states feared that federal control on pesticide use would spoil their industry. Today, very few apple orchards receive FDA routine visits.

2. SEAFOOD

The raw commodities that are most likely to promote the spread of disease are shellfish like clams, shrimp, and oysters. The interstate agreement on supervising these water-grown food items emphasizes that inspectors will pay close attention to points in the harvesting process where the critical health risk vulnerabilities arise. This is the role of HACCP, the system for the "HazardAanalysis of Critical Control Points" in the processing of food. State inspections of sanitation, appearance, and worker protections are augmented by lab testing of samples by the states and the FDA. But the FDA alone could not oversee this aspect of multiple sources, variable season lengths, and variable water conditions. Contaminants from water and field runoff wastes, human, and industrial wastewater discharge, etc., make the seafood industry subject to higher degrees of hazard-based inspection than other commodity food programs. If the state funds an aggressive testing program, it will incur costs but will reduce the safety risks of the products.

3. PESTICIDE RESIDUES ON VEGETABLES AND FRUIT

Raw foods are subject to FDA inspection and state inspection, and there can be significant enforcement problems when pesticide tolerances and exemptions are measured in imported shipments. United States food importers should work with the international suppliers to specifically limit the pesticides that can be used on vegetables and fruit that is to be exported to the American market. Bananas, fresh berries, coffee, and cocoa are among the large-volume imported foods that arrive in their "as-picked" form with minimal processing. If an imported food shipment is detained and then rejected because of an illegal pesticide use, this is a big loss to the exporter who had planned to expand its business with the profits of its sales in the United States. Government evaluation and then destruction of the shipment, probably including fees for inspection and costs of landfill destruction, is a major regulatory enforcement deterrent to the use of less costly, locally available chemicals on food crops that are being grown for export.

Worst of all for the food company, if the FDA determines a pattern of pesticide residue violations came from that company's shipments, an "Import Alert" could be imposed, and that will automatically reject from entry through U.S. Customs any shipments of foods by the suspected violator. Exclusion from the U.S. market may be the death sentence for a company whose plans had anticipated long-term U.S. customer acceptance of their products. But it also causes a short-term crisis for the company's shipments that are already en route. Imagine a set of loaded containers of food, sealed and sent off on a container ship headed toward a U.S. port with the equivalent of a million-dollar fruit shipment. The issuance of an Import Alert by the FDA means the fruit will be condemned upon arrival, "detained without physical examination" in Customs language. The importing company will refuse delivery unless the exporter can convince the FDA to drop the restriction for these container loads. The FDA in turn will refuse unless laboratory testing and other assurances verify that the product is not subject to exclusion. A few of these scenes will persuade a nation that exports food to the United States that its government needs to intervene more closely in agricultural exports and to prevent the use of "rogue" pesticides or excessive amounts of pesticide chemicals in food that is being sent to American customers. So there is a huge leverage for the FDA against foreign food producers.

A shipment from inside the United States that is sampled, tested, and found to have an illegal dose or an illegal chemical will be more immediately dealt with. The FDA will ask the producer to immediately recall, or else the FDA will obtain a court order to seize the "adulterated" food. The food will be quarantined and tested, and then federal EPA pesticide inspectors or state agricultural inspectors will visit the farm or orchard and determine what chemicals were used and whether there should be a large civil penalty imposed against the grower for illegal pesticide application to a crop. Pressure on the grower from a sudden loss of inventory and the anticipated sales income, combined with the expensive penalty for a pesticide violation, will serve as a discipline to induce the firm's compliance with FDA requirements in the future.

4. MEAT PRODUCTS

Animals prepared for slaughter are subject to USDA inspection at the packing plant and to USDA and FDA supervision during the pre-slaughter stages of growth. The FDA supervises medicated feeds, the quality of animal feed used, and any drugs such as antibiotics that are fed to the growing animals. Under its legal authorities, the FDA can take action to stop a farm from shipping to market any animal that has higher rates of drug residues than would be permitted in human meat food products. If a significant residue problem is found at a slaughterhouse, the USDA can shut down a plant, stop movement of animals from a feed lot, or impose penalties.

Animal feed and food contaminants are supervised by the FDA by law, but by state agriculture departments in practice. New food materials for animals that are not drugs or mixes ("medicated feeds") proceed through a state approval process with the American Association of Feed Control Officials. The labels of animal feeds must carry a certified analysis of the feed contents and describe its protein or other vitamin contents. As an example, when domestic animals like dogs began to experience serious illness from feeds contaminated with Chinese melamine, massive recalls were conducted by feed makers, with the oversight of state agriculture and FDA veterinary officials. The protection of animals from contaminated food is less vigorous than the comparable levels of human protection, but the legal punishments are about the same.

Of course, most raw meat will contain some amount of bacteria prior to cooking, and sometimes the illness potential of the meat is quite high if it is not cooked long enough and to a high enough temperature. Government efforts to reduce the spread of meat-related illness have emphasized education of the public to cook meat, especially chicken, to higher temperatures to kill the bacterial content. Raw meat consumption is not recommended because of the substantial risks of infection. Consumer self-preservation is one part of the defense against foodborne illnesses.

5. ORGANIC FOODS

The select minority of food products that are produced with minimal chemicals and pesticides are called "organic foods." The term has an interesting evolution, from a "back to the soil" rejection of mechanized, chemical-supplied agricultural industry to today's highly nuanced regulatory definition. Some of the uses of the term "organic" have not been in what originally might have been considered "back to nature" food items. Competing firms using divergent meanings found the field confusing; this led states to get into the issue, until a federal law was adopted in 1990.

Federal standards defining permissible practices and chemicals have been somewhat controversial since Congress adopted a uniform national organic food label law in 1990. In general, U.S. Department of Agriculture regulations set out the requirements; a USDA-certified group then conducts inspections and grants the right to use organic labels on those products that meet the organic requirements; and the practices and plans for growing produce, meat, etc. must remain within the plan and within the zone of permissible actions. The Code of Federal Regulations, Title 7, Part 205 gives very detailed information about the prerequisites for claiming organic status. The audit checklist is fifty pages when downloaded from the U.S. Department of Agriculture Web site.

Some observers have complained that the USDA allowed non-traditionally "organic" practices to be permissible under the "organic" heading, and that lessens the spirit of the traditional meaning of that term.

In general, consumers can rely on the validity of the "organic" status of food products that bears the USDA seal. A civil penalty of up to $10,000 can be imposed for selling as organic a food product that does not meet the standards. While this penalty has rarely been used, the threat of punishment is an incentive for compliance with non-chemical grower practices.

Examples & Illustrations

Farmers growing cottonseed for use in salad oils must contend with the boll weevil. When cottonseeds are crushed to extract their useful oil, whatever bugs were on the seeds would be crushed as well. The FDA inspected a cotton mill and found weevil remains. That cottonseed oil from the cotton mill had been mixed in with a much larger tank of about a million gallons of salad oil. The FDA condemned the entire tank because it became "adulterated" when the oil affected by weevils' "bug juice" had been intermingled.

Pesticides not approved in the United States should not be used on food crops that are intended for shipment to the United States, because no tolerance or exemption exists for them. After detecting problems over several shipments, the FDA no longer trusted the quality control efforts of the government of "Country X" in monitoring for residues of pesticide chemicals. The FDA subsequently issued an Import Alert calling for Detention Without Physical Examination of raw produce from "Country X." This shut down the extensive harvesting on farms and suddenly interrupted the shipping operations at the key port of the nation, as that country's food exporters could not gain financing once the lenders saw that the products were being automatically rejected at the U.S. ports of entry. The country took a major step forward in oversight of its agriculture by strictly limiting farmers' use of pesticides that had not been on U.S. lists of approved pesticides.

An unscrupulous shipper of nutmeg from "Country X" to the United States learned that weather in "Country X" would ruin the crop, allowing less nutmeg to be marketed here; so he added milk powder and wheat and mixed it with colors and flavors to make it appear to be nutmeg. The crime of economic adulteration of food is a felony; so the FDA responded to a competitor's complaint by opening a criminal investigation and used an undercover sting to discover the extent of the fraudulent shipment and the fraudulent involvement of corrupt government officials.

CHAPTER 5:
REGULATION OF FOOD PROCESSING AND INGREDIENTS

Food for the American table is processed in a wide variety of locations and geographies. The food supply chain into American grocery stores is increasingly global, not simply local. This global trend has accelerated in recent years because of consumer demand for food items ordinarily unavailable in the "off season," driving more purchases to different hemispheres or continents, despite the best educational efforts of local food advocates who call themselves "locavores."

This chapter addresses the safety of the process for making consumer food and the safety of ingredients used in processed foods. Ensuring adequate safety in the food supply is easier for commodity products like grains or rice; a consensus on how to protect the crops exists, and worldwide knowledge of safe handling conditions creates a norm of quality practices to which most U.S. importers will readily subscribe. The issues become more difficult for spices, ethnic food ingredients, or for other special ingredient users who depend on Peru, Mali, Niger, Yemen, etc. for a spice or a specific food material that could be a source of natural contaminants or that produces a vulnerable food item that could be intentionally abused by a potential terrorist or a potential cheater. Use of harmful chemical agents on a restaurant salad bar to frighten away tourists, or use of melamine in infant formula products to cheapen the production costs for that special food, are examples of this context for food safety.

Food security against criminal or terrorist tampering is a significant issue. A major international scare occurred in the early 1990s with news that Chilean grapes were threatened by a phone call made to the U.S. Embassy in Chile by opponents of the nation's military government, and then one grape from a shipment offered for import into the

United States appeared to have been injected with cyanide. There was a major upheaval in import markets that year; the FDA decided to urgently ban all Chilean produce from entry into the United States in response. Fear of poisoned food is so high among consumers and political leaders that a small but discernable risk would not be acceptable for the U.S. government leaders, despite the low actual risk to any particular consumer of the imported shipment.

Problems can occur with imported or mass domestic handling of commingled supplies of food ingredients from various suppliers. The food company's ingredient buyer needs to decide whether, under all the circumstances, he will be able to tolerate uncertainties that may arise when buying from a mixed source of food materials. The protection of the food marketer's reputation, consumer trust in that food, product liability concerns, and stability of sources are all factors that enter into the "food security" decision. Is this threat of contamination, fraudulent dilution, or other cheating a problem that is endemic to all vendors? Or is it specific to one source? Can we as consumers trust the food company's factory mixing operator to reject suspect or visibly bad-quality incoming supplies? Sometimes the importer or U.S. processor of raw ingredients will try to blend off bad or under-performing batches, blending them with good new product to get past the stage of inspection. "Oh, that will burn off" or "Sure, that will wash off in the process" are expressions that were sometimes heard from the purchasing department in the food producer's corporate structure. In today's regulatory climate of reporting potential risks (even those not likely to become actual harms), such an old-fashioned nonchalance would cause penalties and recalls to follow government discovery of the problems.

The public has an interest in knowing how the contaminant got into their food; the news media, the FDA, and the government of the nation from which the food came will be searching for the source of a hazard found after illnesses arise. Finding the source of contaminated food is made more difficult if multiple sources have been intermingled. Blenders of food from multiple sources can affect the ability of the FDA or the food packer to operate a future trace of defective raw material container contents, if such a trace were ever needed. The tracing potential, usually helpful to reduce recalls and product destruction, is also limited by a food vendor's frequent "spot market" purchases of a commodity. This lack of consistent sources will inevitably affect traceability once the problem is identified back to the incoming samples. In 2010, Congress considered legislation that would require U.S. and foreign food producers to adopt tracing systems for foods shipped into or from U.S. facilities. The details of these systems are likely to take several years to evolve because of the diverse nature of our food ingredient markets.

1. REGULATION OF INGREDIENTS AND ADDITIVES

The material used in or with food is regulated along separate lines of government classifications, categorized as food components, food additives, indirect food additives, and incidental additives. Food components include, for example, sugar that is an essential ingredient in candies. Food additives include preservative chemicals added to bread to keep it fresh longer. Indirect food additives include the chemicals added in coating machinery for semiliquid food to help it go through pipes in the factory, but which are expected to be removed before the food processing is completed. Incidental additives are such things as water added to hams to keep them from drying out during the distribution phase to consumer markets.

Because most of this book deals with finished foods and their components, like sweetened carbonated drinks and their sugared ingredients, this chapter will address the additive categories. In 1958 after extensive hearings, Congress required that all additives put into foods would be divided into two categories, "food additive" and "non-additive materials generally recognized as safe." The categories had a distinct consequence: new food additives must show very detailed safety information that satisfies the FDA that the ingredient will cause no harm. The "generally recognized as safe" materials (GRAS) were those so familiar and recognized that they either had extensive consumer experience or extensive scientific awareness of their safe conditions. In later amendments, Congress allowed the subset of food additives that are indirect additives, such as packages and bottles—not intentional ingredients— to be cleared by a "notification" process that was much easier than the detailed approval process.

The food additive clearance process that had been established in 1958 evolved and weakened as FDA career employees for food safety review were pulled away to other tasks. What had been a very technical process for proving safe usage, including the many toxicological and exposure measurements that such food additives could undergo as they reached FDA clearance, gradually weakened as the FDA had fewer scientists and more urgent tasks. At one time, the food additive petition for direct food additives was a very rigorous science process akin to the FDA's review of a new drug. Each element of the potential exposure was probed, with careful scrutiny of the animal and any human study of the food additive. The "Delaney Clause" explicitly barred any ingredient that would cause human cancer after appropriate tests and evaluation, so carcinogenic potential became a critical aspect of review. Over time, food additive approval staff budgets withered, backlogs grew, complaints accelerated, and the process became more difficult to justify without an adequate staffing budget from Congress for the FDA equipment and scientists needed to sustain the process. Europe and Asia cleared materials for food packaging in rapid clearance steps while the U.S. system was bogged down for years.

Congress responded to industry complaints in 1996 by establishing a system of notifications for food contact substances in a new law, Food Drug & Cosmetic Act section 409(h), found in the United States Code at Title 21, section 348. The FDA did not have to spend the scientific review effort necessary to approve the substance, so long as its submitted set of evidence of safety passed an initial screening step with FDA science reviewers. This eliminated the backlog of FDA clearances for plastics, resins, and other indirect materials that were not directly added to foods but that had been delayed for years awaiting FDA examination. This change allowed the FDA the option to file away, without taking action, a food plastics company's notification of a changed or new package material that appeared to present no concern. The 1996 law allowed the FDA to stop a food contact substance that was unusual or potentially troublesome. The product could be halted before it reached the marketplace, and the FDA then could require the filing of a full food additive petition. For example, pipes in a milk plant could be relined with a coating that the resin maker believed would not be released into the milk. The coating would be a food contact substance that could come onto the market for food plant use after notifying FDA, but without specific FDA approval. In the short review period after notification, FDA scientists might tell the resin company to perform all the extensive safety tests that previously had been imposed on such additives. From the FDA's perspective, this optional pathway allowed to FDA by the 1996 amendments frees up science resources for attention to the few cases in which a more intensive review of a novel plastic or metal food wrap would be justified.

2. REGULATION OF SAFE FOOD MANUFACTURING

Stages of the food manufacturing cycle are relatively uniform across all types of foods. The actual steps vary, but we can classify the cycle. This section of the chapter walks through the production steps and then evaluates the regulatory or legal controls that relate to each step.

a. Raw Material Sourcing

Sourcing of food components is the most traditional and most significant phase of assuring clean and safe food. "Sourcing a food ingredient" occurs daily around the world, of course. For our purposes in this book, sourcing is a generic term used to describe a transfer of a food ingredient or component from an original source, such as a grower, to an intermediary, such as a seed mill or grain elevator; this transfer may be done by corn farmers harvesting crops, dairy farmers drawing milk from cows, or ranchers bringing steers to slaughter. Water is the largest component of many food products, so a water well or a screening intake from a river or lake is the source of much of the "raw material" for beverages, sauces, creams, and other food items. Diverse suppliers with diverse problems—beetles in one region, mold in another, cheating on quality or weight in a third—must be taken into account by the prudent food processor. Experience with how to detect various types of food problems is a good foundation, but it is not enough; there must be flexibility, awareness of competitor developments, and intelligence sources to listen and watch for additional threats to the quality of the foods.

Regulatory controls at the sourcing end of foods are of several generic types: evaluation with chemical testing to prevent residues of pesticides in food; mechanical sampling and quality testing of a representative sample of the incoming food, especially for the raw food commodities that require screening or cleaning before importation into the United States; and biological evaluation, attempting to keep out the molds, infections, or pests that would otherwise affect the quality of the crops. Each has a cost, and the production of quality food materials requires that some costs get passed along to the customer.

The 2010 congressional legislation for food safety will force each food facility to prepare a detailed plan of where in its process there are "critical" points at which a safety problem could arise. The safety plan requirements will expand the examination of incoming supplies, and more documentation of the sources will be required. Tracing of components is also required. The food safety plan will be audited by FDA inspectors. In the event that a serious risk is found, the company responsible for the food will be required to notify its supplier about the risk finding, and must inform the distributor to whom the suspect product had been shipped. The 2010 law built upon what was called the Hazard Analysis of Critical Control Points ("HACCP"). HACCP methods had been used for years to find and prevent problems in meat processing plants. The food industry generally knows where in its process the problems are likely to arise; HACCP builds a regulatory planning dimension onto that existing set of knowledge.

b. Preparation

Cleaning and preparation of food is done either in intermediate sites, such as warehouses, or at the loading dock of the food factory. The goal at this stage is to screen out the expected set of contaminant materials, like twigs from cherries, so that the processing steps are easier to operate. Ideally the least desirable units or products are detected and rejected at this stage, if not before.

The regulatory controls at the preparation stage take the form of visual inspection and then physically drawing out samples from random spots in the flow of incoming grain, fruit, etc.. The samples then are tested to assure that the purity claimed for the shipment is actually present. Container loads of Asian or African raw materials are scrutinized at the port of entry to determine the level of purity of the shipment, and the food materials then are compared to the description in the legal documents, typically a bill of lading, which accompanies the container load.

The FDA announced that beginning in 2010 it would intensify its "environmental sampling" by taking samples of air, surface dusts, and possible bacterial sites around the food area, so it is likely that bags and storage containers will be evaluated for the presence of potentially harmful contaminants.

c. Fabrication

The fabrication or mixing step is the addition to the raw food of the liquid, dry, or solid materials that form the "recipe" for the food. For example, flour, sugar, water, and flavorings are "fabricated" into cookies.

Regulatory protection interests of the consumer are less urgent at this stage than is the consumer satisfaction interest: a product badly assembled is not going to produce a desirable end product, like a pizza with half the cheese expected. The company marketing the product has probably run several hundred batches of the recipe before it shipped the first batches of product to its customers. The mixing of ingredients is part art and part science, so the adequacy of the product may depend on the right sequence of addition, right timing and intensity of stirring, and right equalization of heat and moisture conditions in the batch that is being processed. The FDA does not control the problems of poor taste, wrong assembly, or unusual odor, but these consumer satisfaction challenges are part of the food marketer's overall quality assurance concerns.

d. Processing of the Food

The processing step for food may be cooking or steaming vegetables or meats, or chopping raw vegetables for salad bags, or baking, or otherwise converting raw into edible foods. This step is considered the most sensitive to problems due to errors in the factors of time, temperature, sequence of mixing or blending, etc. Especially where the cooking steps are expected to reduce harmful conditions, the processing step makes a great difference in product quality.

Regulatory protection for the public is most acute at this stage; inspection of the process, documentation, and the physical equipment are essential. Countless FDA and USDA enforcement cases have arisen from inspectors' close scrutiny of food factory errors in cooking, steaming, and other processing methods. Botulism grew in soup that was not properly processed; mold was not removed from beans that were undercooked; fish toxins were not cooked away by the proper conditions of time, temperature, and salinity of the cooking of raw fish. For liquids, the plant water supply may have been impure at the source, or there may have been "dead ends" in back-flow water pipes where contaminants could grow and which could be stirred up and then flow back into the liquid product. The food inspector's testing kit includes a thermometer, measuring scale, diagnostic tools appropriate for the particular pathogenic bacteria that could be found, and more. Finding the problem is a key step in correcting the problem for future batches.

e. Post-Processing Handling Steps

Holding the food after processing while it cools or while it is in bulk awaiting packaging is the next step. A large vat of syrup that is cooling from its heat processing in a cold storage area of a factory would be an example of this stage of production. At this stage, the batches that do not appear "good" or do not respond normally to routine screening should be examined carefully to detect any problem that might later manifest itself as a cause of illness.

If the food that regulators are inspecting is one that is susceptible to bacterial or viral contamination, maintenance of proper temperature will be a focus for the food quality inspector's measurements. Conditions that are too warm might allow the harmful bacteria to grow; too cold, and the product may be affected by the same risks that ordinary cooking was expected to alleviate. Sometimes problems appear as the product may turn gritty and chunky, instead of presenting a smooth emulsion, and this could be an aesthetic problem, a signal of unsafe conditions, or both. Cooks know this signal of problems from experience with undercooked or overcooked food in the restaurant setting. FDA and local health inspectors who monitor a wide variety of processing plants have learned this from training and from inspection of records on what were expected to be the conditions of processing for this food. More often than not, the company's planned cooking steps were theoretically adequate to safeguard the food, but a production worker's failure to follow the plan was not detected by the plant supervisor, and the defect was not found because of lax quality control oversight. Then the recall will be embarrassing and expensive.

f. Packaging Foods

Placing the food into packaging involves a long chain of planning, testing the potential containers, studying the retail "shelf life" of one packaged form over another, and so forth. Highly automated machinery transfers bulk food into consumer-size boxes or bags through an array of nozzles, pipes, and rotating disks. Like a precise ballet, the giant vat of precisely cooked tomato juice empties into 6-ounce plastic pouches that are heat-sealed and boxed and tagged and placed on pallets for shipment. Perhaps the simplest food packaging is the casing of sausages or large cheeses inside a food-quality plastic, wax or other container for distribution. What is in the casing or the cheese outer covering should be monitored by federal safety inspectors after appropriate pre-approval.

The regulatory overseer looks for problems upstream and downstream from this packaging step. Upstream, a natural question is why is this food's packaging designed in this way, with this foil or plastic, and can we really expect that the purity intended for this finished product will be protected by this chosen package? Is the can vacuum sealed and will it allow oxygen to enter, causing spoilage? How the particular food's design expectations were satisfied is the important issue; were corners cut in order to save money, and did safety of the finished food suffer from the cheaper, less sturdy packaging choices? Downstream in the factory itself, the inspector examines machinery and output very carefully. The inspector anticipates that holes in the rim of cans of salmon will allow toxins to grow because of the presence of oxygen. The inspector has been taught to look for ink that bleeds through the lining of the package and gets into the food itself. The liquids "cooked in the bag" may have been undercooked and unsafe. The FDA has seen many ways in which package choices and their actual implementation have made food less safe. FDA cannot belatedly find all the problems of particular foods; the work has to be done cooperatively with the responsible manufacturer and packager who has the most to lose if the food causes illnesses.

g. Distribution

The distribution phase of food production is often a vulnerability for foods that depend for their quality on retaining certain ranges of temperature. Spoiled milk, rotted cheese, and melted ice cream are familiar examples. These sensitive phases of cool or heat conditions are a challenge, because they are often contrary to the daily natural weather conditions in some of the distribution area. Ice cream must remain frozen in the storage facility, in the truck, and then in the grocery store's freezer cabinet. Fish for sushi must be kept on ice or otherwise refrigerated.

Local health inspectors and FDA food safety inspection teams bring thermometers and cameras to their task; the consistent cold temperature of the contents of a food delivery truck is a constant summertime challenge for food companies. If the temperature drops below a critical range, the food is ordered off-sale and should be destroyed so that the potential spoilage does not endanger consumers.

h. Rework

Reworking of off-specification batches of product, processing of retail store returns, and evaluation of complaints about product conditions are some components of the final stage of the food processing cycle. It is properly viewed as a cycle, since the rework stage often results in blending off the lesser quality beans, grain, etc. with the incoming raw material, so as not to waste valuable and sometimes expensive ingredients. Food is not treated the same as industrial widgets. Expectations of quality for food products are much higher than for industrial products. To preserve consumer allegiance to the food brand, the food marketer is obliged to accept returns on unsatisfactory food packages. The food processor often has a batch that is not quite right in color, flavor, or other attributes, and the batch is re-blended and diluted with raw materials to be run through the process again. Reducing rework is important to the economics of food manufacturing, so quality must be "built in" to the product. FDA looks at records of production and especially targets those plants that have a high rework ratio. Failure to meet quality standards in the first cycle is an indication of factory or warehouse conditions that are not supportive of the desired levels of quality.

Regulatory protection for the food supply requires safety officials to learn from past problems. Often, the product safety inspector focuses on why a particular component has failed. The re-blending of unsatisfactory finished product would seem to be the right thing to do. A health inspector has to ask whether the reason for rejection was something that reflects badly on the "do-over", for example a serious flaw whose replication in the second-round product would cause illness or injury. So the health inspector would prefer that finished food that was found (by quality control review or by consumer complaints) to have metal shavings should be destroyed. Conversely, if the beans turned yellow rather than pure green, the inspector likely will not object to the reprocessing of the off-specification yellow beans into another production cycle of mixed colored beans. Under the changes made by the FDA and by Congress in 2010, adverse effects from packaging problems may be required to be reported to the FDA and to the suppliers of packaging and the distributors who receive the food.

i. Paperwork or Digital Documentation Controls

Congress has given to the FDA extensive authority for the registration of food sites and producers. The FDA will then ask Congress for the funds to go out to the sites, especially in third-world nations, in order to inspect the safety aspects of food handling and preparation steps at the place of production. Review of procedures, experience of problems or of consistent quality, and close inspection of food processing facilities, is an absolutely essential step to achieving safe food. Quality results should be documented; outages and their follow-up should also be documented.

But collecting records of statistical results alone misses the target. The FDA should be inspecting documentation that the food company has applied HACCP methods the method of problem avoidance known as "Hazard Analysis of Critical Control Points". A well-informed HACCP inspection of the food processing site several times a year is optimal in cost and benefit, compared to the continuous inspection of meats that occurred along the production line of the old traditional USDA-inspected meat factories. The consumer did receive a perceived benefit in the old system of meat packer inspection lines, with some assurance of on-scene government oversight of each meat unit as it passed along the production line. But food experts assure us that the system for screening of plant quality through HACCP checks and audits is as helpful as the old ways. Assuming trustworthy private sector participants, and adequate measurements and timely responses to detected problems, this makes a great deal of sense.

Examples and Illustrations

Deaths among Wisconsin nursing home patients were traced to a peanut butter plant in Georgia that had improperly cleaned its peanut processing equipment. *Salmonella* persisted in the plant, and inadequate cleanout was done. Plant managers did not act upon the positive laboratory test results for *Salmonella*. A national recall eventually reached more than 1200 products made with some peanut component from that factory. The company went bankrupt, and the managers were investigated by the FDA and FBI agents.

A food warehouse had marks from rodent biting and fecal droppings when an FDA inspector visited. Workers with a sick sense of humor had posted a small sign, "Caution: Rat Crossing." The FDA obtained a court order seizing and ordering destruction of hundreds of thousands of dollars of food from that warehouse.

The manager of a commercial bakery was prosecuted for contempt of court after the FDA obtained a court order seizing the bakery's inventory because of unsanitary conditions, but the manager removed cookies from the inventory in violation of the court order. Once a court order is in place, the food is deemed to be under the court's control.

A Virginia ice cream factory was shut down, and a nationwide recall of its ice cream bars was conducted, after *Listeria monocytogenes* contamination was found in its water system, making it possible that backflow could bring contaminants into the water supply. So the desserts might be deadly to persons who were less immune to certain *Listeria*-related infections.

CHAPTER 6:
RESTAURANTS AND FOOD
SERVICE DELIVERY

1. CONSUMER EFFECTS

The restaurant meal that tastes bad usually leads to a lower tip for the server and a decision not to select that dining venue again. But the meal that literally sickens the consumer is likely to lead to a foodborne pathogenic illness event, like a serious bout of *Salmonella* or *E. coli* that causes a hospitalization. At best, a run of diarrhea results; at worst, the food causes choking and possibly death from airway closure, or the particular infection results in a disabling adverse condition like intestinal worms or kidney failure. We have all wondered at one time or another—"was it something I ate that made me sick?"

Choking on an unexpected obstruction in food should, hopefully, be resolved readily by fellow diners' maneuvers, pressing on the diaphragm in a way that forces the airway to expel the blockage. Serious infection that disables a person's immune system or causes other serious reaction should be readily diagnosed but may take a lengthy period to remediate. It is necessary to note the massive number of diarrhea and stomach problems caused by food microbial or physical contaminants that occur "below the radar" of health officials, and those problems cannot be accurately counted. The legal costs of challenging food suppliers tend to deter litigation arising out of suspected bad food situations.

2. FOOD SERVICE FACILITY SANITATION

The operation of the local government's restaurant health inspection system is effective in most urban centers; the most effective systems use posted grade signs, as well as Web site or newspaper ratings of sanitation for each inspected restaurant. Information like this deters misconduct or lax sanitation, as no restaurant can stay afloat if diners fear illness there. What is most important is the certainty for restaurant operators that health inspections will occur.

Sampling and equipment monitoring are standard methods of inspection. Water must be pure enough for cooking. Dishes and utensils are to be cleaned to a certain temperature in the wash; temperatures of the wash water and of the refrigerators that cool sensitive foods are measured during inspections. Each restaurant has generated a health department file of inspection reports and records of complaints, virtually always open to public inspection.

In 2009, the FDA and USDA focused on restaurant protections against *Listeria* infections, which can have serious effects for the elderly, infants, and pregnant women. The FDA will be using more environmental sampling, swabbing kitchen surfaces and testing the swabs for evidence of contaminants. In January 2009, the FDA proposed to change its "zero-tolerance" policy on the presence of *Listeria* in ready-to-eat food. The revised policy would allow a small amount of *Listeria* in cheese, deli meat, and deli salads as long as the food met certain conditions. This move of policy away from total protection was criticized by other agencies and consumer groups.

The FDA's retail-level Model Food Code addresses issues such as refrigeration and food handling, but because it is voluntary, it can be adopted in part or in whole (or not at all) by local health departments when they write their health codes. Voluntary adoption means that inspector training and performance varies among localities; this affects how well *Listeria* growth is gauged. In a January 21, 2009, Federal Register notice, the FDA said it knows little about how *Listeria* contamination occurs in retail establishments. A 2003 *Listeria* assessment found that deli meats present the highest *Listeria* risk, but it did not look at how the contamination occurs. The probable direction of FDA safety standards will be to toughen cleanliness and contaminant prevention requirements, which then would be part of the state, county, or city obligation to actually inspect food service sites.

3. LIABILITY STANDARDS

Every state's reported appellate decisions include cases of restaurant liability for damages arising from illness outbreaks caused by negligent sanitation practices. The law and case decisions will vary slightly, but commonly there is a high burden of care in assuring that the conditions of cooking, cleaning, and storing food will comply with health codes.

The principle underlying each state's actions is the assumption of a high duty of care by a firm that enters the food business. If the harmful event was, for example, a consumer choking on a meat bone, peach pit, or other ingredient that is "naturally present" in the food, it is likely that the lawsuit would be denied; court decisions suggest that some of these items would be expected (unless claims of "boneless," "pitted," etc. had been made about such a risk).

The injured plaintiff who has gone to court without settling is required to show some negligent acts by the food service provider. Considering the normal expectations of reasonable food consumers, claims about "bad" conditions are likely to be dismissed early if the plaintiff did not have support for his argument about the proper standard of care. Judges decide how to define for the jury what the restaurant's duty of care is to its patrons; then the jury may be asked whether that duty has been met in preparing the food that allegedly caused the harm. Facts and particular circumstances make a big difference, especially testimony or messages about the need to clean up bad conditions.

If a health or sanitation law or rule covers a specific obligation of the restaurant operator to perform a certain task, and that task is not performed, the restaurant may be fined or penalized by the local health department. In this situation, a person injured by the food can also sue the restaurant operator and can argue that this sanitation problem was "negligence per se" (an act that is negligent by itself, without need to prove more). In proving the element of negligence in a lawsuit for damages, the fact of the legal violation establishes the finding of negligence in states that use the "negligence per se" reasoning. This quickly delivers the finding of negligence that otherwise would have had to be established, with more witnesses and in more detail, by the injured person who is suing the food vendor.

Liability for a peanut processor, for example, would be shown by proof of a government penalty against that company for shipping infected peanuts, despite the company's awareness of the presence of bacterial contamination in the peanuts. Proof of the government finding of a violation is allowed to serve as a basis for finding negligence. Without a "negligence per se claim," the injured person would have to seek out more extensive technical data in the civil discovery process, paid for with its own funds. Another classic awareness of unsanitary conditions was the FDA penalty after an inspector observed a workers' joke sign "Caution: Rat Crossing" on pallets in a food warehouse. The known infestation was no joke to the FDA, which then condemned the suspect warehouse full of foods.

4. REGULATORY SCENARIO: HEALTH INSPECTION

Temperature, storage, and cooking conditions are important measures of quality in food preparation. Restaurants can expect periodic health inspections from local health inspectors. Awareness of infection controls is one aspect to be tested; another is the ability of the restaurant to maintain its sanitation equipment in good working condition. The risk to the restaurant operator is loss of licensure, and the devastating reputation harm of being "shut down for insanitation" by health officials.

5. PROBLEM INVESTIGATION

Epidemiology, the science of predicting the source of illness, involves the tracing of consumer exposures to potential causal factors and the creation of patterns of localized disease outbreaks. From these patterns of problems and illnesses, a specialist can conclude that the illness was probably related to eating a particular food at a particular restaurant. In a typical county, if forty cases of botulism were reported and all forty patients had eaten salmon sandwiches at the county fair, the salmon would be a primary vector of illness, the "prime suspect."

Health officials have great credibility with news media and the dining public. Publicity about transmission of foodborne disease can be fatal for restaurants and other sellers of foods. Causal connection of the illness and the restaurant are drawn carefully, with investigations coming usually within a week after the wide outbreak of illness is first reported. This pattern is a great incentive for restaurant operators to pay continuing attention to sanitation compliance.

6. PENALTIES

Government restaurant licensing by health departments is customary in every state. The restaurant's license could be revoked for serious or repeated sanitation violations. In addition to license suspension, the issuance of fines or penalties are possible. If a multistate problem arises, as with a chain of Mexican food restaurants whose salsa vegetables were sourced from a single contaminated site, the Centers for Disease Control will coordinate the investigation, and the FDA will use its field investigators to gather samples and to interview each participant in the food chain.

For franchise restaurants, the maintenance of quality control is a term of the contract. Serious adverse publicity about bad conditions at one franchise could harm the perceptions of diners about other sites. So the routine sanitation and compliance inspections by the franchisor will augment the local health officials' inspection cycles.

7. CARRYOUT FOOD SERVICES

There is virtually no difference in regulation of the food service operations for sit-down restaurants and carryout food preparation sites. The maintenance of quality in refrigeration, storage, insect prevention, clean utensils, worker hand washing, etc. are the same.

The difference is in liability related to causation of harm. Sanitation inspections of the carryout food shop are similar, but in the event of a lawsuit, the claims are more difficult to win, as the condition of the food after removal from the store will be disputed. The food was safe when delivered, the defendant shop owner will claim, but it was not maintained properly at a safe temperature after cooking because of poor handling by the purchaser. More of the risk profile of carryout foods depends on compliance by the buyer with reasonable good practices.

8. FOOD HANDLING

Storage and handling issues about food seek to deal with illness and spoilage caused by mishandling of food. Some consumers want an organic food experience with no preservatives. Others disdain vacuum or plastic packaging. The consumer who knowingly accepts risk and does not receive protection, like pasteurization, cannot later sue if the problem was avoidable.

Insects, overheating, or dirt and dust cross-contamination in storage areas are commonplace problems in food storage operations. The scrutiny of storage conditions is on every inspector's checklist. In some areas, truckloads of mixed cargos with foods and chemicals in close proximity may be challenged because of the potential that powdered chemicals got onto broccoli, for example, inside a moving truck. Health standards for ill workers and for prevention of disease transmission must be checked by all health inspectors in the tour of the food facility.

9. TYPES OF PROBLEMS ENCOUNTERED

The FDA's model ordinances and state health requirements for restaurants provide a backdrop for evaluating the safety of dining establishments, First on the list is pest control; next, the mechanical functionality of refrigerators (cold) and dishwashers (hot); then bacterial sampling of surfaces and observation of actual sanitation practices, avoidance of dirt and cross-contamination from one raw material to a finished plate, and so forth. The National Sanitation Foundation standards for clean equipment and clean water are among the norms that are expected to be followed.

Meeting a sanitation standard in an older facility is not easy, but prudent local health officials require the safety of the facility be "brought up to Code" where health could be compromised by ineffective refrigeration, water backflow, or other concerns.

10. TRUCKING AND INTERNET FOOD DELIVERY SERVICES

Some states have adopted laws or regulations that ban the shipment of food in the same vehicle with chemicals to prevent cross contamination. The widespread phenomenon of home delivery of refrigerated food products makes the quality and temperature efforts of the vendor increasingly more important. An expansion of mobile food facility inspections is likely to respond to this phenomenon, where local health officials have the funds to do so.

CHAPTER 7:
FOOD IMPORTATION

The U.S. food supply has become dependent on a constant inflow of food shipments from other nations. Fresh ingredients and produce cross the U.S. border constantly by ship, truck, train, and airplane. Imports of foods are in the millions of shipments each year.

Regulation of imports occurs for economic reasons such as protective tariffs aiding U.S. farmers, and for health reasons screening the contaminants to avoid harm to U.S. consumers. For some nations that export to the United States, a tariff or tax based on the type of goods and their shipment volume or weight will be assessed if the United States wishes to protect its domestic growers from foreign competition, and if treaty obligations permit the protective device to be used. Rice and sugar would be examples of food commodities on which a tariff is placed to shield American farmers, by making the more expensive U.S. production methods equivalent to the net price of the foreign rice per ton imported. The economics of tariffs are important, but are beyond the scope of this book's coverage.

Consumers rarely think about the legal structure that lies behind this remarkable commercial enterprise. Treaties between major trading nations, including the General Agreement on Tariffs and Trade (GATT), which is administered by the Geneva-based World Trade Organization (WTO), govern the limitations that nations can put on the movement of food and other goods across borders. GATT is sometimes referred to as a "free trade" treaty because of its reductions in the tariffs applied when goods are moved from one GATT nation to another, for example when Brazilian oranges are shipped to the United States. There are also "bilateral" trade agreements that give preferences and reduced tariffs to certain partners in two-way trade deals and "regional" agreements, like NAFTA for North America and CAFTA for the Central American and Caribbean nations.

Beyond these economic arrangements, each nation can operate its own food inspection and food quality standards operation. Food safety is a matter of significant national interest. But when food from another nation is excluded, the country that loses sales can file with the World Trade Organization a claim that the receiving nation has unfairly blocked its goods (has illegally imposed a non-tariff trade barrier). Countries that are challenged must appear in Geneva at WTO headquarters, appearing before a dispute panel of three nations' representatives, who will consider whether the exclusion of the imports was permissible because of "sanitary or phytosanitary" issues, i.e., the receiving nation's public health concerns, and whether the exclusion was within the permitted "sanitary" reasons for restricting a particular imported product. The WTO has the power to order the receiving nation to modify its barriers or eliminate them, or to pay a corresponding penalty to the nation affected. Bananas treated with DDT pesticides are excluded from the United States, for example, but the country shipping bananas would probably not win in a WTO challenge, because world safety experts have long concurred that DDT poses serious human health problems for persons exposed to that powerful insecticide. The "SPS" sanitary factor would justify the exclusion.

The safety aspects of incoming shipments of foods can be supervised at the ports of entry by U.S. Customs and Border Protection ("CBP") agents, working with FDA investigators assigned to each port. These are inspections which U.S. Customs coordinates with the FDA's resident Import Specialist who is assigned to that port. FDA import supervision consists of the review of categories of products which the computer system OASIS identifies, among the database of all shipments entering that port, e.g. all cargos of cherries expected to be landed by an air shipper at the Houston airport. A small minority of the flood of imports is inspected by hand or by sampling and laboratory analysis; the majority are passed without FDA action.

1. HOW THE FDA WORKS AGAINST IMPORT PROBLEMS

There are three means by which the FDA acts against problematic food shipments. First, it receives electronic notification of incoming food shipments at a central computer address. These international reports flow into an FDA/Customs central data base office near Dulles International Airport, Virginia. If the computer is programmed properly, it should then signal to FDA import specialists about the imminent arrival of a shipment of a type of food or food from a particular company or region, which may pose a health concern. The FDA then directs the private customs broker or other agent of the importer at the Customs warehouse to physically segregate the incoming load. The FDA then samples the shipment and conducts a lab screening test on a sample of food. During fiscal year 2008, the FDA collected about 22,000 food samples from import shipments. In the cases where prior shipments were deficient or dangerous, the FDA may have issued an Import Alert halting sunsequent imports from the company, the product, or the region. Then the FDA computers can be programmed to "red flag" the incoming shipment, and place an automatic Notice of Detention against it.

The odds of FDA rejection are startlingly small: 17,900 out of 16.2 million entries of FDA-regulated products were rejected in fiscal year 2008. A majority of both statistics were for food entries. (An entry could be a truckload, a bulk cargo, a drum, a box, etc. which has been identified as a specific import item in the Customs paperwork.) To be halted at the port of entry among the one-in-a-thousand of rejected loads, there need not be specific proof by the FDA that this unit is actually harmful or that it would injure consumers. The FDA can sample the food and then reject it as adulterated, or it can place the "DWPE" code against that product in Customs' data system, and it will be Detained Without Physical Examination, an exclusion that is virtually automatic. It is sufficient for DWPE that the FDA has a basis to believe the food does not adequately comply with FDA rules; then the burden is on the importer to show that its detained product complies with the law and rules of the FDA.

From the viewpoint of the non-U.S. company, the situation prior to 9/11 was far simpler. Shipments arrived, FDA sampled a few, most sailed through the port process. Notification by electronic messages before the food arrives is a paperwork burden imposed by Congress in 2002. Legislation that passed the House in 2009, and was pending as this text went to press, would require registration of participants such as farms and processing plants that are engaged in growing and processing food outside the United States for the American market. These sites could be inspected by the FDA overseas investigators, if it chose to do so. The new legislation also would impose tougher standards for importers and would make it easier for the FDA to stop imported shipments with detentions.

2. STATISTICS ON IMPORTED FOODS

The rising wave of food imports into the United States has had dramatic effects. Winter supplies of fruits and vegetables from warmer climates are commonly available. The statistics show that fruit imports (fresh or frozen) exceeded seven and a half million metric tons by 2006. The number of import "lines"—shipments of food products coming through U.S. Customs' ports of entry—is in the multiple millions. The volume exceeded the capacity of the FDA ability to inspect more than a tiny percent of the shipments. In fiscal year 2008, the FDA sampled only 22,000 food imports; the total import lines for all FDA products were over 16.2 million. A decline in the FDA's actual laboratory capacity to evaluate incoming food samples in 2000–2010 reduced the effectiveness of the import screening; without the technical evaluation support capability, field inspectors in the "front line" could not hope to rapidly detect contaminants, counterfeits, and infectious raw materials.

The problem of import food safety came to national headlines with the fraudulent contamination of Chinese food ingredients with melamine, a plastic component that mimics the laboratory profile of natural protein materials. The criminal act of fraudulent substitution of melamine in shipments during (at least) 2006–2008, caused illness and death in some pets and endangered the public's confidence in the safety of imported foods. Recalls and belated criminal convictions disrupted the animal food market and signaled a major vulnerability of protections.

3. EFFECTS OF "JUST-IN-TIME" LOGISTICS

Speed in the supply chain is beneficial in many respects; costs are lowered and inventory levels are reduced, while computerized management of logistics improves the delivery of materials to the food processing plant "just in time" for formulation of the finished food. One of the aspects of the former system that was costly, and was downsized during the recession in 2008–2009, was the routine practice among food processors to conduct a safety evaluation of key ingredients. This was often done by testing selected lots or reserve samples of food materials. The finished food shipments would then be held while tests were conducted to verify identity of the substance (e.g., that no counterfeit ingredients like melamine were present) and the quality of the substance (e.g., that there were no rodent feces or dead flies in the imported sacks of coffee beans). The elimination of this aspect of "delay" in the process saved money for the food processor, but it creates significant safety concerns. As the supply chain speeds up after the recession, the degree of scrutiny at some food plants has diminished to reflect economic conditions and time pressures. Management theorists had expected that suppliers would do more of the quality control work for end-product makers, like producers of canned soup. More dependence on the supplier to verify and assure purity is a noble, "total quality" objective. But if the supplier is a small overseas vendor of specialized foods, as many are, then their assurance of purity has little credibility in the event that illnesses caused by that food were to generate costly recalls and expensive lawsuits from U.S. consumers. By analogy, the importing company that brought defective tires from China to U.S. consumers could not get funding from China to conduct the recall, and it threatened to go bankrupt rather than conduct a required tire recall. The same will almost inevitably occur with food imports from smaller Asian or African exporters. In 2010 legislation FDA was empowered to seek a bond for the cost of the recall.

That quandary of costs-versus-quality is the central problem of post-"global sourcing" implementation. The FDA had built a system that essentially relied upon larger industry quality assurance efforts to augment FDA checkups. Unfortunately for the food consumer, those industry efforts were cut to save money at the same time that appropriations for FDA field resources were being diminished. The FDA assumed the industry's voluntary sampling and laboratory tests would catch any contaminated lots; but fewer voluntary lab testing programs are operational today as a result of cost-control measures in a very competitive and low-margin food industry. The FDA assumed a paper trail of pedigrees for the raw materials could be readily traced; but importers who tried to determine the real sources in foreign nations, like the fatal stories of sourcing the drug heparin that was processed from pig intestines in Chinese shops, found multiple frauds and heard dubious claims of product identity and quality. Congress has considered in 2010 new legislative requirements for the tracing of food ingredient shipments.

Another aspect of the globalization burden is an inherent difficulty in tracing problems of mixed foods back to the sources of each of the raw materials. Blenders of spices and flavors now move their sources of ingredients and the resulting mixed products around the world. So a contaminant in Vietnamese tea leaves may be mingled with Sri Lankan tea and flavors from the Philippines when blended in Taiwan for shipment to Texas. There is no "pedigree" for inspection by the FDA when the Texas-packaged tea causes harm to consumers in North Dakota and Mississippi.

The FDA has struggled with the complexities of the changing marketplace, and it is inherently difficult to trace these blended material concerns back to the source of the problems. More documentation, more registrations, and more inspections outside the United States will help, but there is no way to absolutely prevent some of the defects in foods that have been seen in recent years. Legislation in 2010 may relieve some of these tracing issues, but it will be at a cost to participants in the global supply chain.

4. IMPORT SCREENING ROLES OF THE FEDERAL AGENCIES

U.S. Customs electronic data systems for tracking, evaluating, and collecting tariffs on shipments are the primary means for the FDA to evaluate the need for inspecting incoming food supplies. The Bureau of Customs & Border Protection of the Department of Homeland Security has massive data entry and database screening responsibilities, with the monitoring of data for food safety evaluation being just one of many subordinate tasks.

The FDA designates one or more inspectors in its field offices as "import specialists." These individuals are responsible for tracking the types of foods and drugs that cross the border in their district. A large staff in New Orleans, for example, monitors ship-delivered grain imports, sugar and coffee, fruit, and other cargo from vessels, as well as air cargo coming into the international airport. A very small percentage of incoming foods are actually sampled; the FDA recognizes the mismatch of resources against the flood tide of imports. In 2008, FDA products accounted for 16.2 million "entries," and fewer than 18,000 imports were refused entry. New legislation in 2010 will require each of the foreign sites from which food ingredients were shipped into the United States to have an FDA registration number and to be open to FDA inspections.

The USDA has tighter control on meat, poultry, and egg imports than the FDA has on general food products, because the USDA specifically designates which non-U.S. plants are "eligible sources" that may ship meat into the U.S. market. The USDA has the assurance of quality at those selected plants, with the presence of U.S. inspectors or a national inspection system that is certified by the USDA. In 2009, the USDA imposed tighter controls on imported food that contains more than 2 percent processed eggs as an ingredient; the USDA will now require certification of the factory that is the source of the food.

In unusual circumstances of animal epidemics, the USDA can impose bans on movement of animals and of animal-derived products into the United States from other nations. This reduces the fear of cattle-borne diseases entering U.S. farm areas. In 2008, 3.7 billion pounds of meat and 22 million pounds of eggs and egg products went through the USDA importation system. More than half came from Canadian shippers.

5. ADVANCE NOTIFICATION OF FOOD IMPORTS

After the 9/11 attacks and the anthrax scare, Congress was concerned about screening food imports for potential risks and for terrorism, so in 2002, it established an e-notification system mandating submission of

Internet reports prior to the arrival of the food imports. Advance notice is required for any commercial shipment into the United States of foods (other than meats, which the USDA controls by restricting the permitted shipment sources to a limited set of inspected facilities). All of the electronic data forms flow into a central FDA/Customs processing office near Dulles Airport in Virginia. The system is supposed to "flag" problem shipments and thus bar entry of potentially harmful foods. The weak point of the system is in follow-up by the field inspectors, who cannot search every container and who cannot hope to follow up on every suspicious "lead" developed from the e-notifications.

6. WHEN SAMPLING IS LIKELY

An FDA inspection of incoming products becomes more likely under certain circumstances. FDA headquarters sends out to its field offices an annual list of inspection targets—a "Compliance Program" —requiring specific types of facilities to be inspected and/or amounts of foods to be sampled and tested. In factory inspections, using the HACCP system that looks for Hazard Analysis of Critical Control Points, import scrutiny may be identified as a key safety measure. FDA districts also have inspected on the basis of their past experiences with a particular shipper or with a type of food produced in that region or nation. The FDA may inspect more closely when the product could be a counterfeit, based on experience with cheating in past shipments of foods from that nation or region. Or if the food was re-exported after failing its import screening once, and then the food seller tries to bring it back through another U.S. port of entry, a closer FDA inspection is very likely, and the goods could be destroyed to prevent further re-importation.

The FDA has incentives to inspect more incoming food shipments, but it has to bear the practical downside of limited resources: FDA field offices lack the available laboratory capacity, and they lack sufficient experienced staff to perform all the tests that they would like to have done. About 800 FDA field office positions were cut between 2003 and 2008. Between 2004 and 2008, FDA inspections of imports declined by 6600, to 15,245; of these inspections in 2008, 6788 were food inspections. The numbers for samples declined even more dramatically.

7. WHEN IMPORT ALERTS ARE USED

FDA databases on food are part of its overall computerized import system. The "OASIS" computer system facilitates controls on incoming shipments of imported foods. The purpose of the database is to "flag" a shipment as being potentially high-risk based on past experiences. The FDA then can use the tool called the "import alert" to notify Customs officials and their data system to stop certain incoming shipments that are affected by the alert. If, for example, Nigerian terrorists had threatened to poison jojoba oil, the OASIS system would "flag" a container load of that product, and the FDA could issue an Import Alert that would require a halt to incoming loads while lab samples were taken and physical inspection was conducted at the port.

Companies and their import brokers are likely to object to the issuance of these alerts (except in cases of foreign counterfeiting, which is virtually indefensible), but the use of these alerts is a discretionary act for the FDA. Courts tend to side with the FDA on these highly fact-specific disputes.

The more significant problem for border inspectors was the "gaming" of the import system's information weak points, with multiple reentry efforts being made at various ports. The weak link in the chain is the one border crossing that does not catch the bad food that had been rejected by other ports. Congress responded to this game by allowing the FDA to force the rejected goods to bear a clear marking on the container: "REFUSED BY U.S. FDA" labels are intended to deter attempts at reentry of the product which the FDA has rejected from entry for safety reasons.

8. ENTRY UNDER CUSTOMS BOND

Considering all the problems of contaminants, infectious agents, and residues that incoming food may carry, it is necessary for U.S. Customs to have a system for allowing temporary control by an import-receiving company for the reconditioning, screening, and cleaning of the incoming shipment. A release under Customs Bond provides this system for remedial action. Like bail for an arrested person, the posting of a cash bond assures that the importer will return the goods for a second inspection, so as to avoid loss of money in the amount of the bond. The size of the bond relates to the value of the food import in the shipment. Forfeiture of the amount of the bond occurs if the suspect foods are not returned for a new inspection; steeper penalties by both Customs and the FDA can result if the risky food reaches U.S. consumers.

9. DETENTION OF FOODS AT ENTRY PORTS

The FDA has the power to stop the imported food shipment for thirty days, and during that time, the food cannot be moved without FDA permission. For perishable foods, this thirty-day hold can mean the ruination of a shipment. The detainer action at the port usually involves the company that acts as "import broker" for the shipper; that firm typically negotiates with the FDA on such things as a method of improving the labeling, screening for potential contaminants, and correcting inadequate paperwork. Lab work to evaluate the condition of the incoming shipment is typically required and will be paid for by the importer.

This detention power is separate from the FDA's general authority to detain food (domestic or imported) which it believes by "credible evidence" could be seriously harmful to humans or animals if the suspect food were to be consumed. The import detention is most likely to be used when paperwork such as a prior notification was not submitted, or where an Import Alert has been posted against that shipper or food source.

Proof of danger is not required for the FDA district office's import specialist to place a detainer on a food shipment. The quick response of the broker, its receiving customer, and the shipper will usually result in dissolving the detention.

The FDA likes to act rapidly and informally at the border posts, since many of the incoming foods are perishable. Companies have less room to negotiate against the FDA, and fewer legal rights apply to imported products at the U.S. border, compared to domestic manufacturers. The FDA can provide a quick, informal hearing to the importer, at which the emphasis will be on rapid corrective action of the apparent deficiencies in the imported food. In some cases, competing laboratory analyses clash, and the FDA will negotiate for a third test.

10. FDA POWER TO DETAIN AND DESTROY

The FDA as an institution dislikes taking risks. Risks from bad food include death, so the FDA has the power to destroy dangerous incoming shipments. Some imported food containers show contamination, defects, or potential fraudulent claims, so the FDA responds by detaining the shipment, ordering it to be destroyed or re-exported, and also requiring the containers to be marked "U.S. FDA REFUSED ENTRY." Re-exporting of food and its attempted re-entry into the United States was a problem before the legislation changed in 2002, and some marginal players are still trying to game the system.

Destruction of imported foods, whether through the importer's abandonment or FDA seizure to prevent harm to consumers, is a drastic remedy. The FDA uses this remedy to prevent the worst food from being re-shipped elsewhere. Examples of fatal effects include a shipment of Chinese glycerin, rejected in the United States, which ended up causing deaths in Haiti when used in medicines for children. "Catch and release" may work in fishing, but it has fatal effects in contaminated ingredient importation, so destruction makes more sense than allowing re-exportation.

CHAPTER 8:
ADVERSE EXPERIENCES WITH FOOD
AND THEIR CONSEQUENCES

1. WHAT ARE LIKELY ADVERSE EVENTS FROM FOODS?

Are you feeling sick after yesterday's picnic? Infection with a serious bacterial or viral illness is the most frequent adverse event associated with consumption of foods. The food producer's inability to protect consumers from exposure to toxic strains of *E. coli* or *Salmonella* or *Clostridium difficile* may reflect a company's lack of attention to the details of safety, details that many other food processors have mastered. Food can be made and packed and shipped without exposing consumers to pathogenic contaminants; most food is healthful and unaffected by negative effects of these contaminants. The CDC estimated in 2008, based on recent years' reports, that each year 76 million Americans get sick, more than 300,000 are hospitalized, and 5000 people die from foodborne illnesses.

Illness from spoiled or defective foods is a second issue. The rotten aspect of a fish, for example, should be able to be smelled or seen by the normal adult fish customer. The worst cases are silent killers, infections resulting from unnoticed failures of canning or other packaging, which results in a festering contaminant such as the degraded salmon in poorly sealed cans that exposed many consumers of a certain brand of Alaskan canned salmon to risks from toxins that ordinarily could not grow in a sealed can.

Choking on hard objects in food is a third, and quite avoidable, risk. Fish bones and chicken bone pieces can choke an adult; smaller bones or hard objects can cause a child to stop breathing. The food preparation process should have included a risk analysis that routinely checked for these kinds of "foreign object" risks. Physical defects that could cause injury can be screened out by attentive workers in a prudently planned food manufacturing plant. Doing such a screening saves lives and in the longer term, it saves money for the company on the costs of recalls and regulatory responses.

Contaminants like glass, plastic, dirt, or other materials that get into prepared foods can cause serious harm, since they are unanticipated risks. Crunching down on a roach in a roll, suffering scratches to the mouth from unseen nails or glass, or finding half a dead mouse in one's dinner, are disgusting, scary, and highly litigation-prone moments. The common element is that they are avoidable problems. A food consumer gets the benefit of lower food prices but the expanded risks of exposure to problems that could have been caught by spending more on quality control, supplier education, and planning to detect potential microbial contaminants. Congress in 2010 may adopt laws that compel food firms to have written safety plans, hazard analyses and means of controlling their potential food problems. The more prudent companies already spend their capital and devote personnel time to quality assurance; after several well publicized incidents with imported food contaminants, the 2010 legislation is a response to the public's demand that government should impose more safety controls on all food providers.

2. HOW FOOD CONSUMERS CAN COMPLAIN EFFECTIVELY

Yes, you *should* tell someone in government about this sickness episode! Government employees who receive health complaints about food sellers typically have years of experience. "They've heard it all before", you might think, and so the health inspector or consumer affairs officer can sometimes appear dismissive of a particular complaint if the illness or injury was not serious. Since the government hotline operator has heard a lot about a certain type of food illness, a bad experience that seems surprising and upsetting to a consumer may be just another familiar complaint to the health official. But, yes, you should make the complaint anyway, because patterns and frequency of consumer feedback are important in deciding what steps the government agency will take. Even if the recipient of the phone call does not promise immediate relief, your piece of informed experience will be tallied with others to direct prioritized government inspections and follow-up actions.

What will happen next? Short of a hospitalization or death case, the routine minor comment about illness or injury from food will not result in a sudden government shutdown of the food plant—but all complaints are tracked, using the experience based approximation that for every individual who files a complaint, five to ten others had a similar experience. but did not choose to make an official contact. So a plant whose food causes fifty complaints may have sickened hundreds of consumers. If the food problem with this brand, or this restaurant, suddenly spikes on the curve of frequency of all complaints, something will be done soon. If one fatality or paralysis complaint arrives from a treating physician's suspicion about the food source, a government health inspector will respond immediately.

To be most effective with your complaint, write down some notes before you call. The following questions are frequently asked by the employee who takes these calls:

- What are your symptoms?

- How long have you had these symptoms?

- When did the symptoms appear?

- How long before they appeared did you eat this food?

- Did others who dined with you have the same ill effects?

- Were there other foods consumed at the same time that might have seemed troublesome, for example, off-flavor or off-color in appearance?

- Did a doctor or a clinic run any tests on you as a result of the complaint?

- Has this type of illness been frequent for you in the past?

- Do you have any known food allergies?

- Did you read the food's label before you purchased, cooked, or ate the food?

Writing these items down will prepare you to be less nervous during these typical inquiries. If you and your doctor had discussed possible sources of the illness and you believe it is a food-borne illness, be sure to inform the health official of your doctor's comments about the potential causes.

Focus the complaint on the correct level of government recipient, one that is most likely to take action. Call the local health department first, if the problem is with a restaurant or carryout food location in your city or county. If the food supplier is in your region, but not local, then contact your state health department's food safety office. (In some states this is part of the agriculture agency; in others, it is part of the consumer affairs or attorney general office.) If the problem arose after eating a packaged food sold in mass market grocery retailers, then call the federal Food and Drug Administration district office listed in the white pages phone book or at http://www.fda.gov/, and ask for the consumer complaints representative. FDA has a specialist designated to receive calls about food or drug quality problems.

3. FOOD COMPANY RESPONSES

Adverse events are almost always reported to the company who is identified on the label. Food problems may seem inconsequential, but they will be reported at some point—usually when the individual food consumer's level of concern rises. At some point, the concern about food problems would exceed the "hassle" involved in making the complaint, if a hotline is available. From the viewpoint of the companies receiving complaint calls, a small percentage of the complaints will be dismissed politely because the caller has apparent mental or emotional problems. A small percentage will be actionable, and a refund check will be sent promptly in the mail, while the factory managers search out records of the batch that had defects or contaminants. Most complaint resolutions will be exercises in the preservation of goodwill—the long-term relationship in which the food firm tries to keep the customers happy— with an apology, a coupon or refund, and an empathetic ear. The disappointed consumer usually talks with others, and to the extent she or he can be accommodated, dozens of future sales of that brand can be preserved. Presuming that your food seller wants to keep you as a consumer, there should be an accommodation. Presuming that the food seller wants to stay in business, it will make an accommodation with the government health inspection staff to respond actively to a legitimate complaint.

Within the small number of consumer complaints that seem actionable—appropriate for corrective action by the factory or perhaps a formula change by the product development group—the company's response is a bellwether of how the company itself is operated. Under the federal 2010 legislation and its state counterpart laws, public health officials intended to hold the company accountable for its problems and the companies are expected to communicate risk situations to health officials in a timely manner.

Genuine and prompt responses that show a sincere desire to "make it right" for the consumer will lessen the potential for lawsuits, and certainly will lessen alienation among the group of friends of the complaining person. Bloggers who are vocal consumer advocates thrive on conflict; disarming the conflict early, by an effort to apologize and correct the flaw, is the best way to avoid an Internet perception that the food product is "controversial" or "suspect." No one can guarantee that all consumers will be mollified by the company's response. Veterans of the food industry's consumer response network know that early inter-actions with the consumer will appease a complainer.

4. HOW THE GOVERNMENT TYPICALLY RESPONDS

Some consumers call, e-mail, or write to the food maker with their com-plaints. A smaller percentage of dissatisfied food consumers contact a local health agency to complain. The local inspector may request a sample of the food for analysis, if any remains, and will likely contact the company for results from its own sample evaluations. With some serious illness outbreaks, like Shigella or E. coli 0157, state epidemi-ologists (physicians who track disease occurrence or health risks in state health departments) can connect the numerous outbreaks and form tentative conclusions that the product was "associated with" the illness, or after review of more data, that the product had "caused" the illness. For example, a school's gala party served seafood that was undercooked; the *Shigella* infection suffered by dozens of school par-ents and alumni was evaluated by state officials after numerous calls from hospitals and physicians; and the outbreak was traced back to the sanitation weaknesses of the seafood supplier.

5. HOW THE FDA RESPONDS TO FOOD PROBLEMS

A small number of food consumers will call the FDA hotline for their state, listed on the FDA's Web site under "consumer complaint coordinators" (http://www.fda.gov/Safety/ReportaProblem/Consumer ComplaintCoordinators/default.htm). Those with complaints about meat or poultry will be referred to the USDA at 800-535-4555, to pres-ent a credible health complaint there. FDA coordinators for the state or region will then coordinate the follow-up by inspectors from the FDA district office for that area, with the state health officials who have jurisdiction.

An interview with the consumer will ask about symptoms, timing, other food consumption, and will seek to take a sample for analysis. Samples of the food are taken from the home of the consumer and from the retail supplier. FDA laboratories will check the samples and determine a prob-able causal connection to the illness. After the evidence is evaluated, the FDA may inspect the factory, sample the products, measure the potential sources of contamination, and could take enforcement action if the firm had not been complying with FDA requirements.

If the FDA lab analysis of the samples indicates a causal link, then the FDA's next steps may be to obtain the medical records of the patients who complained and enter summaries of these into a database that allows CDC and FDA epidemiologists to search for causal connections. The voluntary recall or other responses by the prudent food company should follow. Ideally, the company's cooperative aid to the FDA includes responses to the inspector's questions about the experience of the company's designated consumer contact or call center: what were the numbers and patterns of the 800-line and e-mail contacts; how did the call center react to each call; what did the trend analysis show?

The importance of production codes on the side of food packages becomes evident when the need for a possible recall arises. "Use before X date, J23F6" means that the product was produced on a certain date and hour, on a certain production line. Factory records on that particular lot of products can be obtained, and the comparison of the lab findings from the consumer package and the lab results on products as marketed will help the follow-up on the problems.

The powers of the federal Food and Drug Administration to challenge a food firm are significant. A food company's lawyers cannot overcome a challenge by an agency like the FDA unless the FDA staff has made a significant factual mistake; courts will cut a lot of slack for protectors of public health. In virtually all cases, food makers want to "keep the peace" with the FDA, and they willingly participate in follow-up testing of the questioned food items. FDA District office consumer affairs employees track the number and severity of adverse events reported for a particular food company, product, or plant. Headquarters staff reviews trends for national food marketers. Follow-up calls to the company and on-site inspections can be expected, with the speed of follow-up dependent upon the degree of illness or hospitalization alleged to have been associated with that plant's foods.

The worst situation for the company would be a premature denial of any problems, in response to a government call or written inquiry, but which then is followed by a subsequent group of similar complaints. Harm to a company's reputation for honesty is one negative "fallout" from certain statements made during recall situations. "We never knew. . . ." statements recorded at the plant by an FDA inspector might clash with the set of internal quality control records which the FDA later obtains, showing ample knowledge of the specific risk. The worst cases are those with internal company memoranda that demonstrate a calculated risk of non-recall and non-reporting in the face of growing evidence of the injurious nature of a certain formula. Future litigation would be boosted by internal emails at the food company with messages like: "Yeah, we could pull that flavor yogurt off sale, but it would cost us a bundle!"

Imagine the flat denial by Perfect Yogurt Inc. that its yogurt factory could have been the source of any problems. "Foreign materials" contamination, like metal shavings that fall into a yogurt container, for example, might spread pieces of sharp steel into a few hundred containers over a ten-minute production time at that yogurt plant. Here we have an acute risk of mouth or esophageal cuts, from an unexpected contaminant, that is masked from view by the creamy nature of the yogurt. FDA rules require makers of food products to mark a perishable packaged food item with a visible date. Milk carton "best if used by" dating is the most familiar example. Under the 2010 legislation, FDA has the strongest powers in its history to pursue the food company that under-responds to the food safety issues.

The FDA tracks consumer complaint trends constantly. The FDA expects that a company will quickly respond with a targeted product recall if contaminants are suddenly found in the product. The size of the food recall may be small and may reach only a dozen retail outlets that are selling this particular product. Or illness or injury might be a severe risk, in which case the FDA may want a more sweeping protection for consumers by "erring on the side of caution" and holding a nationwide recall of all the marketed units of production.

6. THE RECALL DECISION

A food firm must be ready to identify a pattern of complaints that suggests a health problem with its food and may be required to operate a product recall. The decision to recall is not easy, but it is a cost of doing business in a field where product problems can have an impact human life and health. The first decision the company usually makes is to stop further movement of packaged foods, pending inquiry into causation. Then the firm decides what units to target in its recall. The FDA and USDA have extensive provisions for recalls in their guidance documents and regulations. Several of the appendix materials in this text are useful reading for consumers who want to know more about government's food safety efforts.

7. THE FDA'S REPORTABLE FOOD REGISTRY

Regulatory controls on food safety emergency situations dramatically increased in 2009 with the announcement of an FDA enforcement program to implement portions of the 2007 Food and Drug Administration Amendments Act. The FDAAA had created a "Reportable Foods Registry" in response to slow reporting of problems by some food processors such as the 2008–2009 recalls of peanut products by a small Georgia peanut processor. The implementation of that Registry caused the food industry to pay much closer attention to potential harm situations, and as this text goes to press, there remains some controversy over the new program and its scope. Appendix 4 provides FDA's view of the new Registry.

The FDA's Reportable Food Registry has several elements that consumers of food should appreciate:

• Reporting to FDA is required within twenty-four hours

• Mandatory notice by the food company to its supplier and its direct customer, e.g. the peanut supplier and the distribution warehouse

• FDA required to analyze and send out alerts

• Mandatory reporting if the food has a "probability of causing serious adverse health consequences or death"

• Mandatory investigation of the cause of the serious problem if it occurred at the reporting company (not received as a shipment from elsewhere)

The rules went into effect in September 2009, and the FDA began to use its new powers for the punishment of noncompliance in December 2009. As the FDA explained the working of the new system, its enforcement team screens all incoming notices of the potential contaminants or sources of harm. The FDA began with daily meetings of a cross-functional team of specialists, selecting which inspections needed to be performed, at what levels there should be product recalls, and tracing the potential risks to their sources. Trends are to be examined over time, with special attention to the recurring problems in a particular product area. The FDA was given strong penalty powers in the legislation, and it told the food industry in 2009 that it would aggressively seek to punish companies that knew of a serious food problem which could cause serious illness or injury, but that declined or delayed reporting of that problem to the FDA. (Please refer to Appendix 4 for the Outline, and to Appendix 3 for the internet websites that provide background information.)

8. THE MEDICAL CARE PROVIDER ROLE

Patients who go to physicians, clinics, or hospital emergency rooms with the effects of food "poisoning" offer a treatment opportunity as well as an educational opportunity. Front line health care providers can recognize from experience that symptoms match a particular pattern; and the diagnosis leads to a particular therapy in response. But the nurse or physician should "teach" the patient how to avoid a similar problem in the future. Thorough cooking of meats, refrigeration of creamy salads, and thorough washing of surfaces that hold raw chicken, are among the "how-to" steps that should be recommended at this particular "teaching moment" for the family of the patient. Putting off sanitation or cooking improvements may be normal in the wave of incoming information that everyone sees or could see if they wished; but when the consequence is an injury or illness, the family of the patient is especially "ripe" for this cautionary instruction.

Hospitalization of a patient for treatment by intravenous fluids may be appropriate in more serious cases. Serious infections sometimes require antibiotic therapies; sometimes a surgical response may be needed to deal with the effects of a contaminant.

9. CENTERS FOR DISEASE CONTROL ROLES

Food safety sometimes involves solving mysteries. When groups of people who each had ingested a particular food have developed similar symptoms, analysis of the patterns of illness requires statistical awareness and medical diagnostic skills.

Federal and state officials coordinate their efforts to solve the puzzle of causation. Epidemiologists do their best to find out why illness had occurred in groups of people. The CDC will publish a report via its newsletter, the MMWR, by its Web site, or by press conferences.

10. LAWYERS' ROLES

A tiny percentage of food adverse effect problems result in lawsuits. Companies or attorneys dealing with claims of illness assemble claim files consisting of medical records, technical and historical information about the product, and its similar experiences. To obtain the complaining patient's medical records, attorneys need to first obtain informed consent under the federal HIPAA. After paying the retrieval, processing, and copying fees, the records are sent to an evaluation advisor, who may be a nurse, for an assessment of whether there is a sufficient factual basis for the cause of the illness to be connected to the product, to warrant filing a lawsuit. Most plaintiff lawyers reject many more cases than they accept. The system of paying the lawyer only if the case is won or settled ("contingent fee") acts as a discipline to control the willingness of an attorney to invest time and money in preparing a food injury claim.

Most cases involve a consumer complaint of illness that did not reach the level of a filed lawsuit. Negotiation of the patient's medical payments will be an important task for the company's insurance carrier. The company probably will offer to reimburse medical care costs and to pay a small amount for the consumer's trouble. Corporate "risk managers" seek releases for the settlement payments so that the closure of the file ends the company's liability for that food problem. Diplomatic sensitivity when dealing with an angry parent of a sick child is a learned trait that comes with experience.

Unless a fatal or serious long-term effect occurred, most litigated food cases end with a small payout, commonly with a pretrial settlement and dismissal. Exceptions are the serious illnesses experienced by a class of dozens of consumers in a city or region. For these, a multi-person "class action" lawsuit might be considered. The large pool of funds that a class action could generate will make those lawsuits far more attractive to the lawyer. Class actions make it possible for litigants to justify the expense of researching, managing civil discovery, and dealing with pretrial motions.

11. CONSUMER ORGANIZATION ISSUES

An Oct. 6, 2009 report by the consumer organization, Center for Science in the Public Interest, tabulated the product recall and illness complaints for common foods reported to certain government agencies since 1990. The CSPI report listed ten top categories of foods with problems:

LEAFY GREENS: 363 outbreaks involving 13,568 reported cases of illness

EGGS: 352 outbreaks involving 11,163 reported cases of illness

TUNA: 268 outbreaks involving 2341 reported cases of illness

OYSTERS: 132 outbreaks involving 3409 reported cases of illness

POTATOES: 108 outbreaks involving 3659 reported cases of illness

CHEESE: 83 outbreaks involving 2761 reported cases of illness

ICE CREAM: 74 outbreaks involving 2594 reported cases of illness

TOMATOES: 31 outbreaks involving 3292 reported cases of illness

SPROUTS: 31 outbreaks involving 2022 reported cases of illness

BERRIES: 25 outbreaks involving 3397 reported cases of illness[1]

(Data from www.cspinet.org, Center for Science in the Public Interest Web site)

---

[1]   *Leafy Greens, Eggs, & Tuna Top List of Riskiest FDA-Regulated Foods* (Oct. 6, 2009), *available at* http://www.cspinet.org/new/200910061.html

The CDC and FDA data that was used in compiling the group's report offers an insight into the problem-reporting systems as reported for today's foods. The data might make the uninformed consumer afraid to eat leafy greens, for example. But the reader should note that the reports are a tiny sample of all the food consumed in the U.S. over the 18 year period 1990–2008, and these outbreaks did not all have the same health concerns.

Examples and Illustrations

A bakery supply company receives a shipment of almond paste from Mexico for use in baking pastries. The paste is shipped out the next day to fourteen bakeries and makes it into buns sold to 800 consumers. Several reports of illness come to the bakeries. The local health department contacts the federal Centers for Disease Control, which determines that a bacterial problem in almond paste was likely to have been the cause of illness. The CDC then notifies the FDA, which inspects one of the bakeries, tests some remaining paste, and notifies the bakery supply company. The bakery supply company can then be liable for damages to the consumers in lawsuits, so its insurer and its lawyers become involved. The bakery can be urged by FDA to conduct an immediate recall of the buns containing the suspect almond paste, and to notify the press to advise consumers of these buns that they should not eat any of the almond-flavored pastries. Because the supply company was unaware until the FDA ran the tests to determine contamination, the supply company would probably not be punished by the FDA, though it would have both reputation and commercial-refund losses and would have exposure to new lawsuits from injured pastry consumers. After all the economic losses and potential lawsuits are totalled, the companies may demand that the Mexican supplier reimburse for the losses, but this is unlikely to occur and the insurance rates of the U.S. firms will be increased to recoup the losses incurred by the insurers.

Five parents and three physicians of a national total of twenty-three children, who were reported as being harmed by Cereal X, have complained to the FDA that the cereal's unique size is a choking hazard. The FDA sends a warning letter to the maker of the cereal, who replies that the food is safe for millions of consumers, and refuses to act. The FDA could choose to take action for non-reporting of a potential serious food hazard, but even with powers expanded by the 2010 legislation, FDA does not have enough resources to pursue all of the possible food problem cases. State officials are likely to decline to take enforcement action since the product was nationally sold and "is a federal government problem." Assume that the five parents retain a class action lawyer to sue for negligence; a count in their lawsuit for "violation of the FDA law" is dismissed since there is no private enforcement of the FDA law. The maker of Cereal X argues that different results from each choking incident make these cases unique to each set of facts. The argument defeats class action status and the company then settles the claims for a small amount. The company, without public notification, reduces the size of the cereal pieces.

CHAPTER 9:
DIETARY SUPPLEMENTS

The reader should know at the outset that your author believes in the efficacy of certain dietary supplements and uses them daily. But the advertising for some fraudulent products, with illegal exploitation hiding behind the sound policies that favor honest supplements, has ruined the credibility of all supplements while enriching a few unscrupulous marketers. Much of what follows in this chapter may be perceived as criticism of the field. That may be deserved. Lawyers and lobbyists representing the less honest, less ethical end of the supplements field have profited greatly by constraining government efforts to protect the public. The baseline of medical effectiveness for many dietary supplements is well established, but the baseline of bad marketer conduct has tainted this segment of the food industry in ways that affect its longer-term credibility.

1. FRAUD AND DIETARY SUPPLEMENTS

We begin this chapter with the topic of fraud because that is the experience of most readers: believe the weight loss claim, buy the pills, take the pills, and see no benefit. The credibility of dietary supplement makers has suffered because so many of the consuming public's experiences with peer sellers of supplements have shown some companies to be liars and cheats. Fraud in the marketplace is facilitated by distant sellers' thievery via the Internet. Virtually all adults and many older children have made a purchase or been induced to make a purchase that has turned out to be a waste of money, compared to the anticipated effect. Male enhancement and libido products and diet and weight control products lead the list of fraudulent and profitable scams in the dietary supplement marketplace.

It is unfortunately true that the loudest aggressive claims for quick physiological benefits from dietary supplements are often fraudulent, overstated, or squarely contrary to objective scientific evidence. Optimism about results or "willful blindness" about problems is not enough to make advertising claims lawful. (Appendix 1 provides the Federal Trade Commission's view of what advertising would be lawful.) The industry has experienced some high-profile and well-deserved criminal prosecutions, civil penalties, injunctions, massive disgorgements of profits, seizures, and other forms of bans and constraints. And still the ads arrive—in our e-mail inbox, our newspapers, magazines, and television, billboards, and everywhere.

Dietary supplement benefit claims are visible everywhere. Sexual prowess, thin appearance, younger looks, shinier hair and scalp, better muscles, and the list goes on—are attributed to the tablet, pill, or liquid supplement. The advertising is aimed toward the least-intelligent consumers, who are the most eager for a quick fix. These consumers are those the government should be able to protect. The supplement lobbyists have done the most to constrain consumer protections that can be used in this area.

The legal standard for this category of advertising measures whether the normal, gullible consumer would believe the ad to be truthful. Federal Trade Commission standards for advertising are well understood by reputable companies: *before* the ad is sent out, there should be serious technical support for its claims (not generated solely *after* the credibility of the claim is attacked). Health claims should be supported by human clinical trial data that has been peer-reviewed for publication. See Appendix 1 for more FTC standards information.

The federal challenges to diet supplement marketing can end up in federal courts. Judges do not review the claims as medical or nutritional experts would review them, but they look to the intended audience for a general level of knowledge or awareness. That low level of sophisticated awareness of the limitations of pills and liquids for effecting rapid change in weight or appearance is being exploited by the aggressive sales tactics of the diet supplement marketing companies. Courts have generally sided with the FDA and FTC on disputed questions of consumer perceptions from specific claims.

The dividing line between excessive energetic claims of product benefit and the darker territory of intentional fraud is a very murky separation. "Grow a new bigger brain in a week" is the genre of product benefit claims that will lead some late-night cable viewers to call in for their $49.95 week's supply, subject to automatic renewal. Incredible claims begin with having some apparent potential credence for someone in the audience. Presenters in infomercials may be paid for the value of their exploitation of the presenter, often an older actress or actor. Some Internet sales claims are simply lies and overtly fraudulent efforts to extract money. Government could try to react quickly but there are so many frauds that a "buyer beware" atmosphere is most likely.

It has been said that diet pills sales are a reflection of the "triumph of hope over experience." Willingness to believe in a benefit is high; readiness for disappointment is high; but prosecutors' willingness to challenge is also quite high, when public agency resources permit. The prosecutorial discretion used in diet supplement cases by the FDA, the FTC, and federal and state prosecutors looks for deterrence of crime in the gap between what is promised and what is delivered. Even the seller's most ardent beliefs in its product will not shield a bogus claim from being prosecuted if the belief lacks support in medically valid evidence. Investigation of the background for a claim can probe the company's degree of knowledge and support for its claims. Expressions of intention, self-doubt, or profit potential are captured in the subpoenaed e-mails and memos of the defendant company and will be reviewed as the grand jury develops the indictment for intentional fraud or conspiracy to defraud. The Congress in 2010 considered giving FDA new subpoena authority that could make it possible for detailed access to underlying files of science data, technical support and marketing correspondence of the food and dietary supplement industries. That may be a tool for breaking through the elaborate legal games that have been routinely played by the worst-behaved marketers.

2. CONTENTS

The content of the dietary supplement tablet, pill, or liquid should be expressed on its label. The valid supplement product has some activity, such as a number of International Units of a vitamin or a certain amount of a botanical plant extract. The FDA requires a "Supplement Facts" panel on the labeling of the container which should disclose this information. A "USP" label on the packaging helps the consumer, because it promises the product will specifically conform to a recipe or purity standard set in the encyclopedic pharmacy book called the "United States Pharmacopeia." But in practice, very few of the marketed dietary supplements are being tested for the accuracy and completeness of their labeling. The FDA has a large volume of health-related complaints that take priority, and the industry does not self-police. Relative to pharmaceuticals or medical devices, complaints to the FDA by competing firms are relatively rare, so the consumer is left to rely on the label chosen by the marketer.

Is the factory where the diet supplements are made as clean as a pharmaceutical drug factory would be? Probably not. Enforcement of good manufacturing practices for supplement products was delayed for a decade for lack of resources, until Congress appropriated funds. The FDA now has enacted the required set of practices that guide diet supplement makers. Actual inspectional visits may take longer to become a reality because of the volume of other pressing tasks for FDA resources. Because much of the bulk tablet supply and bulk powder for capsules are made outside the United States, it is much less likely that an FDA inspector will find the problems in the actual formulation and production area, before the diet supplement is packaged. Optimally, FDA and a foreign equivalent agency will inspect the formulation of a mixed botanical product in the Israeli factory and then will inspect the processing of the tablet operations of the Utah plant at which the "all natural botanical benefits" capsules are made.

3. EFFECTIVENESS

Actual results to be achieved with dietary supplements will vary among different consumers. Unlike human new drugs, the new dietary supplement has no burden of advance clearance and no duty to demonstrate before marketing that its contents will actually provide the benefit sought. This was a 1994 lobbying triumph for the dietary supplement industry; but consumers sometimes erroneously assume that if a pill or tablet product is on the market, the FDA must have had some action to clear or approve its contents.

The goal of the diet supplement marketing company is likely to be one of repeated sales to satisfied consumers, so there is a built-in reason for the seller to want its product to deliver results. In 2009, a diet supplement company founder was sentenced to twenty-five years in prison and ordered to forfeit tens of millions of dollars in gains for a fraud scheme that involved forced renewal of orders on callers' credit cards for a falsely promoted "male enhancement" pill. The vast majority of companies are legitimate marketers who actually want the consumer to benefit and reorder the product.

Federal Trade Commission advertising efforts, described in Appendix 1, are a factor in belatedly punishing excessive or misleading claims of benefit. FDA cannot require proof of effective benefits before sale of a dietary supplement. Matching consumer expectations to the dietary supplement's actual effectiveness is a problem if the claims are too vigorous and build too large an anticipated benefit in the minds of the consumer.

4. REMEDIES

If the product does not work as expected, the consumer should first contact the company's hotline and demand a refund. If that is not a satisfactory outcome, the Better Business Bureau (http://www.bbb.org) and the state consumer protection agency, often a state attorney general office, should be contacted about the complaint. Most responsible firms will refund money if the intermediary insists, and most want to keep their records clean at these intermediary agencies.

The Federal Trade Commission's Web site (http://ftc.gov/) has a Web page on dietary supplements where consumers can easily file a complaint online. The huge volume of complaints is studied for trends, and the FTC brings "cease and desist" orders, and sometimes court actions, against companies whose advertising lacks adequate factual support. Appendix 1 explains this process in more detail.

Food and Drug Administration consumer affairs officers can be found through White Pages telephone directories or online, at http://www.fda.gov/ICECI/Inspections/IOM/ucm124008.htm. The FDA will take information about your complaint and will include it in the file for the next scheduled inspection. A sharp increase in complaints will hasten the FDA inspection, sampling, and response to the dietary supplement company. In the normal case, the FDA will write a warning letter to the company, if the claims made are excessive compared to the data support for the claim. Or the FDA could obtain a court order seizing the product, or bring an injunction, or in the most severe cases, could criminally prosecute the company and its executives. In practice, the political strength of the diet supplement companies won 1994 legislation constraining FDA and has acted as a shield that protects the companies from tougher FDA scrutiny. Apart from the efforts of state attorneys general and the Federal Trade Commission Bureau of Consumer Protection, there is very little that consumer advocates can do to protect the public from excesses in the dietary supplement marketplace.

Examples and Illustrations

A male enhancement pill was sold by a company whose sales tactics included automatically resending the pills and rebilling the credit card of the purchaser. The pills' contents probably were closer to pharmaceutical drugs than to vitamins. After a multi-agency investigation and a lengthy and expensive trial, the company founder was sent to prison for twenty-five years, and numerous business associates and the founder's mother were jailed for their part in the mail fraud and other fraudulent conspiracy.

The FDA prosecuted a major chain of vitamin stores after its mall store near Pittsburgh promoted one of its supplement products for uses that no one, even the company, could show had any scientific proof of effectiveness.

CHAPTER 10:
FOODS WITH PESTICIDE RESIDUES

1. CONTEXT IS IMPORTANT

Pesticides are chemicals that intentionally kill, so a rational food consumer does not want to eat these pesticides at any level. The pesticide tolerance system allows a certain amount of "residue", the leftover quantity after cleaning, of the weed-killing and bug-killing chemicals, to be permitted in food eaten by U.S. consumers. That true statement about allowable levels of poison does not mean that consumers are harmed physically or economically. Indeed, the food industry probably could not supply as much food as it does, so cheaply, without the use of chemicals that lessen costs of spoilage and permit longer cycles of transport and storage.

As described in Appendix 2, the pesticide residue control system is complex. The tolerance system also does not mean that consumers are harmed physically; as toxicology science has observed for centuries, the "dose makes the poison," and so long as the residue of chemical left on the food as it is eaten is a low dose, the risk to human health is small. How small? How much tolerance should there be for pesticides? Who should decide?

How small of a risk to human health from pesticides is to be allowed was the core question in food tolerance legislation, adopted in 1954 and updated in 1996. The level of exposure to the food should be so low that there is a *reasonable expectation of no harm*." That was the standard selected by Congress for food safety decisions on pesticide tolerance issues. The actual decision about permissible levels of exposure to residues of the pesticide is made by the scientific staff of the pesticides office within the Environmental Protection Agency. The EPA makes the initial licensing decisions with limitations, and then it is the FDA's task to sample, test, and monitor the quantity of chemicals left on the carrot, wheat, or other food. If the residue of chemical exceeds the tolerance, the food is misbranded.

The pesticide tolerance determination is part of the "product registration" function of the EPA, and approval conditions and limitations will be negotiated with the chemical company that wants to bring a new chemical to the agricultural marketplace. The experimental work done on the chemical includes exposure studies on animals to test the basic toxicology; testing residue levels with or without cooking or washing of the raw commodity; test methods for detecting the presence of the chemical; information on the chemical's environmental fate, breakdown or persistence in soil and water after usel and labeling with specific controls on the usage of the chemical on the crops, e.g. no more than 3 pounds per acre of diluted spray on broccoli crops. Once the registration is issued, the FDA issues a temporary tolerance called an exemption. Later the exemption changes to a final pesticide tolerance rule, which declares food "adulterated" if the harvested food contains a level of the pesticide higher than can be "tolerated." These levels and chemicals are found in the compilation of federal rules in the Code of Federal Regulations. The federal EPA Web sites listed in Appendix 3 also can be searched for pesticide data.

During the EPA review of testing results for the pesticide, samples of corn, tomatoes, or other crops on which the chemical was applied will be taken to a laboratory for sophisticated chemical analysis. The available human data on accidental poisoning from related chemicals or this particular chemical, based on use in other nations, is the baseline level to be avoided. Below that acutely toxic poisoning level, there are gradations of health risks from longer-term exposure, and the EPA intends to get into these variable numbers in order to project a level at which chronic illness like cancer will not be caused by long-term exposure to the chemical. So if we imagine new chemical X intended to be used on lettuce, then the baseline would be health effect reports after a poisoning of field workers who accidentally were sprayed with X in Egypt, for example. That is the level of acute toxicity which serves as the base. Above that threshold amount of exposure, the long-term exposure to X in persons eating lettuce (or any other crop listed on the EPA-approved label of X) is estimated based on animal models (rats fed a correspondingly large dose of X). The chronic toxicity level for exposure to X takes into account a "target" eater who frequently eats lettuce in salads. How much lettuce? How much residue of X will be on the average lettuce consumed by the average adult and child? How much of the chemical X can be on the lettuce, before absorption of X in the body's fatty tissue would begin? Over a lifetime of eating salads with lettuce, would the amount of X that is absorbed be likely to have a harmful effect, such as cancer?

Chemical makers are interested in getting expensive new chemicals from development into market rapidly. They have an incentive to label the product for the easiest food crop to measure, e.g. lettuce, and then to sell the product as a faster or more effective way to deal with lettuce predators, insects, molds, etc. The FDA will have a tolerance listing for the chemical on lettuce. The lab samples of lettuce will be tested for small quantities of residual chemicals of this type, using the analytical methods the chemical company had provided in its registration documents with the EPA. In practice, many of the lettuce growers using the chemical will vary from the quantity the chemical maker states on the product label; the FDA is more concerned with overdoses that result in excessive measurable residues.

2. EXPANDING PESTICIDE USES

In our hypothetical, the pesticide chemical company's sales success with the lettuce growers will lead to work with other crops on which the same chemical can also be effective. Broccoli and lettuce may have similar pest profiles, but their surfaces are different, so more chemicals will reside on the broccoli bunch than on the smooth head of lettuce. This difference matters when the law seeks to calibrate and reduce levels of chemical exposures. Also, new testing methods will be needed to measure the chemical deposited on the broccoli because of its different texture and surface area. User information on broccoli eaters, frequency of use, raw versus cooked, etc. will also be factors when FDA scientists are evaluating what amount of residue should be permitted by a safety margin known as a "tolerance" quantity, e.g. 10 parts per million on leaves of lettuce. The chemical firm returns to the EPA with the request to expand the product's permitted crop uses from lettuce to broccoli, by an amendment in the permissible registered label. So it may be months before approval for use on lettuce is expanded into a supplemental registration for uses on broccoli.

3. EFFECTS FOR CONSUMERS

What does this process mean for consumers? Congress in 1954 feared that chemical residues would harm consumers who were exposed to constant small doses of pesticides on their food. Today, the FDA has a limited amount of money with which to run pesticide assay tests on vegetables and fruits. The FDA may test a vegetable and find an unapproved pesticide, rendering the vegetable shipment subject to recall.

In a few months, the EPA test review may result in approval for the use of this chemical on this crop, but until that occurs, it would not be lawful to spray the lettuce-approved pesticide onto the broccoli, to use that example. The FDA cannot act in isolation; Congress has teamed the agencies together on pesticide residue issues like these.

A common misunderstanding among consumers is that processed foods are somehow cleansed of their pesticide residues. Sometimes, as with the washing of beans to be frozen, some residue is removed and some remains. The EPA's process in setting tolerances takes into account the typical forms of food preparation and ingestion of each of these materials. Listings in the Code of Federal Regulations with limits like "15 parts per million of diazepam residue on cooked beets" are directives that the farmer or food processor must obey. The maker of the generic form of diazepam will be free of blame if the beets arrive at the packing plant with 25 parts per million. But the farmer will be upset at the (probable) rejection of his beets by the quality control reviewers at the packing plant. When this happens more frequently, the label will be "improved" by the chemical maker (with EPA concurrence) to warn the user not to apply the diazepam in a manner that could raise its pesticide residue over 15 parts per million.

This section may be disillusioning to some and disheartening to others. Yes, there will be some level of chemical pesticides in your and your child's dinner. No, there are not enough government enforcers to track and measure what the chemical companies are doing. The best outcome will be to have reason to trust your farmer, and reason to know that the farmer will carefully apply only specifically registered pesticides on the raw crops that produce your food.

Examples and Illustrations

Toggle Farms is a large grower of tangerines in Venezuela, and its products are widely sold throughout the United States. An outbreak of aphids causes severe threats of tree loss, so a Venezuelan version of the imaclopid pesticide, not sold in the United States, is tested on the trees and appears to halt the aphid damage. Toggle loads ten containers with bagged tangerines grown on those trees. When the container ship arrives in Savannah, the FDA takes a sample of 5 pounds and finds a small residue of the pesticide imaclopid. The FDA issued a Notice of Detention and stops movement of the containers. At the hearing, Toggle's attorney requests an exception because the aphid problem is spreading in both the United States and Venezuela, and there is a shortage of tangerines. In the alternative, Toggle asks permission to re-export the containers to the Bahamas. The FDA declines both requests and orders the shipment destroyed. On appeal to federal court, Toggle argues that only a minimal amount of the pesticide is present, so exposure would be low, and that the imaclopid is of the same type of chemical approved for U.S. citrus, so its permission would not be risky. The court rules the FDA has expertise, the statute is discretionary, and so it defers to the FDA's choice of actions on the unapproved pesticide residue.

CHAPTER 11:
BIOTECHNOLOGY AND FOOD

1. HOW BIOTECHNOLOGY IS LIKELY TO TRANSFORM FOOD

Agriculture has known evolutionary adaptations for many centuries. Selective breeding for the biggest bull, the most productive spinach, the longest lasting rice, etc. has been done for many years. Genetics have been at the core of the success with generations of successively stronger, more healthy, or more pest-resistant plants. The science of genetics began with a humble monk who demonstrated the effects of selective breeding on plant attributes. Scientists are optimists about progress; in agriculture, the biological scientists and geneticists believe that the wave of food technology improvements will reduce costs and improve the durability of the crops against predatory insects, thereby benefiting farmers by increasing their yields.

Biotechnology has placed some strains on the government system of uniformity in regulation. The regulatory system for food depends on a process to produce final and binding rules. These rules are not frequently changed or adapted. The food regulatory system, therefore, is static—not dynamic—so regulations are left in place, and government managers make these product or process innovations, for better or worse, fit into the existing regulatory system. An important product norm that the FDA has followed is that the finished product of a biotech process is the focus of attention, not the process that brings that product into being, so a distinctive process to get to that product—biotech versus non-biotech—does not produce a different regulatory outcome. Certainly innovative agricultural firms have argued effectively against new or different controls; there are lobbyists who want no new regulatory controls. Except in unusual cases, the FDA allows these biotech versions of conventional foods to escape the detailed review and preapproval process that they would endure if reviewed as food additives.

Is biotech food harmful? This book cannot answer that controversial question; in general, regulatory scientists believe that the biotech-created versions of the basic protein or seed are not any more harmful than conventional versions used in food, in most instances. Some food changes have produced unexpected bad effects, like Showa Denko's L-tryptophan product, a dietary supplement that caused severe injuries in dozens of users because of an apparent error in biotech formulation.

Harm must be balanced against benefit when making a choice for society at large. Is a particular biotech tomato, grain, or other food much improved from the baseline foods? Yes, in many cases it is hardier against drought or richer in vitamins, when compared to prior food commodities as a baseline. Should consumers be told of the changed source for the seeds that grew their food? Many advocates for disclosure say yes: consumers should have that informed choice. Governments and many farmers tend to say no: it is not relevant to a safety decision since no relatively greater danger exists, and the warnings that are explicit or implicit will deter consumer acceptance of non-harmful biotech crops. Lines have been drawn over this controversy regarding the effects of consumer disclosure about biotech derived food ingredients. Fostering more awareness is portrayed by one side; fostering ignorant biases is portrayed by the other side. A social policy debate has raged for many years about this disclosure issue.

For the last two decades, more and more genetic information about plants and animals has proliferated in scientific literature about genomics. The promise of tailoring crops that are hardier, require less water, and repel disease has been manifested in numerous aspects of modern agricultural research. Greater information has led to experiments with the embryos and offspring of certain living organisms. The Scottish "cloned sheep" named Dolly drew worldwide attention just by being born. Reproducing a living creature was a breakthrough for modern science, beyond the improvements that may be developed from that discovery. Cloning has presented deep ideological and policy divisions and conflicts, so this particular aspect of biotechnology carries a downside for the product developer and marketer.

Food crops that today would have been damaged by predators can be aided by future crop variations derived with further targeted genetic manipulation of seeds. A crop that is resistant to an insect predator is hardier and delivers more income to the farmer. A delicate crop that can be altered to produce hardier, drought-resistant attributes has the prospect of major improvements in yield and reliability. Less fertilizer use, more resistance to mold or insect problems, more durable stalks or higher yields are all benefits to some food products from the use of some biotech additives. The patent system's impact on the private commercial control of these new improved crops poses a lot of social policy questions that are beyond the scope of this text.

Federal research funds have been used for some of the biotech crop experiments with National Science Foundation and USDA Agricultural Research Service grants and experimental programs. Seed modification developments have been pursued into the planting of field crops, yielding new variants on familiar products like soybeans and cotton. The Biotechnology Regulatory Service (BRS) of the U.S. Department of Agriculture has an oversight role in the biotech crop revolution. The BRS, in conjunction with other USDA groups, seeks to stay ahead of animal, plant and seed biotech developments, with the goal that no aberrant crop "monsters" are created in the course of biotech modifications of genetic material. Other nations have expressed some worries about genetically modified organisms, and some have insisted that the U.S. export crop sold to their nation's importers should not include such genetic variants. World attention was drawn to this controversy when Zambia, facing severe agricultural shortfalls, refused a large shipload of U.S. food that had been derived from biotech seeds. Trade barrier disputes, negotiations, and compromises have occurred at the international level.

At the practical level, segregation of the biotech seed plantings will make for some problems with some neighboring farms. The fields planted with experimental modified seeds must be separated from the larger nearby fields of conventional crops, far enough that wind or bees don't carry genetic material into other crops. This separation is needed so that export shipments can strictly comply with any exclusionary "no GMO" (genetically modified organism) restrictions placed on food imports by the governments of some other nations. In the United States, biotech versions of corn that were designed for a particular genetic benefit had been accidentally mixed with conventional corn, and a large scale product recall resulted in the Starlink case.

Examples and Illustrations

Better Butter Inc. sells its product as "traditional old fashioned butter." Consumers Against GMOs tests the butter and finds small amounts of a modified hormone, rbST. CAGMO sues Better Butter for false advertising and infliction of emotional distress on consumers who fear the ingestion of "Frankenstein foods." The court dismisses the claim because no express statement about the minor presence of genetically modified milk was made, and Better Butter had no general duty to keep its product free of rbST, which the FDA had permitted for use in milk. No emotional distress claim could be made in the absence of either a serious risk of harm, a federal prohibition, or a promise of non-GMO status by Better Butter. None of these bases for a lawsuit were present, so the case would be readily dismissed.

Somato Seed Corp. is a dominant corn seed seller. Corn variants have been genetically developed to maximize the ethanol fuel potential of corn kernels, such as "Seed 411." but seed for these ethanol variants are not intended to be consumed as human food. When multiple crops are grown in adjacent properties, planting corn inevitably brings wind drift of seed, and birds carry seeds into adjacent fields. Some cross-fertilization of conventional corn with the biotech 411 version is inevitable. The USDA standards for export corn do not allow this particular variant of corn to be included in shipments of food corn, and the grower using 411 seed must avoid its transmission into other commercial "food corn" grower crops. When corn from neighbor Brownland Farms' property is rejected for export because of a small amount of 411 variant, its value as a food crop drops suddenly, and Brownland sues Somato and its nearby customer. The courts are likely to dismiss the case, as Somato has no duty after giving its instructions to end users of its seed, and the customer will assert that it has not breached any duties, since all the seed spreading occurred by forces of nature.

CHAPTER 12:
CIVIL DAMAGE LAWSUITS FOR FOOD
INJURY OR FRAUD

1. WHAT WILL THE JURY EXPECT?

Civil damage lawsuits settle in most cases; a small percentage reach the jury; but the value of settlements is impacted by what the opposing sides believe that a jury MIGHT do if the case went to a jury decision. What happens in jury deliberations if a court case arises out of a food-related injury? In a food case, any set of randomly selected local residents who sit as the jury in a personal injury claim or, rarely, in an FDA food enforcement case, are likely to come into the courthouse with biases. They eat food, they cook food, they select food, and they are familiar with the variations in food. They can relate to the sense of outrage when an injured person claims an unexpected harm, that a reasonable person eating the food would not have expected the adverse effects from this contaminant. Jurors are repelled by companies that are crooks and cheats who use food as a weapon to steal from consumers.

On the civil side, injured people can and sometimes do sue the food producer when a serious injury results from exposure to harmful food. Three examples of this are:

- Plastic or metal fragments inside a sweet roll cut the mouth;

- Puffer fish in sushi caused an acute poisoning of the diner; or

- *Shigella* organisms infect shrimp-eating consumers, with serious effects on persons who are elderly, physically weak, or "immuno-compromised" cancer patients undergoing chemotherapy.

Unless the injury was obviously tied to a negligent act, and unless that injury could not have happened without an error on the part of the company, the lawsuit might not be viable. Proving the defect in the product, plus proving the condition of a now-destroyed (or now-eaten) food product as of the time of the injury, is not enough. Plaintiffs must also prove a causal connection between the condition of the food and the specific injury. All of the confounding facts and alternate causes must be carefully weighed by the potential litigation advocate before the suit is brought.

The typical civil liability case turns upon a defective food product's failure to meet "consumer expectations." The reasonable food buyer and eater is legally and reasonably entitled to expect that food will not cause harm to the consumer or to vulnerable children or elders in the consumer's family. An expectation of no harm is presumed to exist in legal cases of food injuries.

In the injury lawsuit, the person suing the food vendor will usually allege that he or she was harmed by the actions of one or more among the several different persons who negligently gathered the food and/or negligently processed it, and then served or delivered the food. These plaintiffs try to sue a larger number of participants and then "roll up" or join numerous other defendants in the hope that the smaller ones will settle early, and their awards of settlement dollars can be used to pay for enough experts to be able to go to trial. Experts are costly, and they need to be qualified to testify, over defense objections.

The standard lawsuit has a typical "burden of proof": an injury occurred, proximately caused by bad food, and the defendant had a duty of care, and the duty was breached by inadequate safety measures in the handling or serving of the food. The claim of negligence in exposing that consumer to that bad food has many variations; the primary challenge will be the attribution of fault through knowledge of the risk. The food maker knew its soup could carry an infection, but the plant failed to cook the soup at a temperature hot enough to prevent the growth of bacteria.

The most difficult cases to prove, after the food has been consumed, are claims for conspiracy to cheat the consumer by selling counterfeit food. The sale of counterfeit food, misbranded with the name of another food, is a federal crime. The FDA and the Justice Department can prosecute the crime and seize the falsely labeled food. The government's powers are described in Appendix 8 which contains portions of the Food Drug & Cosmetic Act. But the law does not allow individuals to bring private civil suits to claim damages just because of a violation of the FDA statute. One type of legal action is a public protection through litigation; the public collectively benefits. The other action is a private claim of compensation, and there is not so much of a public need for this plaintiff to recover for her or his losses. So the fact of the violation itself is not a basis for a lawsuit; rather, a lawsuit alleges that the unsafe condition of the food occurred as a result of negligent conduct and caused personal harm.

In today's news media climate, there may be members of a civil jury panel who have been influenced by television and other media that report on the high-tech, elaborate forensic crime labs of "CSI" and similar programs. Compared to the drama of television cases, the typical lawsuit about "food poisoning" is a boring exercise in tracing the detailed history of a shipment lot. Few of these cases get to a jury, but jury trials in this context are less exciting and more often tedious chains of responsibilities for various stages of that food.

Most food disputes are smaller claims, involve transitory illnesses, and settle without litigation. Those that are filed as civil lawsuits rarely reach a jury trial. A complete trial of a food safety case is rare, but not unknown. When a jury case occurs, the very low-key, mundane role of the witnesses who are health inspectors may seem bland and boring to the observer. But a conscientious juror will listen and will give credibility to a respected scientist. If the case is an enforcement case brought by the FDA against a food company, the highlight of the government's case is likely to be a career government scientist who explains the food deficiency and lays out the reasons the FDA chose to attack this particular noncompliance.

Because the food company will fight any serious injury claim, directly or through its insurers, the person who wants to retain a lawyer to sue for a food injury should not expect a quick, easy settlement. Reputation, history, and a desire not to broadcast a "soft target" image all make it likely that the food company will resist the claim. Eventual success will take depositions and document requests, arguments over witness qualifications, disputes about the version of the facts used by the injured person, and intrusive demands for disclosure of medical and other records of the person suing. The prospects of enduring months of such a high-visibility, high-stress lawsuit tend to deter litigation by the persons who have recovered from their foodborne illness.

Most plaintiff's injury cases are accepted by lawyers on a contingent fee basis. The lawyer is investing personal effort and funds, and a loss in the case could jeopardize the lawyer's own money. So the system favors close scrutiny by the lawyer before accepting the case. A contingent fee means the lawyer is "at risk." One who overlooks a fact favoring the defense can waste tens of thousands of dollars if the suit is dismissed or if the jury finds for the defense. Except for the obvious errors—like the "smoking gun" mistakes that put a factory-sized bolt from a packing machine into a frozen ice cream sandwich—most food liability cases tend to favor the company on the defense side. A prudent lawyer screens out these cases early; a prudent judge grants summary judgment on cases that should not take up a jury for weeks of trial. A food illness is not likely to be an easy problem to remedy in the courts.

Examples and Illustrations

Consumer Mary Doe believes that the severe skin rash and eczema she experienced recently was the result of eating a bad batch of lentils from City Market Stores. Her doctor recommended that she stay off work for a month until the severe reaction cleared through her system. Mary sought a lawyer to sue CMS for the $5000 in lost wages and the $2500 cost of her medical tests and treatments. Jane Esquire, a local attorney, did a search of technical literature and found no articles on association of normal lentils with severe dermal problems; the actual lentils have been consumed, so a pesticide residue test is not possible. Jane declines to litigate the case. Weeks later, Mary finds a social network blog entry about a similar case, and after extensive research, finds a pending class action against Beanpot Chemical for skin reactions to its Beanacide spray, a spray used against soil infestations affecting beans. Genna Counsell, a Topeka lawyer specializing in class actions, communicates with Mary. She determines that lentils were likely to have been sprayed with Beanacide one week before they arrived at CMS and brings Mary's case into the class action with thirty-five other individuals who assert bean-associated dermal injuries. Mary eventually receives a $1000 settlement from Beanpot's insurer, a "nuisance settlement", before a trial can be held. Counsell receives $400, and Mary ends up with $600, subject to her health insurer's claim for recovery of insurance-paid medical costs. No one is fully satisfied.

A mistake in formulating the spice mix for brand Y habanero-flavored potato chips led to the company contacting forty customers who had called to complain about severe mouth burns. It was possible that this number could signify that 100 or more consumers had some degree of burns. The maker of brand Y and its insurer meet and decide to pay a small settlement amount, which thirty-five customers accept. Five decide to sue; but three of those cannot find lawyers to take a small case with no permanent injury. Two can find attorneys to actually sue brand Y; both cases are settled soon after filing. No press coverage occurred, and brand Y was unaffected.

CHAPTER 13:
HOW DO FEDERAL AND STATE PROTECTIONS INTERSECT?

No book on food safety can be written solely from a federal perspective. About 80 percent of food inspections in this country are done by state and local officials, according to estimates by the Association of Food and Drug Officials. AFDO favors greater cooperation between state and federal regulators in the food safety field. Coordination, training, and joint project funding has aided the shared responsibility and efforts between state and federal inspectors. The FDA's Center for Food Science and Applied Nutrition devotes some effort to its liaison role with state food enforcers. Cooperative efforts make a significant difference, as extra eyes and ears for the food safety regulation function.

But states and federal regulators sometimes disagree. Because state laws vary so widely, and larger food companies dislike the variability, this idealistic pursuit of cooperative efforts can get sticky at times. This chapter addresses the legal issue of "federal preemption." The term "to preempt," meaning to take over from a subordinate, applies when a court takes a dispute out of the hands of the state courts and decides that the federal power of control on this topic requires the federal courts to rule on the disputed issues.

Congress allows and encourages states to maintain a vital role on food safety issues. Funds to support the state laboratories used for food safety have been appropriated by Congress as a means to build "surge" food safety testing capacity to respond in the event of a sudden need to test the safety of food to detect a potential terrorist attack.

Although Article VI of the Constitution permits the federal government to "preempt" the actions of a state that would clash with a directive from Congress, Congress has been very reluctant to do so in the foods field. Congress said in 1990 that food label descriptions of consumer food ingredients should be uniform in every state. In 2002, Congress prescribed a specific system for allergy warning. But those are label issues, not food safety or food content issues; states have a role in these topical areas.

The narrow power of federal preemption of food label requirements was utilized by Congress in 1990, preempting state label rules in order to reassure industry opponents who had objected to expanded mandatory labeling. The 1990 preemption clause was intended to assure companies that only one uniform method of food label disclosure of nutrition information would be used nationwide. Many industry advocates asked Congress to stop all state enforcement of food safety controls, but their efforts ultimately failed in 2007. They had argued that states interfered with FDA enforcement efforts, but their arguments failed as more news media coverage of food industry problems came to light, and the states rallied their colleagues to oppose preemption. Ultimately, the failure of broad preemption efforts left the states in about the same position as before 1990, though states are forbidden by the 1990 law to adopt nutrition label variations in addition to the federal Nutrition Facts panel. Appendix 7 addresses the 1990 NLEA amendments.

In practice, the FDA and state food safety agencies work together frequently. Politics of headquarters-level disputes are put aside at the operating level when each agency admits that it needs the other to get the job done for the benefit of food consumers. States call the FDA when interstate shipments appear to have been contaminated in transit or appear questionable as imports. The FDA can call on a state to send inspectors to a local plant when the FDA lacks the personnel to reach that site quickly, to stop the suspect product. (Sometimes the FDA deputizes the state health official as an official agent of the FDA for these limited purposes.) States call on the FDA's network to trace back the source of suspect products, especially when the state is responding to an assertion that consumers were harmed by shipments from distant locations. The FDA sometimes asks its state counterpart to send a state agent with an embargo notice to hold suspect food shipments until a federal seizure order can be obtained.

The federal Centers for Disease Control works with states to isolate where a foodborne illness originated, and then CDC physicians aid the FDA and state officials to find the restaurant, production plant, or shipping point at which the illness first appeared. Lab skills and equipment used in certain kinds of analysis are in short supply, and federal funds are added to the state funds when needed. A state land grant university lab that supports its state's food safety group might be able to rapidly detect a certain residue and deliver results today rather than next week. Homeland Security legislation gave the FDA the funding needed to support state laboratory expertise and operating equipment for testing of potentially contaminated foods.

An area of potential conflict appears when the state takes an enforcement action that the federal FDA chooses not to take, or vice versa. A federal case in northern New York involved *Geotrichum* mold on factory equipment used to process green beans. The FDA brought a major enforcement case against the bean packer; but state inspectors had seen the mold on machines and had passed the factory as sufficiently clean. The state provided a witness for the company against the FDA's claim that the mold was a risk, and George Burditt, the attorney for the bean packer, literally ate the moldy beans in front of the jury to convince the jurors of their safety. The defense won the case, but by that time, the company had fully cleaned its facility. Deterrence worked, as the FDA had hoped. Others in the business had also been affected by the news of the court case and improved their cleaning processes.

Legal barriers to state action are collectively called "preemption issues." Express preemption means that Congress has blocked the state action through words used in the federal law: "No state shall adopt a rule on X." Implied preemption means Congress did not speak precisely about this topic, but by implication the two systems would clash; obeying one would violate the other, and so it is implied that the federal viewpoint will prevail. For the consumer, this constitutional defense by industry in court cases is more than a legal curiosity. It can block the injured food consumer who is asserting that company negligence caused his personal injury from winning a court case. The food company may escape paying a jury verdict for damages if the court agrees that federal preemption blocks the jury from deciding that the standard of care was not met. Even if Congress did not expressly take away standard-setting from the state courts, arguments for the defense of federal preemption will continue to be asserted.

Examples and Illustrations

Texas state food officials inspected a trucking company warehouse and found extensive rat and insect problems in the area used for food shipments. The company was prosecuted in state court for unsanitary conditions in a food establishment. Its defense was that the FDA had visited the site and had not found a problem, and therefore there could not be a valid legal basis for state findings of food adulteration. The court denied the claim because each of the inspecting authorities had its own powers and its own standards, with no express preemption applicable.

The FDA set good manufacturing practice standards for dietary supplement products in 2007. A diet supplement manufacturing plant in Georgia was inspected in 2009 and was found to be using inadequate equipment, and the FDA ordered the plant to change its processing equipment. The company responded that Georgia law since 1980 had allowed the equipment under state regulations for all makers of "foods." The FDA insisted that the specific rules for dietary supplements superseded the older, more general state requirements, and the firm conceded and made the changes.

CHAPTER 14:
FOOD ADVERTISING

Why did you buy that snack, that dinner, that soda? Were you conditioned to do so by effective advertisements? Would the food we consume today look very different without any advertising? Would we be healthier with less "junk food"? Does the food advertising industry help or hurt consumers? These are questions that psychologists, sociologists, and economists can argue for years. Should food advertising be regulated? Most lawyers will agree that it should; the legal community's conservative and libertarian factions argue for wider "freedoms," and no single answer fits all situations.

The regulation of food advertising is a dynamic, not a simple, process for oversight of the commercial creativity of marketers. If a food package had claimed to help your body to live forever, we all would universally condemn the claims as factually unsupportable. In the 1950s, the government challenged a product claim that eating this "will put off death to the very last minute." While it may be laughable in retrospect, it shows the marketer's optimistic belief in the gullibility of the food-consuming public. How to stop the most outrageous false advertising is reasonably well understood by federal and state regulators, so the "baseline" of policing food frauds is relatively strong.

Benign, happy depictions of children eating fresh fruit or drinking milk will probably be welcomed by any consumer/parent as an ideal reminder of the parental responsibility to select "good" foods. If a food advertisement shows the picture of the type of food and a price, and nothing else, we would universally find the advertising to be unobjectionable. So there is much that could be said in food advertising that the law would welcome or, at least, not condemn. In between these two poles of malignant falsehood and benign truths, we find many interesting variations.

Some percentage of today's national and local advertisements for foods and dietary supplements are false or misleading—and quite profitable. Government officials have limited resources and can challenge only a small fraction of those ads, and the advertisers know that weakness and "place their bets" accordingly. Consumers can sue, filling the gap of government shortcomings, but these private suits rarely occur. By the time the costs of the lawsuit are recovered, the consumer has wasted time and money to pursue a minor irritating scoundrel; government uses its available resources to take down the worst actors and to deter others from following in the footsteps of fraudsters.

Why don't more consumers sue about misleading ads for foods? The reality underlying food marketing regulation is that each food decision is a small-dollar purchase, so no single individual consumer loses so much by a food fraud that the consumer could have a reasonable incentive to pay a lawyer and to sue the corporate defendant for damages. Unlike automobile "lemons" and homes with hidden damage, the purchase of food that does not live up to its advertising is usually "chalked up to a lesson learned." Ham with excessive water adding weight, diet supplements that do not reduce body fat, and bogus packaging that conceals defects will dissatisfy the consumer but will not usually justify a lawsuit for $10 or $25 in damages.

That does not mean consumers don't complain; of course they do. It is traditionally seen as the government's role to act for all consumers, when no single consumer loses enough to warrant the expensive effort to challenge a fraudulent ad. The ads can be challenged in several ways, and this chapter shows how the bad claims can be brought to light and hopefully brought to a favorable conclusion.

Regulation of nationwide food advertising is done by the Federal Trade Commission (FTC), see Appendix 1, and to a lesser extent by state consumer protection entities, often the state attorney general's consumer protection section. It takes a serious commitment of resources for a public enforcement team to litigate against the deep pockets of a food corporation. It takes a forecast of future judicial deference—acceptance of the agency's expertise in defining ambiguous terms—to apply tough legal standards as a basis for punishing the misleading ad. And it takes the supervisory role of experienced prosecutors to do battle with the better paid and more experienced counsel who will be retained by the food marketer. Every time the industry is cornered, its lobbying efforts produce a piece of legislation like the 1994 Dietary Supplement law, which avoids strong controls. So it is an uphill battle to enforce advertising laws in the food and especially in the diet supplement industry.

The first legal issue in food advertising cases will be: "was it false?" The government agency sends an inquiry letter to the food marketing company asking about the basis of support for the claim. An ad that says "Contains 20% juice" should be based on an analysis of the finished product that shows 20 percent juice content. If the claim was more subjective than quantitative—"smoothest" or "most creamy"— the government will request the supporting comparative details. If the company lacks supporting data for the claim (such as a human health study of equivalent consumers fed a diet with and without the food), then the FTC treats the claim as false, if the claimed fact is not generally accepted and well known, e.g. beef contains protein and oranges contain vitamin C. Claims in advertising that "beef cures cancer" or "oranges prevent diabetes" would be considered false for lack of evidence unless there was adequate human study data in the advertiser's hands before the claim is made. Data must satisfy scientific standards of methodology and quality that are appropriate for the type of message being given to consumers. (An advertiser cannot defend an FTC case with anecdotes, routine consumer opinions, or data it develops after it is charged.)

The second legal issue will be "is it misleading, though literally true?" The claim of benefit could mislead the average, non-sophisticated food eater to think that the benefit will actually occur to his health if he eats the food. A rare positive result is not enough to support "good for you" claims. If a qualifier phrase is needed, it should be used. Measuring who is misled requires some consumer research or focus group work, unless it is very obvious to the judge and the lawyers involved that an average person would expect this particular benefit. "Younger skin," "lower weight," "more hair", etc. may occur in a few people but not in the majority of users; the claim would be deemed to be misleading if it were so open-ended or so without qualifications that the average reader would be led to assume that the benefit would come to him as well. Benefits to health must be supported by data, and then if the benefit will not be seen by a large percentage of buyers, a qualifier or limiting phrase is expected to be used.

The ability of consumers and competitors to use the federal law of false advertising, the Lanham Act, is in some transition in the courts. A recent Supreme Court decision, eBay v.MercExchange, threatens to change the long-standing presumption that there will be irreparable harm, once there is a showing of deception in Lanham Act advertising cases.The Court's reasoning in eBay may also affect the presumptions arising from literal falsity, express comparative claims, willfulness, "establishment claims", and puffery. These legal issues will be developed in later court decisions.

The third legal issue will be, "did the advertising violate a specific law or a specific binding regulation?" If it did, the penalty in that law will be applied, and the case can be resolved quickly. Constitutional First Amendment "commercial speech" advocates have been well paid in recent years for arguing against restraints on free expression, but courts have been cautious in allowing misleading marketing claims to be treated as if they are a special class of shielded "free speech." There is no "freedom to mislead." A careful analysis of Supreme Court decisions under the commercial speech doctrine will be done by courts if a state law or a regulation is challenged "on its face" before the dispute relates to a specific ad claim. When the challenge arises after the company has made a bogus health benefit claim, courts are reluctant to shield misleading forms of expression as being protected by "free speech" rights. The degree of scientific consensus and factual support will have an impact on how receptive a court is to the claim of the food marketer's freedom to assert a product benefit.

The final legal issue will be, "if the ad is false or misleading, what remedy will be effective?" Corrective advertising rarely works to communicate to those general consumers who were persuaded by the misleading ads to buy the product. But disgorgement (refunds at the full retail price paid) bites hard against the fraud if the company had retained database lists of its defrauded buyers. More often in recent years, a court injunction against the company, its executive, and its ad agency, together with a substantial penalty fine, will deter the prudent company from future use of these excessive claims. State attorneys general sometimes amass a group of states to share the cost of a challenge; they seek a penalty that deters future violations by the company and its officers (to avoid seeing those officers later reissuing a similar bogus claim, but under another company's name).

A special set of advertising issues arises in states that have adopted the controversial "Food Libel" laws. These laws allow damage awards after a jury trial, for the benefit of farmers, against persons who alleged the farm produced unsafe or less desirable food. A state statute allowed Texas cattlemen to sue television star Oprah Winfrey for statements about the safety of beef, which the cattlemen argued were defamatory about their product, though without any specific mention by Oprah of a specific rancher or farmer. Oprah won, and in more cases, defendants will prevail—but only after expensive lawyering on their side against the farm industry's trial counsel. As the 2009 documentary film "Food Inc." showed, the effect of criminalizing or using laws to punish opinions expressed about food has been to restrain critics of the safety of certain food products. Criticism of all beef is not normally libelous for one beef producer; yet the "food libel" laws subject critics to litigation in dozens of states, so they deter the critics with the threat of bearing litigation costs, acting as a kind of gag on critics.

A portion of the "policing" of food advertising never reaches the public consciousness. Major marketers who are members of the Better Business Bureau can file a complaint against their competitor with the BBB's National Advertising Division (NAD). Their Web site provides detailed background at http://www.narcpartners.org/index.aspx NAD acts like a neutral reviewer of claims, requesting that the supporting data for the ad that is being challenged be shared with NAD staff. The staff and their expert advisers then evaluate what is claimed to be wrong with the ad. If the NAD finds the ad misleading or false, the firm that used the ad is expected to withdraw it, or the firm may appeal to the National Advertising Review Board of the BBB. No penalties are paid and no fines imposed. This private dispute resolution mechanism is quicker, cheaper, and less visible than a federal or state investigation. Its downside is that the NAD process is used only by the reputable national firms, and not by purveyors of bogus products or hustlers with excessive claims of benefit. Food claims by major companies can be challenged and defended; food claims by the less well-established marketers are left to government enforcers.

Examples and Illustrations

"Quilties Taste Great, Have Zero Calories, and Help You Lose 10 Pounds in Your First Week!" The first claim is subjective "puffery" with no objective scale of good or bad taste, so no regulator will act on it. The caloric count is measured under FDA standards[1] a standard serving or the recommended amount to be consumed is measured, and if it produces 5 calories or less under standard caloric count methodology, then the number can be rounded down to zero. Quilties is required to have the lab caloric measurements on file when an inspector asks for them. "Help You" is a conditional qualifier; it implies that the consumer must take some action such as exercise. "Lose 10 Pounds" is a specific numerical benefit, so data must show this is reasonably to be expected over the first seven days after eating the Quilties for the first time. If only a small minority of Quilties users in a scientifically valid study had lost 10 pounds, the claim would be vulnerable to serious challenges.

---

1   21 CFR § 101.60 (2009), *available at* http://ecfr.gpoaccess.gov/cgi/t/text/text-id x?c=ecfr&rgn=div8&view=text&node=21:2.0.1.1.2.4.1.3&idno=21 (2009).

CHAPTER 15:
FOOD PACKAGING ISSUES

The law's use of definitions sometimes generates unusual results. It is hard to imagine buying a pizza in a cardboard box and then eating the box. But chemically treated cardboard is often used by restaurants to prevent seepage of oil from hot pizzas. The chemicals used come into direct contact with the food. So the FDA argued, and the courts agreed, that pizza boxes are a kind of package that could interact with the pizza; some chemicals could pass from the box into the food; and therefore the treated paperboard used in the box was regulated by the FDA as a subcategory of "food." The logic seems clear as a legal matter, though the average pizza eater will not be dining on the cardboard of the box. Food packagers therefore have to pay special attention to the health effects of the materials that they utilize that come in contact with food.

The purpose of food packaging is simple: deliver the food securely to the consumer, with a maximum attractiveness and a minimum of damage to the food. The purpose of government regulating food packaging is to assure that chemicals in the package do not transfer ("leach out") into the food. Leaching means the action of drawing out of a chemical from the container wall, into the food that is kept inside that wall. When a new soft drink bottle was developed by Monsanto in the 1970s, the FDA concluded (and the court agreed) that since it was technically possible for the bottle chemical to pass into warm carbonated beverages, the FDA could regulate the bottle. The science of toxicity had uncertainties about the leaching from the plastic bottle into the food. The science was uncertain; the FDA exists to protect the public from harm; so the FDA presumed the chemical would pass into the food because of a principle of physics dealing with chemical migration from one object into another. The court deferred to the special expertise of the FDA about that bottle. As a result, the plastics company did not proceed with the factories to make these plastic bottles, and instead it took a huge loss.

The first issue consumers have with packaging is "will a packaging problem affect the food?" If the new and empty container is partly full of dirt when the bottle reaches the filling point at the dairy, the bottle's problem certainly will make the milk that is placed into that bottle less attractive. But a lack of cleanliness is overtly visible, while chemical exposures are more subtle. Does the food package's plastic give off an odor that makes the pasta smell bad when cooked? Is the cardboard carton for cereal one that was made with recycled paper, which may give off chemical odors and may impart undesired flavors to the cereal inside that box? The FDA has standards for the movement of plastic packaging materials into foods of various kinds. The well-informed food maker will perform a food package stress test, in heat or cold conditions, to determine the long-term durability of the package in its relation to the food.

Indirect food additives, as packaging materials are known, required specific FDA approval for four decades, 1958-1996. These were once the slowest moving files in the FDA's safety evaluation in-box, and industry lobbied hard for a change in the law which could speed up progress. The FDA consciously stopped close examination of packaging materials after 1996 amendments allowing easier clearance were adopted by Congress. Most package materials are now marketed after a simple submission of a "notification" to the FDA. Unless there is a reason to believe the packaging material contains something that is dramatically new, and that food could be affected by contact, the FDA does not stop the marketing. Under the post-1996 norms, the FDA will not force the food packager or plastic supplier to conduct extensive safety testing, as had been required prior to the 1996 amendments.

A food consumer's second question would be, "does the product leak out or become vulnerable to entry by crawling or flying insects?" Physical ability of the package to protect the contents is essential to the safety of the contents. This package choice requires some attention to security. Terrorist attacks by poisoning food would be a concern. The wave of food criminal tampering cases in the 1980s led to the use of more "tamper-evident" packaging (skilled criminals have dispelled the notion of "tamper-proof" food packaging). Air tight food packaging with vacuum seals may be optimal for safety, but may be prohibitively expensive for a small size container of a low-cost, low-risk food. A balance of food security, food safety, and food affordability must be made.

Third, how much cost does this choice of packaging add to the price of the food? A bulk purchase of 10 pounds of generic macaroni is made at a low price, which we can call X dollars. How much more is the consumer willing to pay for plastic-wrapped, single-serving, ready-to-cook microwave spaghetti? The consumer can make the choice by everyday shopping decisions. If the consumer is on a tighter budget, larger wholesale unpackaged food for cook-it-yourself use becomes more attractive. Seeing one's sales trending away from expensive packaged versions would be a signal to the food maker to re-orient its packaging approaches. Gold-plated food packages could exist, but consumers would not pay for them.

Fourth, "is this packaging deceptive?" When a small food unit is placed inside a large box hanging on the shelf, a charge could be made that consumers are misled to believing that there is a larger food unit inside. The company could respond that delicate fragile food items need to be safeguarded against damage or theft. If the packaging of meat is vacuum sealed with a gas that makes the meat look better than it would, or appear good for days after its normal spoilage, then the package choice can be criticized. It is unlikely that government agencies would go beyond a warning letter to a court case where there was not an obvious deception of the consumer.

Finally, "what is the remedy?" If the packaging inadvertently violates a rule, it should be changed on a reasonable timetable. If the chemical that leaks from packaging could make the food inside more hazardous, then it should be recalled and changed on a tight timeline. If the package creates a false impression of size or weight or volume, then the corrective step is for government to negotiate a settlement in which the company will offer refunds or reduce prices for a limited time to compensate for its inappropriate sales practices, and will make the needed changes with government approval of the more honest packaging.

Examples and Illustrations

A colorful display of a 3 x 7-inch plastic wrapped container for a very small 1 x 2-inch chocolate egg would be subject to criticism by regulators as potentially deceptive to consumers. The company would respond with results of drop tests, showing the chocolate egg needed to have a surrounding physical support structure and that a broken egg will not be saleable. The company will also argue that the special eggs needed appropriate safeguards against shoplifters, and the larger hard plastic shield deterred thieves from trying to pocket the product.

Chemicals used for lining soft drink cans are particularly volatile combinations. They are directly in contact with a liquid and with carbon dioxide, under various conditions of heat in storage. The FDA may require the specific approval of data, as well as reporting safety tests done on the can liner chemical mixture, before the cans are permitted to be used.

Recycling service trucks pick up used cardboard containers for chemicals at a home improvement center; the collected scrap cardboard is mixed with chemicals and water and "repulped" into new cardboard; as it dries some of the odors of the original chemical boxes are evident in the cardboard. If the boxes are not rejected by the cardboard box plant, the food they contain may smell like the original chemicals. A recall is likely or there may be an FDA inquiry into the food factory's set of quality control standards.

CHAPTER 16:
ENVIRONMENTAL ASPECTS OF
FOOD PRACTICES

Part of the public debate over food policy in recent years has addressed environmental issues, especially industrial food growers' "carbon footprint" and the difficult issues of water uses. Other sources cover these issues in vast detail, but they deserve to be mentioned here for completeness.

1. ENERGY

Energy use and diesel exhaust are related environmental issues for food industry consideration. Modern industrial-scale farming is very energy-intensive. Growing a large, uniform crop will require abundant pumped water, fertilizers, harvesting equipment that burns diesel, and the ubiquitous fuel for machinery, lubricants for tractors, etc. Food crops will need to be harvested and prepared for sale, and this takes mechanical equipment with adequate fuel for all the diesel equipment needed. We could not have today's accessible, economical food choices if the energy were not available to mechanize our agricultural practices. Federal standards for diesel exhaust emissions have focused on the particulates, tiny flakes that are blown out of the carbon being combusted with ignition of diesel fuel. As the permissible air pollution levels are lowered and new diesel engines are forced to burn cleaner fuels, farm use of fuels will be one of the sectors likely to be greatly affected by costs to replace older, smoky engines with new ones. When in 2010 the Congress debated climate change legislation, the agricultural industry lobbied for exemptions and exclusions.

2. WASTEWATER

Animal waste ponds and manure piles from Concentrated Animal Feeding Operations (CAFOs) are a severe blight on the land and water of some states. A river full of liquid chicken fecal matter is a prospect that no mayor wants to confront on the edge of town. Smell, flies attracted, and undesirable effects on local fishing make the ponds nasty in warmer weather. Land disposal of the CAFO "output" as crop fertilizer or just as waste spread on patches of soil are alternate means of disposal. Incineration has many technical challenges, and there would be large environmental issues for persons downwind.

Concentrating and stressing cows, pigs, or chickens with feed mixed with antibitics, to grow the animals faster inside a CAFO without major disease risks, is a decision made on cost grounds. The economic need for jobs and revenues tends to induce the state environmental authorities to accept CAFO locations, sometimes under pressure of state lawmakers who want economic development opportunities. Other resources have gone into great detail about these environmental waste problems. Philosophically, the debate is over the external effect of waste on nearby communities, compared to the external benefits on the state economy of having producers paying taxes in poorer areas. For some, the analysis is one of "environmental justice" for the down-trodden. For others, job creation justifies the CAFO, and those whose homes are affected have had plenty of notice, so they should relocate. The complexities of a "free range" debate will continue to intensify.

3. WATER UTILIZATION

Water use is a significant issue with crop irrigation, animal drinking stations, washing at food processing plants, water use in slaughter-house operations, etc. Public debate in arid states about farm use of water and city water needs often contests the relative value of irrigation diversion of water. Riparian rights, downstream owner entitlement to water, or other powers can be traded or combined in some situations.

4. AIR EMISSIONS AND NUISANCES

Air quality benefits of growing crops are sometimes cited in the debates over global warming. Others assert that the diesel exhausts used in planting and harvesting exceed the oxygen creation benefits of the growing plants. Tree fruit and nut growers may assert that their trees absorb carbon dioxide; a series of environmental assessments would be needed to generate an accurate balance of emission effects.

5. RESIDUES OF PESTICIDE USE

Pesticide use on the crops, the storage bins, and on the land causes a variety of environmental concerns. The long-term effect of the wide use of chemical plant poisons on the soil can be debated from many different perspectives, including runoff, soil degradation, seed issues, etc.

CHAPTER 17:
HOW THE "LOCAL FOOD" MOVEMENT
RELATES TO FOOD SAFETY

Whether it is a fad or a long-lasting trend, advocates for "local food" have been able to draw notice to their viewpoint, and some public debates have expressed support for "close-to-home" food supplies.

Proponents for locally grown food make several arguments. Less energy is burned to move the crop from a distant area to the local consumer. Food is produced more carefully by actual farmers—persons who either sell at a farmer's market or whose identities are known to repeat customers in their local community. Preservation of agricultural traditions is a desirable "connection to the land." Retaining the capacity to sustain ourselves despite the globalization of commerce has a long-term cultural attractiveness. The contrary view is that mass grower and mass distribution processes save costs per unit, making more food more available to more people. Those who wish to pay more for local products can do so, but most will not opt to do so.

The baseline of any evaluation of local food must be what crops can be grown in our climate with our soil, in light of the difficulties of productive food growing, within the natural constraints of our sunlight and warmth season for nurturing plant growth? What crop predators are likely to be encountered here, and is enough land available for the desired crops in light of other commercial and residential use patterns? And which Americans will survive without that quintessential "non-local staple," coffee, tea, or cola?

Local farmers' markets sell produce that the consumer can see along with the grower who literally stands behind the safe condition of her crop. It has not yet been documented whether "local food" sourcing makes a safety difference. The FDA and other agencies do not categorically regard transported food products as being any less valuable or secure. The geographic source of food, so long as the food is safe, should make no difference in the acceptability of the ultimate food by consumers.

What is likely to be missing among local crops sold locally is extensive laboratory evaluation of these crops. In rich agricultural regions, testing labs and soil evaluation systems are well in place. One who does not have nearby scientific support for questions of food safety must depend on either shipping samples to distant university labs or asking regulatory agencies to perform their standard evaluative testing. So the assumption that a crop grown locally contains less cadmium or lead, for example, than a crop grown in southern California, might not be verifiable. The scale of the growing space and the costs of testing might be such that the local farmer would ask the consumer to "take on faith" that the local food is better for you.

CHAPTER 18:
PRICING, COMPETITION, AND MONOPOLY

Why should this book on consumers and food deal with esoteric legal and economic issues like monopoly power? Pricing really matters to food consumers in all nations of the world. Because if food is not affordable, its safety is less relevant, because consumers will be less likely to be eating quantities of that food. One could aspire to have fresh, whole grains and locally grown fruit, but if one is unable to afford those foods, their availability is of little real value to the consumer. For example, imported Russian caviar from the Caspian Sea sturgeon is so expensive that a book on food safety addressing its safety issues would be irrelevant to the vast majority of readers. But affordability of corn flour matters to the less affluent consumers. The diversion of U.S. corn to ethanol production has a consequence for U.S. consumers of products made with corn and worldwide economies that depend on shipments of affordable corn from the U.S. surplus.

Prices tend to fall when many sellers compete in a marketplace with the same goods. Monopoly power is the ability of a seller to control availability of goods so as to keep prices of those goods higher in a particular marketplace than would be the situation if all sellers could freely compete. By analogy, on an island with one fishing boat, the price of the fish to land-based consumers could be dictated by the boat owner. Centuries of consumer and government complaints have not produced any ideal way to safeguard the food pricing system from excessive manipulation. Weather, distribution problems, environmental contamination and other reasons for scarcity will inevitably drive up prices,

By the nature of the food industry, concentration of the movement of food to the marketplace is a source of great power. The costs of food logistics and distribution are likely to be greater with the globalization of remote sourcing of foods like tea and spices. Distribution cost can be reduced by having a smaller number of food cargo suppliers and by integrating shipping modes like cargo vessels, container ports, trains, trucking, etc. The historical pattern is that a smaller number of players are more tempted to arrange commodity prices that favor their profitability. In response, Congress and state legislatures have adopted prohibitions that have made certain tactics for the dominant control of supplies into a clear violation of antitrust laws, if that control occurs.

Dominance in food distribution allows control on pricing in many commodities; a Midwestern ice sales conspiracy led to criminal prosecutions in 2009 against companies that divided the nation and declined to bid for sales in a territory that was secretly allocated to its competing ice distributors. A whistleblower exposed significant antitrust violations by a huge Illinois food conglomerate, which led to multiple criminal penalties against corporate officials. And sometimes the crop-growing stage is where the competition problems are seen. For example, particular varieties of biotechnology seeds may be patented after expensive product research. The use of lawful monopoly power from valid patents may be employed to exclude other sellers of the patented food material for the twenty-year life of that patent. Seeds, plants, variations on certain genetic attributes of food animals, etc. can be modified by genetic engineering that discovers a new way to produce a benefit. Of course, the social policy issues of "engineering lives" can be debated. Should the legal system allow a monopoly to be created through patenting forms of plant or animal life, or should patents in cloning, biotech changes to chickens, etc. be off-limits to the commercial exclusivity of the patent system?

To date, the answer has been to allow patents on living organisms, and with that trend, the patent system has had an important beneficial role in rewarding and stimulating agricultural research. A better tomato, like the bar code reader that the retailer uses to track tomato sales, or the satellite tracking device that is used to monitor movements of tomato-carrying trucks, is able to be patented if the inventor qualifies under the law of patents for the twenty-year term of exclusivity. More details of this debate can be found in many articles or books on antitrust enforcement and competition.

Another form of non-patent monopoly is control of supplies of food ingredients such as spices. This dominant control is less favored in American law. If the dominant food seller has such a strong control of the supply, its pricing decision can hurt the consumer without relief from the competitive marketplace of smaller sellers. For example, the strongest marketer of hay in a remote agricultural corner of the West could agree with the next-largest hay seller to price each seller's hay at an inflated price, and cattle ranchers in January would need to pay more for the hay to save their cattle from snow-caused starvation. Illegal restraints occasionally occur in the food marketplace by the use of monopoly pricing power among very large participants. With imports of specialized food ingredients, the potential exists that exporters from a certain nation might get together to decide how much of their crop is exported at what prices; international antitrust law is not as effective a tool as it could be in preventing such collusive price moves.

Beyond price fixing, there are "tying agreements" for favored products and certain forms of franchising, which are suspected of driving up prices and reducing competition with other producers. These are such detailed legal issues as to go beyond our scope in this book. But the reader should recognize that pricing of food involves factors of market power and competitive power. These elements enter into the consideration of how effectively consumers can be protected from economic misconduct.

Down at the local level, price competition can be directly restrained by agreements among the sellers to limit discounts, to reject coupons, to prefer one milk supplier who is willing to pay secret rebates, etc. These decisions cut out the consumer from a choice of vendors of food—at least a choice based on price—so this kind of restraint is likely to be challenged when and if it comes to light. Given the nature of the current culture favoring whistleblowers, it seems likely that restraints that overtly control a market will come to light from ex-employees and others who learn of the illegal agreements.

Is food any different from other markets that have antitrust problems? Yes, it is. In one way, local food suppliers of perishable materials like milk benefit from geographic advantages when there are few alternate sources for a necessary commodity. The urgency of need for a fresh milk product empowers them in ways that shippers of steel, tires, plastic sheeting, etc. do not enjoy. In another way, food has a great advantage. The agricultural industry has lobbied successfully for federal price control programs. The USDA establishes Marketing Orders for certain commodities such as milk and uses price support payments to support continued production when the food product has temporarily become more expensive to produce than its market sale price. Congress has for decades been receptive to the voting population of farm states, who assert that the price support program "saves the family farm" and produces a more secure chain of supply. What the food consumer needs to know is that political support for price supports is still alive and well, despite the demographic shift toward urban areas and away from small food production. The shift has been a well-understood trend in recent decades, and the congressional decision to retain food subsidies that add to the consumer price of food is a clear political choice, whether wise or not.

CHAPTER 19:
THE FUTURE OF FOOD SAFETY

Technology can be a blessing or a curse, and food technology presents a very public series of choices which some may bless and some may curse. Most consumers embrace new technologies in television, phone service, etc. but might be hesitant about changes in their food choices. Food selection is a choice for those with funds to purchase a variety of foods. As this book has repeatedly described, choices that we make as consumers are the marketplace's choices. And choices that our legislators and regulators make are the central policy decisions for our nation's food supply.

The future involves more elaborate, less expensive safety monitoring and measurement of bacteria and viruses in the food supply. Future diagnostic tools will allow food producers to detect the presence of a pathogenic problem, like *E. coli* 0157:H7, and if enough money is spent on research and recordkeeping, the diagnostic tools will show where the contaminant came into the food system. Sadly, technology has added so much speed and homogeneity to food processing that we may never be able to retrospectively determine which of several sources was the particular antecedent of a particular illness for a person. The closer we look at pathogens in all of our locations in the food chain, the more of the infectious agents we may find there.

Individual health choices govern all key decisions about foods. With affluence comes choice. The purchase of a higher-priced food that has a known origin, which complies with organic standards of non-chemical treatment during growing, is a choice that some consumers make. As more opt for foods with an organic production background, farmers will respond to meet the market desires. If consumers decline to eat the meat harvested from cloned sheep, the marketplace will respond by declining to use that technology. What is significant is that the marketplace of consumer perceptions is far stronger in its impacts than the impact of the occasional government regulatory effort. If consumers boycott a food they believe to be unsafe, its sales will collapse rapidly. But a marketplace trend is seen in proprietary sales statistics over time, not so much in broadcast news.

Consumer perceptions, good or bad, are a subtle consumer message or signal. Companies must comply if they wish to retain competitive position. That subtlety explains why the relatively few government regulatory enforcement actions inevitably get publicity, while the companies' reactions to sales trends usually escape the press and media coverage.

The future of food frauds can be stated more bluntly: no change will be able to stop all of the excessive claims. Deterrence by penalties or jail time or orders to disgorge (give back) money will not halt this bad behavior. Human nature will lead some firms to continue the hype that offers attractiveness through miracle diets, and human folly will continue to lead some to believe it. The future of food safety is that more vigilance and tougher controls will produce more protections but at a higher cost. At the end, we recognize that in both food safety and food frauds, it is our individual efforts that are the solution to these interrelated problems.

APPENDIX 1:
FEDERAL TRADE COMMISSION WEBSITE CAUTION WEIGHING THE EVIDENCE IN DIET ADS

Flip through a magazine, scan a newspaper, or channel surf and you see them everywhere: Ads that promise quick and easy weight loss without diet or exercise. Wouldn't it be nice if—as the ads claim—you could lose weight simply by taking a pill, wearing a patch, or rubbing in a cream? Too bad claims like that are almost always false.

Doctors, dieticians, and other experts agree that the best way to lose weight is to eat fewer calories and increase your physical activity so you burn more energy. A reasonable goal is to lose about a pound a week. For most people, that means cutting about 500 calories a day from your diet, eating a variety of nutritious foods, and exercising regularly.

When it comes to evaluating claims for weight loss products, the Federal Trade Commission (FTC) recommends a healthy portion of skepticism. Before you spend money on products that promise fast and easy results, weigh the claims carefully. Think twice before wasting your money on products that make any of these false claims:

"Lose weight without diet or exercise!"

Achieving a healthy weight takes work. Take a pass on any product that promises miraculous results without the effort. Buy one and the only thing you'll lose is money.

"Lose weight no matter how much you eat of your favorite foods!"

Beware of any product that claims that you can eat all you want of high-calorie foods and still lose weight. Losing weight requires sensible food choices. Filling up on healthy vegetables and fruits can make it easier to say no to fattening sweets and snacks.

"Lose weight permanently! Never diet again!"

Even if you're successful in taking the weight off, permanent weight loss requires permanent lifestyle changes. Don't trust any product that promises once-and-for-all results without ongoing maintenance.

"Block the absorption of fat, carbs, or calories!"

Doctors, dieticians, and other experts agree that there's simply no magic non-prescription pill that will allow you to block the absorption of fat, carbs, or calories. The key to curbing your craving for those "downfall foods" is portion control. Limit yourself to a smaller serving or a slimmer slice.

"Lose 30 pounds in 30 days!"

Losing weight at the rate of a pound or two a week is the most effective way to take it off and keep it off. At best, products promising lightning-fast weight loss are false. At worst, they can ruin your health.

"Everybody will lose weight!"

Your habits and health concerns are unique. There is simply no one-size-fits-all product guaranteed to work for everyone. Team up with your health care provider to design a personalized nutrition and exercise program suited to your lifestyle and metabolism.

"Lose weight with our miracle diet patch or cream!"

You've seen the ads for diet patches or creams that claim to melt away the pounds. Don't believe them. There's nothing you can wear or apply to your skin that will cause you to lose weight.

For more information, visit the FTC's website at www.ftc.gov. Additional information on nutrition and weight loss is available through the National Institute of Diabetes and Digestive and Kidney Diseases' Weight-control Information Network (1-800-WIN-8098). To report fraudulent weight loss product claims, contact your state Attorney General, local consumer protection office, or Better Business Bureau.

The FTC works for the consumer to prevent fraudulent, deceptive, and unfair business practices in the marketplace and to provide information to help consumers spot, stop, and avoid them. To file a complaint or to get free information on consumer issues, visit ftc.gov or call toll-free, 1-877-FTC-HELP (1-877-382-4357); TTY: 1-866-653-4261. The FTC enters consumer complaints into the Consumer Sentinel Network, a secure online database and investigative tool used by hundreds of civil and criminal law enforcement agencies in the U.S. and abroad.

APPENDIX 2:
PESTICIDE RESIDUES

FDA Compliance Policy Guide 575.100 (emphasis added)

http://www.fda.gov/ICECI/ComplianceManuals/CompliancePolicy GuidanceManual/ucm123236.htm

Tolerances for Pesticides:

Section 408 of the FFDCA authorizes the Environmental Protection Agency (EPA) to establish a tolerance for the maximum amount of a pesticide residue that may be legally present in or on a raw agricultural commodity. This section also authorizes EPA to exempt a pesticide residue in a raw agricultural commodity from the requirement of a tolerance. A tolerance or tolerance exemption is required when EPA grants registration under the Federal Insecticide, Fungicide, and Rodenticide Act (FIFRA) for the use of a pesticide in food and feed production in the United States. Registration of a pesticide is not, however, a prerequisite for establishing a tolerance. For example, EPA may establish a temporary tolerance under section 408(j) to permit the experimental use of a non-registered pesticide, or *EPA may establish a tolerance for a pesticide residue resulting from the use of the pesticide in food or feed production in a foreign country*.

Tolerances and exemptions from tolerances established by EPA for pesticide residues in a raw agricultural commodities are listed in 40 CFR Part 180.

Food Additive Regulations for Pesticides:

A tolerance or tolerance exemption for a pesticide residue in a raw agricultural commodity also applies to the processed form of the commodity when ready to eat. (See section 402(a)(2)(C) of the FFDCA.) However, *if a pesticide is to be used on a processed food or feed, or if conformity with residue present in or on a raw agricultural commodity in conformity with its tolerance under section 408 concentrates during processing to a level when ready to eat that is greater than the tolerance for the raw agricultural commodity, a food additive regulation is required.* In either instance, EPA is authorized under section 409 of the FFDCA to establish a food additive regulation for the maximum amount of a pesticide residue that may be legally present in a processed food or feed.

Food additive regulations issued by EPA for pesticide residues in processed food and feed appear in 21 CFR Part 193 and in 21 CFR Part 561, respectively.

Enforcement of Tolerances and Food Additive Regulations for Pesticides:

The Food and Drug Administration (FDA) is responsible for the enforcement of pesticide tolerances and food additive regulations established by EPA. This enforcement authority is derived from section 402(a)(2)(B) and of the FFDCA. Under this section a raw agricultural commodity or a processed food or feed is deemed to be adulterated and subject to FDA enforcement action if it contains either:

– A pesticide residue at a level greater than that specified by a tolerance or food additive regulation; or

– A pesticide residue for which there is no tolerance, tolerance exemption, or food additive regulation.

There are exceptions to FDA enforcing an adulteration charge under section 402 for a pesticide residue in a food or feed that is not subject to a tolerance, tolerance exemption, or food additive regulation. The exceptions include:

– Unavoidable Pesticide Residues: Food or feed may contain a pesticide residue from sources of contamination that cannot be avoided by good agricultural or manufacturing practices, such as contamination by a pesticide that persists in the environment. *In the absence of a tolerance, tolerance exemption, or food additive regulation, FDA may establish an "action level" for such unavoidable pesticide residues. An action level specifies the level below which FDA exercises its discretion not to take enforcement action.* An action level established by FDA is based on EPA's recommendation, which follows the criteria of Section 406 of the FFDCA. (See 21 CFR Parts 109 and 509 for information on FDA policy and procedures for establishing action levels for unavoidable food and feed contaminants.) Food or feed found to contain an unavoidable pesticide residue at a level that is at or greater than an action level is subject to FDA enforcement action. FDA action levels currently in effect for unavoidable pesticide residues in food and feed are listed in Attachment B.

– EPA Emergency Exemptions: EPA is authorized by section 18 of FIFRA to grant an exemption from the registration requirements for the use of a non-registered pesticide under emergency conditions. (See 40 CFR Part 166.) Neither FIFRA nor the FFDCA have explicit provisions for establishing an "emergency tolerance" for a pesticide residue resulting from an emergency exemption granted-by EPA for food or feed use. Under a formal agreement between the U.S. Department of Agriculture, EPA, and FDA (50 FR 2304), however, EPA will recommend an enforcement level for residues of a pesticide granted an emergency exemption. FDA will use the recommended enforcement level to determine compliance with the FFDCA. (See FDA Field Management Directive No. 136.)

FDA will also consider taking enforcement action for violation of sections 402(a)(2)(B) or 402(a)(2)(C) in the following situations:

– A food or feed contains residues of two or more pesticides of the same chemical class and the total amount of such residues when added together exceeds the lowest numerical tolerance for residues of one of the pesticides found in that class as set forth in 40 CFR 180.3(e)(1). (Note: In applying the criteria in this regulation, the residues to be added together must be at or above the analytical limit of quantitation as specified in the Pesticide Analytical Manual (PAM), Volume I, section 143.21.).

– A processed food or feed was derived from a raw agricultural commodity that contained a pesticide residue that did not conform to an established tolerance or tolerance exemption.

– In the absence of a food additive regulation and in accordance with 21 CFR 170.19 or 21 CFR 570.19, a pesticide residue in a processed food or feed when ready to eat is greater than the tolerance prescribed for the raw agricultural commodity.

Imports:

The requirements of section 402 of the FFDCA apply equally to domestically produced and imported food and feed found to contain pesticide residues. Therefore, *even though the use of a pesticide in a foreign country is not subject to EPA registration requirements under FIFRA, a pesticide residue in imported food or feed must be in conformity with a tolerance, tolerance exemption, or food additive regulation established by EPA* or, if the pesticide residue is unavoidable, an action level established by FDA.

APPENDIX 3:
FEDERAL FOOD SAFETY RESOURCE WEBSITES

- Food & Drug Administration (fda.gov)

- Food Safety and Inspection Service (U.S. Department of Agriculture)

- www.FoodSafety.gov (Managed by Food and Drug Administration) *Gateway to Government Food Safety Information*

- National Food Safety Programs (www.foodsafety.gov) *Produce and Import Initiative/Eggs/Fruit Juice Sprouts / Listeria /Research/ Risk Assessment*

- Food Defense and Terrorism (Food and Drug Administration) fda.gov

- Food Safety Office (Centers for Disease Control and Prevention) cdc.gov

- Food Safety (Environmental Protection Agency) epa.gov

- U.S. Customs and Border Protection

APPENDIX 4:
REPORTABLE FOOD

OUTLINE OF FOOD CONTAMINATION RESPONSE PLAN AS SEEN BY U.S. FDA UNDER ITS "REPORTABLE FOOD REGISTRY" REQUIREMENTS AFTER 2009

1. Food company registers its site as a food establishment, e.g. peanut factory, cookie bakery, juice plant.

2. Food company is a "responsible party" for reporting under section 1005 of FDA Amendments Act.

3. Food company learns of contamination or other significant food concern with incoming food, processed food on site, or food shipped out to distribution. If the concern entails a probability of serious adverse health consequences or death, the company must notify FDA within 24 hours by website submission to FDA "Electronic Portal" for reports and must notify suppliers and direct customers (option: all customers, public alert, etc.).

4. Food company has all the usual legal obligations of product recall and customer notification, in addition to reportable food registry actions.

5. FDA will coordinate with state and the Center for Disease Control, and will conduct inspection and request records.

6. FDA may choose to issue a public alert via news media re health risks.

7. Inspection and records search may lead the FDA to charge the company for delays in reporting should the company have known about serious risks.

8. Companies anticipate extensive adverse publicity from use of the report by attorneys, who will seek potential claimants potentially affected by healthy issues post-food consumption.

9. Companies anticipate refund for claimants, and the subsequent product reputational concerns.

APPENDIX 5:
FEDERAL MEAT INSPECTION ACT (FMIA)

TITLE 21 – FOOD AND DRUGS

CHAPTER 12 – MEAT INSPECTION

SUBCHAPTER I—INSPECTION REQUIREMENTS; ADULTERATION
AND MISBRANDING

§601. Definitions.

As used in this chapter, except as otherwise specified, the following terms shall have the meanings stated below:

(a) The term "Secretary" means the Secretary of Agriculture of the United States or his delegate.

(b) The term "firm" means any partnership, association, or other unincorporated business organization.

(c) The term "meat broker" means any person, firm, or corporation engaged in the business of buying or selling carcasses, parts of carcasses, meat, or meat food products of cattle, sheep, swine, goats, horses, mules, or other equines on commission, or otherwise negotiating purchases or sales of such articles other than for his own account or as an employee of another person, firm, or corporation.

(d) The term "renderer" means any person, firm, or corporation engaged in the business of rendering carcasses or parts or products of the carcasses, of cattle, sheep, swine, goats, horses, mules, or other equines, except rendering conducted under inspection or exemption under this subchapter.

(e) The term "animal food manufacturer" means any person, firm, or corporation engaged in the business of manufacturing or processing animal food derived wholly or in part from carcasses, or parts of products of the carcasses, of cattle, sheep, swine, goats, horses, mules, or other equines.

(f) The term "State" means any State of the United States and the Commonwealth of Puerto Rico.

(g) The term "Territory" means Guam, the Virgin Islands of the United States, American Samoa, and any other territory or possession of the United States, excluding the Canal Zone.

(h) The term "commerce" means commerce between any State, any Territory, or the District of Columbia, and any place outside thereof; or within any Territory not organized with a legislative body, or the District of Columbia.

(i) The term "United States" means the States, the District of Columbia, and the Territories of the United States.

(j) The term "meat food product" means any product capable of use as human food which is made wholly or in part from any meat or other portion of the carcass of any cattle, sheep, swine, or goats, excepting products which contain meat or other portions of such carcasses only in a relatively small proportion or historically have not been considered by consumers as products of the meat food industry, and which are exempted from definition as a meat food product by the Secretary under such conditions as he may prescribe to assure that the meat or other portions of such carcasses contained in such product are not adulterated and that such products are not represented as meat food products. This term as applied to food products of equines shall have a meaning comparable to that provided in this paragraph with respect to cattle, sheep, swine, and goats.

(k) The term "capable of use as human food" shall apply to any carcass, or part or product of a carcass, of any animal, unless it is denatured or otherwise identified as required by regulations prescribed by the Secretary to deter its use as human food, or it is naturally inedible by humans.

(l) The term "prepared" means slaughtered, canned, salted, rendered, boned, cut up, or otherwise manufactured or processed.

(m) The term "adulterated" shall apply to any carcass, part thereof, meat or meat food product under one or more of the following circumstances:

- (1) if it bears or contains any poisonous or deleterious substance which may render it injurious to health; but in case the substance is not an added substance, such article shall not be considered adulterated under this clause if the quantity of such substance in or on such article does not ordinarily render it injurious to health;

- (2)
  - (A) if it bears or contains (by reason of administration of any substance to the live animal or otherwise) any added poisonous or added deleterious substance (other than one which is
    - (i) a pesticide chemical in or on a raw agricultural commodity;
    - (ii) a food additive; or
    - (iii) a color additive) which may, in the judgment of the Secretary, make such article unfit for human food;
  - (B) if it is, in whole or in part, a raw agricultural commodity and such commodity bears or contains a pesticide chemical which is unsafe within the meaning of section 346a of this title,
  - (C) if it bears or contains any food additive which is unsafe within the meaning of section 348 of this title,
  - (D) if it bears or contains any color additive which is unsafe within the meaning of section 379e of this title: Provided, That an article which is not adulterated under clause (B), (C), or (D) shall nevertheless be deemed adulterated if use of the pesticide chemical, food additive, or color additive in or on such article is prohibited by regulations of the Secretary in establishments at which inspection is maintained under this subchapter
  - (3) if it consists in whole or in part of any filthy, putrid, or decomposed substance or is for any other reason unsound, unhealthful, unwholesome, or otherwise unfit for human food;
- (4) if it has been prepared, packed, or held under insanitary conditions whereby it may have become contaminated with filth, or whereby it may have been rendered injurious to health;
- (5) if it is, in whole or in part, the product of an animal which has died otherwise than by slaughter;
- (6) if its container is composed, in whole or in part, of any poisonous or deleterious substance which may render the contents injurious to health;
- (7) if it has been intentionally subjected to radiation, unless the use of the radiation was in conformity with a regulation or exemption in effect pursuant to section 348 of this title;
- (8) if any valuable constituent has been in whole or in part omitted or abstracted therefrom; or if any substance has been substituted, wholly or in part therefor; or if damage or inferiority has been

concealed in any manner; or if any substance has been added thereto or mixed or packed therewith so as to increase its bulk or weight, or reduce its quality or strength, or make it appear better or of greater value than it is; or

- (9) if it is margarine containing animal fat and any of the raw material used therein consisted in whole or in part of any filthy, putrid, or decomposed substance.

(n) The term "misbranded" shall apply to any carcass, part thereof, meat or meat food product under one or more of the following circumstances:

- (1) if its labeling is false or misleading in any particular;
- (2) if it is offered for sale under the name of another food;
- (3) if it is an imitation of another food, unless its label bears, in type of uniform size and prominence, the word "imitation" and immediately thereafter, the name of the food imitated;
- (4) if its container is so made, formed, or filled as to be misleading;
- (5) if in a package or other container unless it bears a label showing (A) the name and place of business of the manufacturer, packer, or distributor; and (B) an accurate statement of the quantity of the contents in terms of weight, measure, or numerical count: Provided, That under clause (B) of this subparagraph (5), reasonable variations may be permitted, and exemptions as to small packages may be established, by regulations prescribed by the Secretary;
- (6) if any word, statement, or other information required by or under authority of this chapter to appear on the label or other labeling is not prominently placed thereon with such conspicuousness (as compared with other words, statements, designs, or devices, in the labeling) and in such terms as to render it likely to be read and understood by the ordinary individual under customary conditions of purchase and use;
- (7) if it purports to be or is represented as a food for which a definition and standard of identity or composition has been prescribed by regulations of the Secretary under section 607 of this title unless (A) it conforms to such definition and standard, and (B) its label bears the name of the food specified in the definition and standard and, insofar as may be required by such regulations, the common names of optional ingredients (other than spices, flavoring, and coloring) present in such food;

- (8) if it purports to be or is represented as a food for which a standard or standards of fill of container have been prescribed by regulations of the Secretary under section 607 of this title, and it falls below the standard of fill of container applicable thereto, unless its label bears, in such manner and form as such regulations specify, a statement that it falls below such standard;

- (9) if it is not subject to the provisions of subparagraph (7), unless its label bears (A) the common or usual name of the food, if any there be, and (B) in case it is fabricated from two or more ingredients, the common or usual name of each such ingredient; except that spices, flavorings, and colorings may, when authorized by the Secretary, be designated as spices, flavorings, and colorings without naming each: Provided, That to the extent that compliance with the requirements of clause (B) of this subparagraph (9) is impracticable, or results in deception or unfair competition, exemptions shall be established by regulations promulgated by the Secretary;

- (10) if it purports to be or is represented for special dietary uses, unless its label bears such information concerning its vitamin, mineral, and other dietary properties as the Secretary, after consultation with the Secretary of Health and Human Services, determines to be, and by regulations prescribes as, necessary in order fully to inform purchasers as to its value for such uses;

- (11) if it bears or contains any artificial flavoring, artificial coloring, or chemical preservative, unless it bears labeling stating that fact: Provided, That, to the extent that compliance with the requirements of this subparagraph (11) is impracticable, exemptions shall be established by regulations promulgated by the Secretary; or

- (12) if it fails to bear, directly thereon or on its container, as the Secretary may by regulations prescribe, the inspection legend and, unrestricted by any of the foregoing, such other information as the Secretary may require in such regulations to assure that it will not have false or misleading labeling and that the public will be informed of the manner of handling required to maintain the article in a wholesome condition.

(o) The term "label" means a display of written, printed, or graphic matter upon the immediate container (not including package liners) of any article.

(p) The term "labeling" means all labels and other written, printed, or graphic matter (1) upon any article or any of its containers or wrappers, or (2) accompanying such article.

(q) The term "Federal Food, Drug, and Cosmetic Act (21 U.S.C. 301 et seq.)" means the Act so entitled, approved June 25, 1938 (52 Stat. 1040), and Acts amendatory thereof or supplementary thereto.

(r) The terms "pesticide chemical," "food additive," "color additive," and "raw agricultural commodity" shall have the same meanings for purposes of this chapter as under the Federal Food, Drug, and Cosmetic Act (21 U.S.C. 301 et seq.).

(s) The term "official mark" means the official inspection legend or any other symbol prescribed by regulations of the Secretary to identify the status of any article or animal under this chapter.

(t) The term "official inspection legend" means any symbol prescribed by regulations of the Secretary showing that an article was inspected and passed in accordance with this chapter.

(u) The term "official certificate" means any certificate prescribed by regulations of the Secretary for issuance by an inspector or other person performing official functions under this chapter.

(v) The term "official device" means any device prescribed or authorized by the Secretary for use in applying any official mark.

§602. Congressional statement of findings.

Meat and meat food products are an important source of the Nation's total supply of food. They are consumed throughout the Nation and the major portion thereof moves in interstate or foreign commerce. It is essential in the public interest that the health and welfare of consumers be protected by assuring that meat and meat food products distributed to them are wholesome, not adulterated, and properly marked, labeled, and packaged. Unwholesome, adulterated, or misbranded meat or meat food products impair the effective regulation of meat and meat food products in interstate or foreign commerce, are injurious to the public welfare, destroy markets for wholesome, not adulterated, and properly labeled and packaged meat and meat food products, and result in sundry losses to livestock producers and processors of meat and meat food products, as well as injury to consumers. The unwholesome, adulterated, mislabeled, or deceptively packaged articles can be sold at lower prices and compete unfairly with the wholesome, not adulterated, and properly labeled and packaged articles, to the detriment of consumers and the public generally. It is hereby found that all articles and animals which are regulated under this chapter are either in interstate or foreign commerce or substantially affect such commerce, and that regulation by the Secretary and cooperation by the States and other jurisdictions as contemplated by this chapter are appropriate to prevent and eliminate burdens upon such commerce, to effectively regulate such commerce, and to protect the health and welfare of consumers.

§603. Inspection of meat and meat food products.

- **(a) Examination of animals before slaughtering; diseased animals slaughtered separately and carcasses examined**

For the purpose of preventing the use in commerce of meat and meat food products which are adulterated, the Secretary shall cause to be made, by inspectors appointed for that purpose, an examination and inspection of all cattle, sheep, swine, goats, horses, mules, and other equines before they shall be allowed to enter into any slaughtering, packing, meat-canning, rendering, or similar establishment, in which they are to be slaughtered and the meat and meat food products thereof are to be used in commerce; and all cattle, sheep, swine, goats, horses, mules, and other equines found on such inspection to show symptoms of disease shall be set apart and slaughtered separately from all other cattle, sheep, swine, goats, horses, mules, or other equines, and when so slaughtered the carcasses of said cattle, sheep, swine, goats, horses, mules, or other equines shall be subject to a careful examination and inspection, all as provided by the rules and regulations to be prescribed by the Secretary, as provided for in this subchapter.

- **(b) Humane methods of slaughter**

For the purpose of preventing the inhumane slaughtering of livestock, the Secretary shall cause to be made, by inspectors appointed for that purpose, an examination and inspection of the method by which cattle, sheep, swine, goats, horses, mules, and other equines are slaughtered and handled in connection with slaughter in the slaughtering establishments inspected under this chapter. The Secretary may refuse to provide inspection to a new slaughtering establishment or may cause inspection to be temporarily suspended at a slaughtering establishment if the Secretary finds that any cattle, sheep, swine, goats, horses, mules, or other equines have been slaughtered or handled in connection with slaughter at such establishment by any method not in accordance with the Act of August 27, 1958 (72 Stat. 862; 7 U.S.C. 1901–1906) until the establishment furnishes assurances satisfactory to the Secretary that all slaughtering and handling in connection with slaughter of livestock shall be in accordance with such a method.

§604. Post mortem examination of carcasses and marking or labeling; destruction of carcasses condemned; reinspection.

For the purposes hereinbefore set forth the Secretary shall cause to be made by inspectors appointed for that purpose a post mortem examination and inspection of the carcasses and parts thereof of all cattle, sheep, swine, goats, horses, mules, and other equines to be prepared at any slaughtering, meat-canning, salting, packing, rendering, or similar establishment in any State, Territory, or the District of Columbia as articles of commerce which are capable of use as human food; and the carcasses and parts thereof of all such animals found to be not adulterated shall be marked, stamped, tagged, or labeled as "Inspected and passed"; and said inspectors shall label, mark, stamp, or tag as "Inspected and condemned" all carcasses and parts thereof of animals found to be adulterated; and all carcasses and parts thereof thus inspected and condemned shall be destroyed for food purposes by the said establishment in the presence of an inspector, and the Secretary may remove inspectors from any such establishment which fails to so destroy any such condemned carcass or part thereof, and said inspectors, after said first inspection, shall, when they deem it necessary, reinspect said carcasses or parts thereof to determine whether since the first inspection the same have become adulterated, and if any carcass or any part thereof shall, upon examination and inspection subsequent to the first examination and inspection, be found to be adulterated, it shall be destroyed for food purposes by the said establishment in the presence of an inspector, and the Secretary may remove inspectors from any establishment which fails to so destroy any such condemned carcass or part thereof.

§605. Examination of carcasses brought into slaughtering or packing establishments, and of meat food products issued from and returned thereto; conditions for entry.

The foregoing provisions shall apply to all carcasses or parts of carcasses of cattle, sheep, swine, goats, horses, mules, and other equines or the meat or meat products thereof which may be brought into any slaughtering, meat-canning, salting, packing, rendering, or similar establishment, and such examination and inspection shall be had before the said carcasses or parts thereof shall be allowed to enter into any department wherein the same are to be treated and prepared for meat food products; and the foregoing provisions shall also apply to all such products, which, after having been issued from any slaughtering, meat-canning, salting, packing, rendering, or similar establishment, shall be returned to the same or to any similar establishment where such inspection is maintained. The Secretary may limit the entry of carcasses, parts of carcasses, meat and meat food products, and other materials into any establishment at which inspection under this subchapter is maintained, under such conditions as he may prescribe to assure that allowing the entry of such articles into such inspected establishments will be consistent with the purposes of this chapter.

§606. Inspectors of meat food products; marks of inspection; destruction of condemned products; products for export.

For the purposes hereinbefore set forth the Secretary shall cause to be made, by inspectors appointed for that purpose, an examination and inspection of all meat food products prepared for commerce in any slaughtering, meat-canning, salting, packing, rendering, or similar establishment, and for the purposes of any examination and inspection and inspectors shall have access at all times, by day or night, whether the establishment be operated or not, to every part of said establishment; and said inspectors shall mark, stamp, tag, or label as "Inspected and passed" all such products found to be not adulterated; and said inspectors shall label, mark, stamp, or tag as "Inspected and condemned" all such products found adulterated, and all such condemned meat food products shall be destroyed for food purposes, as hereinbefore provided, and the Secretary may remove inspectors from any establishment which fails to so destroy such condemned meat food products: *Provided*, That subject to the rules and regulations of the Secretary the provisions of this section in regard to preservatives shall not apply to meat food products for export to any foreign country and which are prepared or packed according to the specifications or directions of the foreign purchaser, when no substance is used in the preparation or packing thereof in conflict with the laws of the foreign country to which said article is to be exported; but if said article shall be in fact sold or offered for sale for domestic use or consumption then this proviso shall not exempt said article from the operation of all the other provisions of this chapter.

§607. Labeling, marking, and container requirements.

- **(a) Labeling receptacles or coverings of meat or meat food products inspected and passed; supervision by inspectors.**

When any meat or meat food product prepared for commerce which has been inspected as hereinbefore provided and marked "Inspected and passed" shall be placed or packed in any can, pot, tin, canvas, or other receptacle or covering in any establishment where inspection under the provisions of this chapter is maintained, the person, firm, or corporation preparing said product shall cause a label to be attached to said can, pot, tin, canvas, or other receptacle or covering, under the supervision of an inspector, which label shall state that the contents thereof have been "inspected and passed" under the provisions of this chapter; and no inspection and examination of meat or meat food products deposited or inclosed in cans, tins, pots, canvas, or other receptacle or covering in any establishment where inspection under the provisions of this chapter is maintained shall be deemed to be complete until such meat or meat food products have been sealed or inclosed in said can, tin, pot, canvas, or other receptacle or covering under the supervision of an inspector.

- **(b) Information on articles or containers; legible form.**

All carcasses, parts of carcasses, meat and meat food products inspected at any establishment under the authority of this subchapter and found to be not adulterated, shall at the time they leave the establishment bear, in distinctly legible form, directly thereon or on their containers, as the Secretary may require, the information required under paragraph (n) of section 601 of this title.

- **(c) Labeling: type styles and sizes; definitions and standards of identity or composition; standards of fill of container; consistency of Federal and Federal-State standards.**

The Secretary, whenever he determines such action is necessary for the protection of the public, may prescribe: (1) the styles and sizes of type to be used with respect to material required to be incorporated in labeling to avoid false or misleading labeling in marketing and labeling any articles or animals subject to this subchapter or subchapter II of this chapter; (2) definitions and standards of identity or composition for articles subject to this subchapter and standards of fill of container for such articles not inconsistent with any such standards established under the Federal Food, Drug, and Cosmetic Act (21 U.S.C. 301 et seq.), and there shall be consultation between the Secretary and the Secretary of Health and Human Services prior to the issuance of such standards under either Act relating to articles subject to this chapter to avoid inconsistency in such standards and possible impairment of the coordinated effective administration of these Acts. There shall also be consultation between the Secretary and an appropriate advisory committee provided for in section 661 of this title, prior to the issuance of such standards under this chapter, to avoid, insofar as feasible, inconsistency between Federal and State standards.

- **(d) Sales under false or misleading name, other marking or labeling or in containers of misleading form or size; trade names, and other marking, labeling, and containers approved by Secretary.**

No article subject to this subchapter shall be sold or offered for sale by any person, firm, or corporation, in commerce, under any name or other marking or labeling which is false or misleading, or in any container of a misleading form or size, but established trade names and other marking and labeling and containers which are not false or misleading and which are approved by the Secretary are permitted.

- **(e) Use withholding directive respecting false or misleading marking, labeling, or container; modification of false or misleading matter; hearing; withholding use pending proceedings; finality of Secretary's action; judicial review; application of section 194 of title 7.**

If the Secretary has reason to believe that any marking or labeling or the size or form of any container in use or proposed for use with respect to any article subject to this subchapter is false or misleading in any particular, he may direct that such use be withheld unless the marking, labeling, or container is modified in such manner as he may prescribe so that it will not be false or misleading. If the person, firm, or corporation using or proposing to use the marking, labeling or container does not accept the determination of the Secretary, such person, firm, or corporation may request a hearing, but the use of the marking, labeling, or container shall, if the Secretary so directs, be withheld pending hearing and final determination by the Secretary. Any such determination by the Secretary shall be conclusive unless, within thirty days after receipt of notice of such final determination, the person, firm, or corporation adversely affected thereby appeals to the United States court of appeals for the circuit in which such person, firm, or corporation has its principal place of business or to the United States Court of Appeals for the District of Columbia Circuit. The provisions of section 194 of title 7 shall be applicable to appeals taken under this section.

§608. Sanitary inspection and regulation of slaughtering and packing establishments; rejection of adulterated meat or meat food products.

The Secretary shall cause to be made, by experts in sanitation or by other competent inspectors, such inspection of all slaughtering, meat canning, salting, packing, rendering, or similar establishments in which cattle, sheep, swine, goats, horses, mules and other equines are slaughtered and the meat and meat food products thereof are prepared for commerce as may be necessary to inform himself concerning the sanitary conditions of the same, and to prescribe the rules and regulations of sanitation under which such establishments shall be maintained; and where the sanitary conditions of any such establishment are such that the meat or meat food products are rendered adulterated, he shall refuse to allow said meat or meat food products to be labeled, marked, stamped or tagged as "inspected and passed."

§609. Examination of animals and food products thereof, slaughtered and prepared during nighttime.

The Secretary shall cause an examination and inspection of all cattle, sheep, swine, goats, horses, mules and other equines, and the food products thereof, slaughtered and prepared in the establishments hereinbefore described for the purposes of commerce to be made during the nighttime as well as during the daytime when the slaughtering of said cattle, sheep, swine, goats, horses, mules, and other equines, or the preparation of said food products is conducted during the nighttime.

§610. Prohibited acts.

No person, firm, or corporation shall, with respect to any cattle, sheep, swine, goats, horses, mules, or other equines, or any carcasses, parts of carcasses, meat or meat food products of any such animals—

- **(a) Slaughtering animals or preparation of articles capable of use as human food**

Slaughter any such animals or prepare any such articles which are capable of use as human food at any establishment preparing any such articles for commerce, except in compliance with the requirements of this chapter;

- **(b) Humane methods of slaughter**

Slaughter or handle in connection with slaughter any such animals in any manner not in accordance with the Act of August 27, 1958 (72 Stat. 862; 7 U.S.C. 1901–1906);

- **(c) Sales, transportation, and other transactions**

Sell, transport, offer for sale or transportation, or receive for transportation, in commerce, (1) any such articles which (A) are capable of use as human food and (B) are adulterated or misbranded at the time of such sale, transportation, offer for sale or transportation, or receipt for transportation; or (2) any articles required to be inspected under this subchapter unless they have been so inspected and passed;

- **(d) Adulteration or misbranding**

Do, with respect to any such articles which are capable of use as human food, any act while they are being transported in commerce or held for sale after such transportation, which is intended to cause or has the effect of causing such articles to be adulterated or misbranded.

§611. Devices, marks, labels, and certificates; simulations.

• (a) Devices to be made under authorization of Secretary

No brand manufacturer, printer, or other person, firm, or corporation shall cast, print, lithograph, or otherwise make any device containing any official mark or simulation thereof, or any label bearing any such mark or simulation, or any form of official certificate or simulation thereof, except as authorized by the Secretary.

• (b) Other misconduct

No person, firm, or corporation shall—

- (1) forge any official device, mark, or certificate;

- (2) without authorization from the Secretary use any official device, mark, or certificate, or simulation thereof, or alter, detach, deface, or destroy any official device, mark, or certificate;

- (3) contrary to the regulations prescribed by the Secretary, fail to use, or to detach, deface, or destroy any official device, mark, or certificate;

- (4) knowingly possess, without promptly notifying the Secretary or his representative, any official device or any counterfeit, simulated, forged, or improperly altered official certificate or any device or label or any carcass of any animal, or part or product thereof, bearing any counterfeit, simulated, forged, or improperly altered official mark;

- (5) knowingly make any false statement in any shipper's certificate or other nonofficial or official certificate provided for in the regulations prescribed by the Secretary; or

- (6) knowingly represent that any article has been inspected and passed, or exempted, under this chapter when, in fact, it has, respectively, not been so inspected and passed, or exempted.

§612. Inspection of animals for export.

The Secretary shall cause to be made a careful inspection of all cattle, sheep, swine, goats, horses, mules, and other equines intended and offered for export to foreign countries at such times and places, and in such manner as he may deem proper, to ascertain whether such cattle, sheep, swine, goats, horses, mules, and other equines are free from disease.

§613. Inspectors of animals for export; certificates of condition.

For the purpose of section 612 of this title the Secretary may appoint inspectors who shall be authorized to give an official certificate clearly stating the condition in which such cattle, sheep, swine, goats, horses, mules, and other equines are found.

§614. Clearance prohibited to vessel carrying animals for export without inspector's certificate.

No clearance shall be given to any vessel having on board cattle, sheep, swine, goats, horses, mules, or other equines for export to a foreign country until the owner or shipper of such cattle, sheep, swine, goats, horses, mules, or other equines has a certificate from the inspector authorized to be appointed, stating that the said cattle, sheep, swine, goats, horses, mules, or other equines are sound and healthy, or unless the Secretary shall have waived the requirement of such certificate for export to the particular country to which such cattle, sheep, swine, goats, horses, mules, or other equines are to be exported.

§615. Inspection of carcasses, meat of which is intended for export.

The Secretary shall also cause to be made a careful inspection of the carcasses and parts thereof of all cattle, sheep, swine, goats, horses, mules, and other equines, the meat of which, fresh, salted, canned, corned, packed, cured, or otherwise prepared, is intended and offered for export to any foreign country, at such times and places and in such manner as he may deem proper.

§616. Inspectors of carcasses, etc., meat of which is intended for export; certificates of condition.

For the purpose of section 615 of this title the Secretary may appoint inspectors who shall be authorized to give an official certificate stating the condition in which said cattle, sheep, swine, goats, horses, mules, or other equines, and the meat thereof, are found.

§617. Clearance prohibited to vessel carrying meat for export without inspector's certificate.

No clearance shall be given to any vessel having on board any fresh, salted, canned, corned, or packed beef, mutton, pork, goat or equine meat for export to and sale in a foreign country from any port in the United States, until the owner or shipper thereof shall obtain from an inspector appointed under the provisions of this chapter a certificate that the said cattle, sheep, swine, goats, horses, mules, and other equines were sound and healthy at the time of inspection, and that their meat is sound and wholesome, unless the Secretary shall have waived the requirements of such certificate for the country to which said cattle, sheep, swine, goats, horses, mules, and other equines or meats are to be exported.

§618. Delivery of inspectors' certificates, and of copies.

The inspectors provided for under this subchapter shall be authorized to give official certificates of the condition of the cattle, sheep, swine, goats, horses, mules, and other equines, their carcasses and products as described in this subchapter; and one copy of every certificate granted under the provisions of this chapter shall be filed in the Department of Agriculture, another copy shall be delivered to the owner or shipper, and when the cattle, sheep, swine, goats, horses, mules, and other equines, or their carcasses and products are sent abroad, a third copy shall be delivered to the chief officer of the vessel on which the shipment shall be made.

§619. Marking, labeling, or other identification of kinds of animals of articles' derivation; separate establishments for preparation and slaughtering activities.

No person, firm, or corporation shall sell, transport, offer for sale or transportation, or receive for transportation, in commerce, any carcasses of horses, mules, or other equines or parts of such carcasses, or the meat or meat food products thereof, unless they are plainly and conspicuously marked or labeled or otherwise identified as required by regulations prescribed by the Secretary to show the kinds of animals from which they were derived. When required by the Secretary, with respect to establishments at which inspection is maintained under this subchapter, such animals and their carcasses, parts thereof, meat and meat food products shall be prepared in establishment separate from those in which cattle, sheep, swine, or goats are slaughtered or their carcasses, parts thereof, meat or meat food products are prepared.

§620. Imports.

- **(a) Adulteration or misbranding prohibition; compliance with inspection, building construction standards, and other provisions; humane methods of slaughter; treatment as domestic articles subject to this chapter and food, drug, and cosmetic provisions; marking and labeling; personal consumption exemption.**

No carcasses, parts of carcasses, meat or meat food products of cattle, sheep, swine, goats, horses, mules, or other equines which are capable of use as human food, shall be imported into the United States if such articles are adulterated or misbranded and unless they comply with all the inspection, building, construction standards, and all other provisions of this chapter and regulations issued thereunder applicable to such articles in commerce within the United States. No such carcasses, parts of carcasses, meat or meat food products shall be imported into the United States unless the livestock from which they were produced was slaughtered and handled in connection with slaughter in accordance with the Act of August 27, 1958 (72 Stat. 862; 7 U.S.C. 1901–1906). All such imported articles shall, upon entry into the United States, be deemed and treated as domestic articles subject to the other provisions of this chapter and the Federal Food, Drug, and Cosmetic Act (21 U.S.C. 301 et seq.): *Provided*, That they shall be marked and labeled as required by such regulations for imported articles: *Provided* further, That nothing in this section shall apply to any individual who purchases meat or meat products outside the United States for his own consumption except that the total amount of such meat or meat products shall not exceed fifty pounds.

- **(b) Terms and conditions for destruction.**

The Secretary may prescribe the terms and conditions for the destruction of all such articles which are imported contrary to this section, unless (1) they are exported by the consignee within the time fixed therefor by the Secretary, or (2) in the case of articles which are not in compliance with the chapter solely because of misbranding, such articles are brought into compliance with the chapter under supervision of authorized representatives of the Secretary.

- **(c) Payment of storage, cartage, and labor charges by owner or consignee; liens.**

All charges for storage, cartage, and labor with respect to any article which is imported contrary to this section shall be paid by the owner or consignee, and in default of such payment shall constitute a lien against such article and any other article thereafter imported under this chapter by or for such owner or consignee.

- **(d) Prohibition.**

The knowing importation of any article contrary to this section is prohibited.

- **(e) Reports to Congressional committees.**

Not later than March 1 of each year the Secretary shall submit to the Committee on Agriculture of the House of Representatives and the Committee on Agriculture, Nutrition, and Forestry of the Senate a comprehensive and detailed written report with respect to the administration of this section during the immediately preceding calendar year. Such report shall include, but shall not be limited to the following:

- (1)(A) A certification by the Secretary that foreign plants exporting carcasses or meat or meat products referred to in subsection (a) of this section have complied with requirements that achieve a level of sanitary protection equivalent to that achieved under United States requirements with regard to all inspection, building construction standards, and all other provisions of this chapter and regulations issued under this chapter.

- (B) The Secretary may treat as equivalent to a United States requirement a requirement described in subparagraph (A) if the exporting country provides the Secretary with scientific evidence or other information, in accordance with risk assessment methodologies determined appropriate by the Secretary, to demonstrate that the requirement achieves the level of sanitary protection achieved under the United States requirement. For the purposes of this subsection, the term "sanitary protection" means protection to safeguard public health.

- (C) The Secretary may—

  o (i) determine, on a scientific basis, that a requirement of an exporting country does not achieve the level of protection that the Secretary considers appropriate; and

  o (ii) provide the basis for the determination to the exporting country in writing on request.

- (2) The names and locations of plants authorized or permitted to have imported into the United States therefrom carcasses or meat or meat products referred to in subsection (a) of this section.

- (3) The number of inspectors employed by the Department of Agriculture in the calendar year concerned who were assigned to inspect plants referred to in paragraph (e)(2) (FOOTNOTE 1) hereof and the frequency with which each such plant was inspected by such inspectors. (FOOTNOTE 1) See References in Text note below.

- (4) The number of inspectors licensed by each country from which any imports subject to the provisions of this section were imported who were assigned, during the calendar year concerned, to inspect such imports and the facilities in which such imports were handled and the frequency and effectiveness of such inspections.

- (5) The total volume of carcasses or meat or meat products referred to in subsection (a) of this section which was imported into the United States during the calendar year concerned from each country, including a separate itemization of the volume of each major category of such imports from each country during such year, and a detailed report of rejections of plants and products because of failure to meet appropriate standards prescribed by this chapter.

- (6) The name of each foreign country that applies standards for the importation of meat articles from the United States that are described in subsection (h)(2) of this section.

- **(f) Inspection and other standards; applicability, enforcement, etc.; certifications.**

Notwithstanding any other provision of law, all carcasses, parts of carcasses, meat, and meat food products of cattle, sheep, swine, goats, horses, mules, or other equines, capable of use as human food, offered for importation into the United States shall be subject to the inspection, sanitary, quality, species verification, and residue standards applied to products produced in the United States. Any such imported meat articles that do not meet such standards shall not be permitted entry in to the United States. The Secretary shall enforce this provision through (1) the imposition of random inspections for such species verification and for residues, and (2) random sampling and testing of internal organs and fat of the carcasses for residues at the point of slaughter by the exporting country in accordance with methods approved by the Secretary. Each foreign country from which such meat articles are offered for importation into the United States shall obtain a certification issued by the Secretary stating that the country maintains a program using reliable analytical methods to ensure compliance with the United States standards for residues in such meat articles. No such meat article shall be permitted entry into the United States from a country for which the Secretary has not issued such certification. The Secretary shall periodically review such certifications and shall revoke any certification if the Secretary determines that the country involved is not maintaining a program that uses reliable analytical methods to ensure compliance with United States standards for residues in such meat articles. The consideration of any application for a certification under this subsection and the review of any such certification, by the Secretary, shall include the inspection of individual establishments to ensure that the inspection program of the foreign country involved is meeting such United States standards.

- **(g) Administration of animal drugs or antibiotics; terms and conditions; entry order violations.**

The Secretary may prescribe terms and conditions under which cattle, sheep, swine, goats, horses, mules, and other equines that have been administered an animal drug or antibiotic banned for use in the United States may be imported for slaughter and human consumption. No person shall enter cattle, sheep, swine, goats, horses, mules, and other equines into the United States in violation of any order issued under this subsection by the Secretary.

- **(h) Reciprocal meat inspection requirement**
  - (1) As used in this subsection:
    - (A) The term "meat articles" means carcasses, meat and meat food products of cattle, sheep, swine, goats, horses, mules, or other equines, that are capable of use as human food.
    - (B) The term "standards" means inspection, building construction, sanitary, quality, species verification, residue, and other standards that are applicable to meat articles.
  - (2) On request of the Committee on Agriculture or the Committee on Ways and Means of the House of Representatives or the Committee on Agriculture, Nutrition, and Forestry or the Committee on Finance of the Senate, or at the initiative of the Secretary, the Secretary shall, as soon as practicable, determine whether a particular foreign country applies standards for the importation of meat articles from the United States that are not related to public health concerns about end-product quality that can be substantiated by reliable analytical methods.
  - (3) If the Secretary determines that a foreign country applies standards described in paragraph (2)—
    - (A) the Secretary shall consult with the United States Trade Representative; and
    - (B) within 30 days after the determination of the Secretary under paragraph (2), the Secretary and the United States Trade Representative shall recommend to the President whether action should be taken under paragraph (4).
  - (4) Within 30 days after receiving a recommendation for action under paragraph (3), the President shall, if and for such time as the President considers appropriate, prohibit imports into the United States of any meat articles produced in such foreign country unless it is determined that the meat articles produced in that country meet the standards applicable to meat articles in commerce within the United States.
  - (5) The action authorized under paragraph (4) may be used instead of, or in addition to, any other action taken under any other law.

§621. Inspectors to make examinations provided for; appointment; duties; regulations.

The Secretary shall appoint from time to time inspectors to make examination and inspection of all cattle, sheep, swine, goats, horses, mules, and other equines, inspection of which is hereby provided for and of all carcasses and parts thereof, and of all meats and meat food products thereof, and of the sanitary conditions of all establishments in which such meat and meat food products hereinbefore described are prepared; and said inspectors shall refuse to stamp, mark, tag, or label any carcass or any part thereof, or meat food product therefrom, prepared in any establishment hereinbefore mentioned, until the same shall have actually been inspected and found to be not adulterated; and shall perform such other duties as are provided by this chapter and by the rules and regulations to be prescribed by said Secretary; and said Secretary shall, from time to time, make such rules and regulations as are necessary for the efficient execution of the provisions of this chapter, and all inspections and examinations made under this chapter, shall be such and made in such manner as described in the rules and regulations prescribed by said Secretary not inconsistent with provisions of this chapter.

§622. Bribery of or gifts to inspectors or other officers and acceptance of gifts.

Any person, firm, or corporation, or any agent or employee of any person, firm, or corporation, who shall give, pay, or offer, directly or indirectly, to any inspector, deputy inspector, chief inspector, or any other officer or employee of the United States authorized to perform any of the duties prescribed by this chapter or by the rules and regulations of the Secretary any money or other thing of value, with intent to influence said inspector, deputy inspector, chief inspector, or other officer or employee of the United States in the discharge of any duty provided for in this chapter, shall be deemed guilty of a felony, and, upon conviction thereof, shall be punished by a fine not less than $5,000 nor more than $10,000 and by imprisonment not less than one year nor more than three years; and any inspector, deputy inspector, chief inspector, or other officer or employee of the United States authorized to perform any of the duties prescribed by this chapter who shall accept any money, gift, or other thing of value from any person, firm, or corporation, or officers, agents, or employees thereof, given with intent to influence his official action, or who shall receive or accept from any person, firm, or corporation engaged in commerce any gift, money, or other thing of value, given with any purpose or intent whatsoever, shall be deemed guilty of a felony and shall, upon conviction thereof, be summarily discharged from office and shall be punished by a fine not less than $1,000 nor more than $10,000 and by imprisonment not less than one year nor more than three years.

§ 623. Exemptions from inspection requirements.

- **(a) Personal slaughtering and custom slaughtering for personal, household, guest, and employee uses.**

The provisions of this subchapter requiring inspection of the slaughter of animals and the preparation of the carcasses, parts thereof, meat and meat food products at establishments conducting such operations for commerce shall not apply to the slaughtering by any person of animals of his own raising, and the preparation by him and transportation in commerce of the carcasses, parts thereof, meat and meat food products of such animals exclusively for use by him and members of his household and his nonpaying guests and employees; nor to the custom slaughter by any person, firm, or corporation of cattle, sheep, swine or goats delivered by the owner thereof for such slaughter, and the preparation by such slaughterer and transportation in commerce of the carcasses, parts thereof, meat and meat food products of such animals, exclusively for use, in the household of such owner, by him and members of his household and his nonpaying guests and employees; nor to the custom preparation by any person, firm, or corporation of carcasses, parts thereof, meat or meat food products, derived from the slaughter by any person of cattle, sheep, swine, or goats of his own raising, or from game animals, delivered by the owner thereof for such custom preparation, and transportation in commerce of such custom prepared articles, exclusively for use in the household of such owner, by him and members of his household and his nonpaying guests and employees: *Provided*, That in cases where such person, firm, or corporation engages in such custom operations at an establishment at which inspection under this subchapter is maintained, the Secretary may exempt from such inspection at such establishment any animals slaughtered or any meat or meat food products otherwise prepared on such custom basis: *Provided* further, That custom operations at any establishment shall be exempt from inspection requirements as provided by this section only if the establishment complies with regulations which the Secretary is hereby authorized to promulgate to assure that any carcasses, parts thereof, meat or meat food products wherever handled on a custom basis, or any containers or packages containing such articles, are separated at all times from carcasses, parts thereof, meat or meat food products prepared for sale, and that all such articles prepared on a custom basis, or any containers or packages containing such articles, are plainly marked "Not for Sale" immediately after being prepared and kept so identified until delivered to the owner and that the establishment conducting the custom operation is maintained and operated in a sanitary manner.

- **(b) Territorial exemption; refusal, withdrawal, or modification.**

The Secretary may, under such sanitary conditions as he may by regulations prescribe, exempt from the inspection requirements of this subchapter the slaughter of animals, and the preparation of carcasses, parts thereof, meat and meat food products, by any person, firm, or corporation in any Territory not organized with a legislative body solely for distribution within such Territory when the Secretary determines that it is impracticable to provide such inspection within the limits of funds appropriated for administration of this chapter and that such exemption will otherwise facilitate enforcement of this chapter. The Secretary may refuse, withdraw, or modify any exemption under this subsection in his discretion whenever he determines such action is necessary to effectuate the purposes of this chapter.

- **(c) Pizzas containing meat food products.**

  - (1) Under such terms and conditions as the Secretary shall prescribe through rules and regulations issued under section 624 of this title that may be necessary to ensure food safety and protect public health such as special handling procedures, the Secretary shall exempt pizzas containing a meat food product from the inspection requirements of this chapter if—

    - (A) the meat food product components of the pizzas have been prepared, inspected, and passed in a cured or cooked form as ready-to-eat in compliance with the requirements of this chapter; and

    - (B) the pizzas are to be served in public or private nonprofit institutions.

  - (2) The Secretary may withdraw or modify any exemption under this subsection whenever the Secretary determines such action is necessary to ensure food safety and to protect public health. The Secretary may reinstate or further modify any exemption withdrawn or modified under this subsection.

- **(d) Adulteration and misbranding provisions applicable to inspection-free articles.**

The adulteration and misbranding provisions of this subchapter, other than the requirement of the inspection legend, shall apply to articles which are exempted from inspection or not required to be inspected under this section.

§624. Storage and handling regulations; violations; exemption of establishments subject to non-Federal jurisdiction.

The Secretary may by regulations prescribe conditions under which carcasses, parts of carcasses, meat, and meat food products of cattle, sheep, swine, goats, horses, mules, or other equines, capable of use as human food, shall be stored or otherwise handled by any person, firm, or corporation engaged in the business of buying, selling, freezing, storing, or transporting, in or for commerce, or importing, such articles, whenever the Secretary deems such action necessary to assure that such articles will not be adulterated or misbranded when delivered to the consumer. Violation of any such regulation is prohibited. However, such regulations shall not apply to the storage or handling of such articles at any retail store or other establishment in any State or organized Territory that would be subject to this section only because of purchases in commerce, if the storage and handling of such articles at such establishment is regulated under the laws of the State or Territory in which such establishment is located, in a manner which the Secretary, after consultation with the appropriate advisory committee provided for in section 661 of this title, determines is adequate to effectuate the purposes of this section.

SUBCHAPTER II—MEAT PROCESSORS AND RELATED INDUSTRIES

§641. Prohibition of subchapter I inspection of articles not intended for use as human food; denaturation or other identification prior to distribution in commerce; inedible articles.

Inspection shall not be provided under subchapter I of this chapter at any establishment for the slaughter of cattle, sheep, swine, goats, horses, mules, or other equines, or the preparation of any carcasses or parts or products of such animals, which are not intended for use as human food, but such articles shall, prior to their offer for sale or transportation in commerce, unless naturally inedible by humans, be denatured or otherwise identified as prescribed by regulations of the Secretary to deter their use for human food. No person, firm, or corporation shall buy, sell, transport, or offer for sale or transportation, or receive for transportation, in commerce, or import, any carcasses, parts thereof, meat or meat food products of any such animals, which are not intended for use as human food unless they are denatured or otherwise identified as required by the regulations of the Secretary or are naturally inedible by humans.

§642. Recordkeeping requirements.

- **(a) Classes of persons bound; scope of disclosure; access to places of business; examination of records, facilities, and inventories; copies; samples.**

The following classes of persons, firms, and corporations shall keep such records as will fully and correctly disclose all transactions involved in their businesses; and all persons, firms, and corporations subject to such requirements shall, at all reasonable times upon notice by a duly authorized representative of the Secretary, afford such representative access to their places of business and opportunity to examine the facilities, inventory, and records thereof, to copy all such records, and to take reasonable samples of their inventory upon payment of the fair market value therefor—

- (1) Any persons, firms, or corporations that engage, for commerce, in the business of slaughtering any cattle, sheep, swine, goats, horses, mules, or other equines, or preparing, freezing, packaging, or labeling any carcasses, or parts or products of carcasses, of any such animals, for use as human food or animal food;

- (2) Any persons, firms, or corporations that engage in the business of buying or selling (as meat brokers, wholesalers or otherwise), or transporting in commerce, or storing in or for commerce, or importing, any carcasses, or parts or products of carcasses, of any such animals;

- (3) Any persons, firms, or corporations that engage in business, in or for commerce, as renderers, or engage in the business of buying, selling, or transporting, in commerce, or importing, any dead, dying, disabled, or diseased cattle, sheep, swine, goats, horses, mules, or other equines, or parts of the carcasses of any such animals that died otherwise than by slaughter.

- **(b) Period of maintenance.**

Any record required to be maintained by this section shall be maintained for such period of time as the Secretary may by regulations prescribe.

§643. Registration of business, name of person, and trade names.

No person, firm, or corporation shall engage in business, in or for commerce, as a meat broker, renderer, or animal food manufacturer, or engage in business in commerce as a wholesaler of any carcasses, or parts or products of the carcasses, of any cattle, sheep, swine, goats, horses, mules, or other equines, whether intended for human food or other purposes, or engage in business as a public warehouseman storing any such articles in or for commerce, or engage in the business of buying, selling, or transporting in commerce, or importing, any dead, dying, disabled, or diseased animals of the specified kinds, or parts of the carcasses of any such animals that died otherwise than by slaughter, unless, when required by regulations of the Secretary, he has registered with the Secretary his name, and the address of each place of business at which, and all trade names under which, he conducts such business.

§644. Regulation of transactions, transportation, or importation of 4-D animals to prevent use as human food.

No person, firm, or corporation engaged in the business of buying, selling, or transporting in commerce, or importing, dead, dying, disabled, or diseased animals, or any parts of the carcasses of any animals that died otherwise than by slaughter, shall buy, sell, transport, offer for sale or transportation, or receive for transportation, in commerce, or import, any dead, dying, disabled, or diseased cattle, sheep, swine, goats, horses, mules or other equines, or parts of the carcasses of any such animals that died otherwise than by slaughter, unless such transaction, transportation or importation is made in accordance with such regulations as the Secretary may prescribe to assure that such animals, or the unwholesome parts or products thereof, will be prevented from being used for human food purposes.

§645. Federal provisions applicable to State or Territorial business transactions of a local nature and not subject to local authority.

The authority conferred on the Secretary by section 642, 643, or 644 of this title with respect to persons, firms, and corporations engaged in the specified kinds of business in or for commerce may be exercised with respect to persons, firms, or corporations engaged, in any State or organized Territory, in such kinds of business but not in or for commerce, whenever the Secretary determines, after consultation with an appropriate advisory committee provided for in section 661 of this title, that the State or territory does not have at least equal authority under its laws or such authority is not exercised in a manner to effectuate the purposes of this chapter including the State providing for the Secretary or his representative being afforded access to such places of business and the facilities, inventories, and records thereof, and the taking of reasonable samples, where he determines necessary in carrying out his responsibilities under this chapter; and in such case the provisions of section 642, 643, or 644 of this title, respectively, shall apply to such persons, firms, and corporations to the same extent and in the same manner as if they were engaged in such business in or for commerce and the transactions involved were in commerce.

SUBCHAPTER III—FEDERAL AND STATE COOPERATION

§661. Federal and State cooperation.

- **(a) Congressional statement of policy.**

It is the policy of the Congress to protect the consuming public from meat and meat food products that are adulterated or misbranded and to assist in efforts by State and other Government agencies to accomplish this objective. In furtherance of this policy—

- (1) Development and administration of State meat inspection program equal to subchapter I ante and post mortem inspection, reinspection, and sanitation requirements The Secretary is authorized, whenever he determines that it would effectuate the purposes of this chapter, to cooperate with the appropriate State agency in developing and administering a State meat inspection program in any State which has enacted a State meat inspection law that imposes mandatory ante mortem and post mortem inspection, reinspection and sanitation requirements that are at least equal to those under subchapter I of this chapter, with respect to all or certain classes of persons engaged in the State in slaughtering cattle, sheep, swine, goats, or equines, or preparing the carcasses, parts thereof, meat or meat food products, of any such animals for use as human food solely for distribution within such State.

- (2) Development and administration of State program with authorities equal to subchapter II authorities; cooperation with Federal agencies The Secretary is further authorized, whenever he determines that it would effectuate the purposes of this chapter, to cooperate with appropriate State agencies in developing and administering State programs under State laws containing authorities at least equal to those provided in subchapter II of this chapter; and to cooperate with other agencies of the United States in carrying out any provisions of this chapter.

- (3) Scope of cooperation: advisory assistance, technical and laboratory assistance and training, and financial and other aid; limitation on amount; equitable allocation of Federal funds; adequacy of State program to obtain Federal cooperation and payments Cooperation with State agencies under this section may include furnishing to the appropriate State agency (i) advisory assistance in planning and otherwise developing an adequate State program under the State law; and (ii) technical and laboratory assistance and training (including necessary curricular and instructional materials and equipment), and financial and other aid for administration of such a program. The amount to be contributed to any State by the Secretary under this section from Federal funds for any year shall not exceed 50 per centum of the estimated total cost of the cooperative program; and the Federal funds shall be allocated among the States desiring to cooperate on an equitable basis. Such cooperation and payment shall be contingent at all times upon the administration of the State program in a manner which the Secretary, in consultation with the appropriate advisory committee appointed under paragraph (4), deems adequate to effectuate the purposes of this section.

- (4) Advisory committees The Secretary may appoint advisory committees consisting of such representatives of appropriate State agencies as the Secretary and the State agencies may designate to consult with him concerning State and Federal programs with respect to meat inspection and other matters within the scope of this chapter, including evaluating State programs for purposes of this chapter and obtaining better coordination and more uniformity among the State programs and between the Federal and State programs and adequate protection of consumers.

- **(b) Single State agency; subordinate governmental unit as part of State agency**

The appropriate State agency with which the Secretary may cooperate under this chapter shall be a single agency in the State which is primarily responsible for the coordination of the State programs having objectives similar to those under this chapter. When the State program includes performance of certain functions by a municipality or other subordinate governmental unit, such unit shall be deemed to be a part of the State agency for purposes of this section.

- **(c) State meat inspection requirements**

  - (1) Notice to Governor of nondevelopment or nonenforcement; designation of State as subject to subchapters I and IV; delay and revocation of designation; publication in Federal Register; notice of production of adulterated meat or meat food products; designation of State If the Secretary has reason to believe, by thirty days prior to the expiration of two years after December 15, 1967, that a State has failed to develop or is not enforcing, with respect to all establishments within its jurisdiction (except those that would be exempted from Federal inspection under subparagraph (2)) at which cattle, sheep, swine, goats, or equines are slaughtered, or their carcasses, or parts or products thereof, are prepared for use as human food, solely for distribution within such State, and the products of such establishments, requirements at least equal to those imposed under subchapter I and IV of this chapter, he shall promptly notify the Governor of the State of this fact. If the Secretary determines, after consultation with the Governor of the State, or representative selected by him, that such requirements have not been developed and activated, he shall promptly after the expiration of such two-year period designate such State as one in which the provisions of subchapters I and IV of this chapter shall apply to operations and transactions wholly within such State: *Provided,* That if the Secretary has reason to believe that the State will activate such requirements within one additional year, he may delay such designation for said period, and not designate the State, if he determines at the end of the year that the State then has such requirements in effective operation. The Secretary shall publish any such designation in the Federal Register and, upon the expiration of thirty days after such publication, the provisions of subchapters I and IV shall apply to operations and transactions and to persons, firms, and corporations engaged therein in the State to the same extent and in the same manner as if such operations and transactions were conducted in or for commerce. Thereafter, upon request of the Governor, the Secretary shall revoke such designation if the Secretary determines that such State has developed and will enforce requirements at least equal to those imposed under subchapter I and subchapter IV of this chapter: And provided further, That, notwithstanding any other provision of this section, if the Secretary determines that any establishment within a State is producing adulterated meat or meat food products for distribution within such State which would clearly endanger the public health he shall notify the Governor of the State and the appropriate Advisory Committee provided by section 661 of this title of such fact for effective action under State or local law. If the State does not take action to prevent such endangering of the public health within a reasonable time after such notice, as determined by the Secretary, in light of the risk to public health, the Secretary may forthwith designate any such establishment as subject to the provisions of subchapters I and IV of this chapter, and thereupon the establishment and operator thereof shall be subject to such provisions as though engaged in commerce until such time as the Secretary determines that such State has developed and will enforce requirements at least equal to those imposed under subchapter I and subchapter IV of this chapter.

○ (2) Exemptions of retail stores, restaurants, and similar retail-type establishments; operations conducted at a restaurant central kitchen facility The provisions of this chapter requiring inspection of the slaughter of animals and the preparation of carcasses, parts thereof, meat and meat food products shall not apply to operations of types traditionally and usually conducted at retail stores and restaurants, when conducted at any retail store or restaurant or similar retail-type establishment for sale in normal retail quantities or service of such articles to consumers at such establishments if such establishments are subject to such inspection provisions only under this paragraph (c). For the purposes of this subparagraph, operations conducted at a restaurant central kitchen facility shall be considered as being conducted at a restaurant if the restaurant central kitchen prepares meat or meat food products that are ready to eat when they leave such facility and are served in meals or as entrees only to customers at restaurants owned or operated by the same person, firm, or corporation owning or operating such facility: *Provided,* That such facility shall be subject to the provisions of section 642 of this title: *Provided further,* That the facility may be subject to the inspection requirements under subchapter I of this chapter for as long as the Secretary deems necessary, if the Secretary determines that the sanitary conditions or practices of the facility or the processing procedures or methods at the facility are such that any of its meat or meat food products are rendered adulterated.

○ (3) Termination of designation of State upon development and enforcement of minimum requirements; redesignation; designation for nonenforcement of minimum requirements: notice and publication in Federal Register Whenever the Secretary determines that any State designated under this paragraph (c) has developed and will enforce State meat inspection requirements at least equal to those imposed under subchapters I and IV of this chapter with respect to the operations and transactions within such State which are regulated under paragraph (1), he shall terminate the designation of such State under this paragraph (c), but this shall not preclude the subsequent redesignation of the State at any time upon thirty days notice to the Governor and publication in the Federal Register in accordance with this paragraph, and any State may be designated upon such notice and publication at any time after the period specified in this paragraph whether or not the State has theretofore been designated upon the Secretary determining that it is not effectively enforcing requirements at least equal to those imposed under subchapters I and IV of this chapter.

- (4) Periodic review; report to Congressional committees The Secretary shall promptly upon December 15, 1967, and periodically thereafter, but at least annually, review the requirements, including the enforcement thereof, of the several States not designated under this paragraph (c), with respect to the slaughter, and the preparation, storage, handling and distribution of carcasses, parts thereof, meat and meat food products, of such animals, and inspection of such operations and annually report thereon to the Committee on Agriculture of the House of Representatives and the Committee on Agriculture, Nutrition, and Forestry of the Senate in the report required under section 691 of this title.

- **(d) "State" defined**

As used in this section, the term "State" means any State (including the Commonwealth of Puerto Rico) or organized Territory.

SUBCHAPTER IV—AUXILIARY PROVISIONS

§671. Inspection services; refusal or withdrawal; hearing; business unfitness based upon certain convictions; other provisions for withdrawal of services unaffected; responsible connection with business; finality of Secretary's actions; judicial review; record.

The Secretary may (for such period, or indefinitely, as he deems necessary to effectuate the purposes of this chapter) refuse to provide, or withdraw, inspection service under subchapter I of this chapter with respect to any establishment if he determines, after opportunity for a hearing is accorded to the applicant for, or recipient of, such service, that such applicant or recipient is unfit to engage in any business requiring inspection under subchapter I because the applicant or recipient, or anyone responsibly connected with the applicant or recipient, has been convicted, in any Federal or State court, of (1) any felony, or

(2) more than one violation of any law, other than a felony, based upon the acquiring, handling, or distributing of unwholesome, mislabeled, or deceptively packaged food or upon fraud in connection with transactions in food. This section shall not affect in any way other provisions of this chapter for withdrawal of inspection services under subchapter I from establishments failing to maintain sanitary conditions or to destroy condemned carcasses, parts, meat or meat food products.

For the purpose of this section a person shall be deemed to be responsibly connected with the business if he was a partner, officer, director, holder, or owner of 10 per centum or more of its voting stock or employee in a managerial or executive capacity.

The determination and order of the Secretary with respect thereto under this section shall be final and conclusive unless the affected applicant for, or recipient of, inspection service files application for judicial review within thirty days after the effective date of such order in the appropriate court as provided in section 674 of this title. Judicial review of any such order shall be upon the record upon which the determination and order are based.

§672. Administrative detention; duration; pending judicial proceedings; notification of governmental authorities; release.

Whenever any carcass, part of a carcass, meat or meat food product of cattle, sheep, swine, goats, horses, mules, or other equines, or any product exempted from the definition of a meat food product, or any dead, dying, disabled, or diseased cattle, sheep, swine, goat, or equine is found by any authorized representative of the Secretary upon any premises where it is held for purposes of, or during or after distribution in, commerce or otherwise subject to subchapter I or II of this chapter, and there is reason to believe that any such article is adulterated or misbranded and is capable of use as human food, or that it has not been inspected, in violation of the provisions of subchapter I of this chapter or of any other Federal law or the laws of any State or Territory, or the District of Columbia, or that such article or animal has been or is intended to be, distributed in violation of any such provisions, it may be detained by such representative for a period not to exceed twenty days, pending action under section 673 of this title or notification of any Federal, State, or other governmental authorities having jurisdiction over such article or animal, and shall not be moved by any person, firm, or corporation from the place at which it is located when so detained, until released by such representative. All official marks may be required by such representative to be removed from such article or animal before it is released unless it appears to the satisfaction of the Secretary that the article or animal is eligible to retain such marks.

§673. Seizure and condemnation.

- **(a) Proceedings in rem; libel of information; jurisdiction; disposal by destruction or sale; proceeds into the Treasury; sales restrictions; bond; court costs and fees, storage, and other expenses against claimants; proceedings in admiralty; jury trial; United States as plaintiff.**

  - (1) Any carcass, part of a carcass, meat or meat food product of cattle, sheep, swine, goats, horses, mules or other equines, or any dead, dying, disabled, or diseased cattle, sheep, swine, goat, or equine, that is being transported in commerce or otherwise subject to subchapter I or II of this chapter, or is held for sale in the United States after such transportation, and that (A) is or has been prepared, sold, transported, or otherwise distributed or offered or received for distribution in violation of this chapter, or (B) is capable of use as human food and is adulterated or misbranded, or (C) in any other way is in violation of this chapter, shall be liable to be proceeded against and seized and condemned, at any time, on a libel of information in any United States district court or other proper court as provided in section 674 of this title within the jurisdiction of which the article or animal is found.

  - (2) If the article or animal is condemned it shall, after entry of the decree, (A) be distributed in accordance with paragraph (5), or (B) be disposed of by destruction or sale as the court may direct and the proceeds, if sold, less the court costs and fees, and storage and other proper expenses, shall be paid into the Treasury of the United States, but the article or animal shall not be sold contrary to the provisions of this chapter, or the laws of the jurisdiction in which it is sold: *Provided,* That upon the execution and delivery of a good and sufficient bond conditioned that the article or animal shall not be sold or otherwise disposed of contrary to the provisions of this chapter, or the laws of the jurisdiction in which disposal is made, the court may direct that such article or animal be delivered to the owner thereof subject to such supervision by authorized representatives of the Secretary as is necessary to insure compliance with the applicable laws.

  - (3) When a decree of condemnation is entered against the article or animal and it is released under bond, or destroyed, court costs and fees, and storage and other proper expenses shall be awarded against the person, if any, intervening as claimant of the article or animal.

○ (4) The proceedings in such libel cases shall conform, as nearly as may be, to the proceedings in admiralty, except that either party may demand trial by jury of any issue of fact joined in any case, and all such proceedings shall be at the suit of and in the name of the United States.

○ (5)

▪ (A) An article that is condemned under paragraph (1) may as the court may direct, after entry of the decree, be distributed without charge to nonprofit, private entities or to Federal, State, or local government entities engaged in the distribution of food without charge to individuals, if such article—

▪ (i) has been inspected under this chapter and found to be wholesome and not to be adulterated within the meaning of paragraphs (1) through (7) and (9) of section 601(m) of this title and a determination is made at the time of the entry of the decree that such article is wholesome and not so adulterated; and

▪ (ii) is plainly marked "Not for Sale" on such article or its container.

▪ (B) The United States may not be held legally responsible for any article that is distributed under subparagraph (A) to a nonprofit, private entity or to a Federal, State, or local government entity, if such article—

▪ (i) was found after inspection under this chapter to be wholesome and not adulterated within the meaning of paragraphs (1) through (7) and (9) of section 601(m) of this title and a determination was made at the time of the entry of the decree that such article was wholesome and not so adulterated; and

▪ (ii) was plainly marked "Not for Sale" on such article or its container.

▪ (C) The person from whom such article was seized and condemned may not be held legally responsible for such article, if such article—

▪ (i) was found after inspection under this chapter to be wholesome and not adulterated within the meaning of paragraphs (1) through (7) and (9) of section 601(m) of this title and a determination was made at the time of the entry of the decree that such article was wholesome and not so adulterated; and

- (ii) was plainly marked "Not for Sale" on such article or its container.

- **(b) Condemnation or seizure under other provisions unaffected.**

The provisions of this section shall in no way derogate from authority for condemnation or seizure conferred by other provisions of this chapter, or other laws.

§674. Federal court jurisdiction of enforcement and injunction proceedings and other kinds of cases; limitations of section 607(e) of this title.

The United States district courts, the District Court of Guam, the District Court of the Virgin Islands, the highest court of American Samoa, and the United States courts of the other Territories, are vested with jurisdiction specifically to enforce, and to prevent and restrain violations of, this chapter, and shall have jurisdiction in all other kinds of cases arising under this chapter, except as provided in section 607(e) of this title.

§675. Assaulting, resisting, or impeding certain persons; murder; protection of such persons.

Any person who forcibly assaults, resists, opposes, impedes, intimidates, or interferes with any person while engaged in or on account of the performance of his official duties under this chapter shall be fined not more than $5,000 or imprisoned not more than three years, or both. Whoever, in the commission of any such acts, uses a deadly or dangerous weapon, shall be fined not more than $10,000 or imprisoned not more than ten years, or both. Whoever kills any person while engaged in or on account of the performance of his official duties under this chapter shall be punished as provided under sections 1111 and 1114 of title 18.

§676. Violations.

- **(a) Misdemeanors; felonies: intent to defraud and distribution of adulterated articles; good faith.**

Any person, firm, or corporation who violates any provision of this chapter for which no other criminal penalty is provided by this chapter shall upon conviction be subject to imprisonment for not more than one year, or a fine of not more than $1,000, or both such imprisonment and fine; but if such violation involves intent to defraud, or any distribution or attempted distribution of an article that is adulterated (except as defined in section 601(m)(8) of this title), such person, firm, or corporation shall be subject to imprisonment for not more than three years or a fine of not more than $10,000, or both: *Provided,* That no person, firm, or corporation, shall be subject to penalties under this section for receiving for transportation any article or animal in violation of this chapter if such receipt was made in good faith, unless such person, firm, or corporation refuses to furnish on request of a representative of the Secretary the name and address of the person from whom he received such article or animal, and copies of all documents, if any there be, pertaining to the delivery of the article or animal to him.

- **(b) Minor violations; written notice of warning of criminal and civil proceedings.**

Nothing in this chapter shall be construed as requiring the Secretary to report for prosecution or for the institution of libel or injunction proceedings, minor violations of this chapter whenever he believes that the public interest will be adequately served by a suitable written notice of warning.

§677. Other Federal laws applicable for administration and enforcement of chapter; location of inquiries; jurisdiction of Federal courts.

For the efficient administration and enforcement of this chapter, the provisions (including penalties) of sections 46, 48, 49 and 50 of title 15 (except paragraphs (c) through (h) of section 46 and the last paragraph of section 49 (FOOTNOTE 1) of title 15), and the provisions of section 409(l) (FOOTNOTE 1) of title 47; are made applicable to the jurisdiction, powers, and duties of the Secretary in administering and enforcing the provisions of this chapter and to any person, firm, or corporation with respect to whom such authority is exercised. The Secretary, in person or by such agents as he may designate, may prosecute any inquiry necessary to his duties under this chapter in any part of the United States, and the powers conferred by said sections 49 and 50 of title 15 on the district courts of the United States may be exercised for the purposes of this chapter by any court designated in section 674 of this title.

(FOOTNOTE 1) The last paragraph of section 49 of title 15, and the provisions of section 409(l) of title 47, referred to in text, which related to immunity of witnesses, were repealed by sections 211 and 242, respectively, of Pub. L. 91-452, Oct. 15, 1970, title II, 84 Stat. 929, 930. For provisions relating to immunity of witnesses, see section 6001 et seq. of Title 18, Crimes and Criminal Procedure.

§678. Non-Federal jurisdiction of federally regulated matters; prohibition of additional or different requirements for establishments with inspection services and as to marking, labeling, packaging, and ingredients; recordkeeping and related requirements; concurrent jurisdiction over distribution for human food purposes of adulterated or misbranded and imported articles; other matters.

Requirements within the scope of this chapter with respect to premises, facilities and operations of any establishment at which inspection is provided under subchapter I of this chapter, which are in addition to, or different than those made under this chapter may not be imposed by any State or Territory or the District of Columbia, except that any such jurisdiction may impose recordkeeping and other requirements within the scope of section 642 of this title, if consistent therewith, with respect to any such establishment. Marking, labeling, packaging, or ingredient requirements in addition to, or different than, those made under this chapter may not be imposed by any State or Territory or the District of Columbia with respect to articles prepared at any establishment under inspection in accordance with the requirements under subchapter I of this chapter, but any State or Territory or the District of Columbia may, consistent with the requirements under this chapter, exercise concurrent jurisdiction with the Secretary over articles required to be inspected under said subchapter I, for the purpose of preventing the distribution for human food purposes of any such articles which are adulterated or misbranded and are outside of such an establishment, or, in the case of imported articles which are not at such an establishment, after their entry into the United States. This chapter shall not preclude any State or Territory or the District of Columbia from making requirement (FOOTNOTE 1) or taking other action, consistent with this chapter, with respect to any other matters regulated under this chapter.

(FOOTNOTE 1) So in original. Probably should be "requirements".

§679. Application of Federal Food, Drug, and Cosmetic Act.

- **(a) Authorities under food, drug, and cosmetic provisions unaffected.**

Notwithstanding any other provisions of law, including section 902(b) of the Federal Food, Drug, and Cosmetic Act (21 U.S.C. 392(a)), the provisions of this chapter shall not derogate from any authority conferred by the Federal Food, Drug, and Cosmetic Act (21 U.S.C. 301 et seq.) prior to December 15, 1967.

- **(b) Enforcement proceedings; detainer authority of representatives of Secretary of Health and Human Services.**

The detainer authority conferred by section 672 of this title shall apply to any authorized representative of the Secretary of Health and Human Services for purposes of the enforcement of the Federal Food, Drug, and Cosmetic Act (21 U.S.C. 301 et seq.) with respect to any carcass, part thereof, meat, or meat food product of cattle, sheep, swine, goats, or equines that is outside any premises at which inspection is being maintained under this chapter, and for such purposes the first reference to the Secretary in section 672 of this title shall be deemed to refer to the Secretary of Health and Human Services.

§680. Authorization of appropriations.

There are hereby authorized to be appropriated such sums as may be necessary to carry out the provisions of this chapter.

SUBCHAPTER V—MISCELLANEOUS PROVISIONS

§691. Reports to Congressional committees.

The Secretary shall annually report to the Committee on Agriculture of the House of Representatives and the Committee on Agriculture, Nutrition, and Forestry of the Senate with respect to the slaughter of animals subject to this Act, and the preparation, storage, handling and distribution of carcasses, parts thereof, meat and meat food products, of such animals, and inspection of establishments operated in connection therewith, including the operations under and effectiveness of this Act.

§692. Inspection extended to reindeer.

The provisions of the meat inspection law may be extended to the inspection of reindeer.

§693. Inspection of dairy products for export.

The act of March 3, 1891, as amended, for the inspection of live cattle and products thereof, shall be deemed to include dairy products intended for exportation to any foreign country, and the Secretary of Agriculture may apply, under rules and regulations to be prescribed by him, the provisions of said act for inspection and certification appropriate for ascertaining the purity and quality of such products, and may cause the same to be so marked, stamped, or labeled as to secure their identity and make known in the markets of foreign countries to which they may be sent from the United States their purity, quality, and grade;

and all the provisions of said act relating to live cattle and products thereof for export shall apply to dairy products so inspected and certified.

§694. Authorization of appropriations.

Annual appropriations of the sum of $3,000,000 from the general fund of the Treasury are authorized for the expenses of the inspection of cattle, sheep, swine, and goats and the meat and meat food products thereof which enter into interstate or foreign commerce and for all expenses necessary to carry into effect the provisions of this Act relating to meat inspection, including rent and the employment of labor in Washington and elsewhere, for each year, and in addition there is authorized to be appropriated such other sums as may be necessary in the enforcement of the meat inspection laws.

§695. Payment of cost of meat-inspection service; exception.

The cost of inspection rendered on and after July 1, 1948, under the requirements of laws relating to Federal inspection of meat and meat food products shall be borne by the United States except the cost of overtime pursuant to section 394 of title 7.

APPENDIX 6:
FAIR PACKAGING AND LABELING ACT

TITLE 15 - COMMERCE AND TRADE

CHAPTER 39 - FAIR PACKAGING AND LABELING PROGRAM

§1451. Congressional Delegation of Policy.

Informed consumers are essential to the fair and efficient functioning of a free market economy. Packages and their labels should enable consumers to obtain accurate information as to the quantity of the contents and should facilitate value comparisons. Therefore, it is hereby declared to be the policy of the Congress to assist consumers and manufacturers in reaching these goals in the marketing of consumer goods.

§1452. Unfair and Deceptive Packaging and Labeling: Scope of Prohibition.

• (a) Nonconforming labels

It shall be unlawful for any person engaged in the packaging or labeling of any consumer commodity (as defined in this chapter) for distribution in commerce, or for any person (other than a common carrier for hire, a contract carrier for hire, or a freight forwarder for hire) engaged in the distribution in commerce of any packaged or labeled consumer commodity, to distribute or to cause to be distributed in commerce any such commodity if such commodity is contained in a package, or if there is affixed to that commodity a label, which does not conform to the provisions of this chapter and of regulations promulgated under the authority of this chapter.

• (b) Exemptions

The prohibition contained in subsection (a) of this section shall not apply to persons engaged in business as wholesale or retail distributors of consumer commodities except to the extent that such persons (1) are engaged in the packaging or labeling of such commodities, or (2) prescribe or specify by any means the manner in which such commodities are packaged or labeled.

§1453. Requirements of Labeling; Placement, Form, and Contents of Statement of Quantity; Supplemental Statement of Quantity.

- **(a) Contents of label**

No person subject to the prohibition contained in section 1452 of this title shall distribute or cause to be distributed in commerce any packaged consumer commodity unless in conformity with regulations which shall be established by the promulgating authority pursuant to section 1455 of this title which shall provide that—

- (1) The commodity shall bear a label specifying the identity of the commodity and the name and place of business of the manufacturer, packer, or distributor;

- (2) The net quantity of contents (in terms of weight or mass, measure, or numerical count) shall be separately and accurately stated in a uniform location upon the principal display panel of that label, using the most appropriate units of both the customary inch/pound system of measure, as provided in paragraph (3) of this subsection, and, except as provided in paragraph (3)(A)(ii) or paragraph (6) of this subsection, the SI metric system;

- (3) The separate label statement of net quantity of contents appearing upon or affixed to any package—

  o (A)

    • (i) if on a package labeled in terms of weight, shall be expressed in pounds, with any remainder in terms of ounces or common or decimal fractions of the pound; or in the case of liquid measure, in the largest whole unit (quarts, quarts and pints, or pints, as appropriate) with any remainder in terms of fluid ounces or common or decimal fractions of the pint or quart;

    • (ii) if on a random package, may be expressed in terms of pounds and decimal fractions of the pound carried out to not more than three decimal places and is not required to, but may, include a statement in terms of the SI metric system carried out to not more than three decimal places;

    • (iii) if on a package labeled in terms of linear measure, shall be expressed in terms of the largest whole unit (yards, yards and feet, or feet, as appropriate) with any remainder in terms of inches or common or decimal fractions of the foot or yard;

- (iv) if on a package labeled in terms of measure of area, shall be expressed in terms of the largest whole square unit (square yards, square yards and square feet, or square feet, as appropriate) with any remainder in terms of square inches or common or decimal fractions of the square foot or square yard;

  o (B) shall appear in conspicuous and easily legible type in distinct contrast (by topography, layout, color, embossing, or molding) with other matter on the package;

  o (C) shall contain letters or numerals in a type size which shall be

    - (i) established in relationship to the area of the principal display panel of the package, and

    - (ii) uniform for all packages of substantially the same size; and

  o (D) shall be so placed that the lines of printed matter included in that statement are generally parallel to the base on which the package rests as it is designed to be displayed; and

- (4) The label of any package of a consumer commodity which bears a representation as to the number of servings of such commodity contained in such package shall bear a statement of the net quantity (in terms of weight or mass, measure, or numerical count) of each such serving.

- (5) For purposes of paragraph (3)(A)(ii) of this subsection the term "random package" means a package which is one of a lot, shipment, or delivery of packages of the same consumer commodity with varying weights or masses, that is, packages with no fixed weight or mass pattern.

- (6) The requirement of paragraph (2) that the statement of net quantity of contents include a statement in terms of the SI metric system shall not apply to foods that are packaged at the retail store level.

- **(b) Supplemental statements**

No person subject to the prohibition contained in section 1452 of this title shall distribute or cause to be distributed in commerce any packaged consumer commodity if any qualifying words or phrases appear in conjunction with the separate statement of the net quantity of contents required by subsection (a) of this section, but nothing in this subsection or in paragraph (2) of subsection (a) of this section shall prohibit supplemental statements, at other places on the package, describing in nondeceptive terms the net quantity of contents: *Provided,* That such supplemental statements of net quantity of contents shall not include any term qualifying a unit of weight or mass, measure, or count that tends to exaggerate the amount of the commodity contained in the package.

§1454. Rules and Regulations.

- **(a) Promulgating authority**

The authority to promulgate regulations under this chapter is vested in (A) the Secretary of Health and Human Services (referred to hereinafter as the "Secretary") with respect to any consumer commodity which is a food, drug, device, or cosmetic, as each such term is defined by section 321 of title 21; and (B) the Federal Trade Commission (referred to hereinafter as the "Commission") with respect to any other consumer commodity.

- **(b) Exemption of commodities from regulations**

If the promulgating authority specified in this section finds that, because of the nature, form, or quantity of a particular consumer commodity, or for other good and sufficient reasons, full compliance with all the requirements otherwise applicable under section 1453 of this title is impracticable or is not necessary for the adequate protection of consumers, the Secretary or the Commission (whichever the case may be) shall promulgate regulations exempting such commodity from those requirements to the extent and under such conditions as the promulgating authority determines to be consistent with section 1451 of this title.

- **(c) Scope of additional regulations**

Whenever the promulgating authority determines that regulations containing prohibitions or requirements other than those prescribed by section 1453 of this title are necessary to prevent the deception of consumers or to facilitate value comparisons as to any consumer commodity, such authority shall promulgate with respect to that commodity regulations effective to—

- (1) establish and define standards for characterization of the size of a package enclosing any consumer commodity, which may be used to supplement the label statement of net quantity of contents of packages containing such commodity, but this paragraph shall not be construed as authorizing any limitation on the size, shape, weight or mass, dimensions, or number of packages which may be used to enclose any commodity;

- (2) regulate the placement upon any package containing any commodity, or upon any label affixed to such commodity, of any printed matter stating or representing by implication that such commodity is offered for retail sale at a price lower than the ordinary and customary retail sale price or that a retail sale price advantage is accorded to purchasers thereof by reason of the size of that package or the quantity of its contents;

- (3) require that the label on each package of a consumer commodity (other than one which is a food within the meaning of section 321(f) of title 21) bear (A) the common or usual name of such consumer commodity, if any, and (B) in case such consumer commodity consists of two or more ingredients, the common or usual name of each such ingredient listed in order of decreasing predominance, but nothing in this paragraph shall be deemed to require that any trade secret be divulged; or

- (4) prevent the nonfunctional-slack-fill of packages containing consumer commodities. For purposes of paragraph (4) of this subsection, a package shall be deemed to be nonfunctionally slack-filled if it is filled to substantially less than its capacity for reasons other than (A) protection of the contents of such package or (B) the requirements of machines used for enclosing the contents in such package.

- **(d) Development by manufacturers, packers, and distributors of voluntary product standards**

Whenever the Secretary of Commerce determines that there is undue proliferation of the weights or masses, measures, or quantities in which any consumer commodity or reasonably comparable consumer commodities are being distributed in packages for sale at retail and such undue proliferation impairs the reasonable ability of consumers to make value comparisons with respect to such consumer commodity or commodities, he shall request manufacturers, packers, and distributors of the commodity or commodities to participate in the development of a voluntary product standard for such commodity or commodities under the procedures for the development of voluntary products standards established by the Secretary pursuant to section 272 of this title. Such procedures shall provide adequate manufacturer, packer, distributor, and consumer representation.

- **(e) Report and recommendations to Congress upon industry failure to develop or abide by voluntary product standards**

If (1) after one year after the date on which the Secretary of Commerce first makes the request of manufacturers, packers, and distributors to participate in the development of a voluntary product standard as provided in subsection (d) of this section, he determines that such a standard will not be published pursuant to the provisions of such subsection (d), or (2) if such a standard is published and the Secretary of Commerce determines that it has not been observed, he shall promptly report such determination to the Congress with a statement of the efforts that have been made under the voluntary standards program and his recommendation as to whether Congress should enact legislation providing regulatory authority to deal with the situation in question.

§1455. Procedures for Promulgation of Regulations.

• (a) Hearings by Secretary of Health and Human Services

Regulations promulgated by the Secretary under section 1453 or 1454 of this title shall be promulgated, and shall be subject to judicial review, pursuant to the provisions of subsections (e), (f), and (g) of section 371 of title 21. Hearings authorized or required for the promulgation of any such regulations by the Secretary shall be conducted by the Secretary or by such officer or employees of the Department of Health and Human Services as he may designate for that purpose.

• (b) Judicial review; hearings by Federal Trade Commission

Regulations promulgated by the Commission under section 1453 or 1454 of this title shall be promulgated, and shall be subject to judicial review, by proceedings taken in conformity with the provisions of subsections (e), (f), and (g) of section 371 of title 21 in the same manner, and with the same effect, as if such proceedings were taken by the Secretary pursuant to subsection (a) of this section. Hearings authorized or required for the promulgation of any such regulations by the Commission shall be conducted by the Commission or by such officer or employee of the Commission as the Commission may designate for that purpose.

• (c) Cooperation with other departments and agencies

In carrying into effect the provisions of this chapter, the Secretary and the Commission are authorized to cooperate with any department or agency of the United States, with any State, Commonwealth, or possession of the United States, and with any department, agency, or political subdivision of any such State, Commonwealth, or possession.

• (d) Returnable or reusable glass containers for beverages

No regulation adopted under this chapter shall preclude the continued use of returnable or reusable glass containers for beverages in inventory or with the trade as of the effective date of this Act, nor shall any regulation under this chapter preclude the orderly disposal of packages in inventory or with the trade as of the effective date of such regulation.

§1456. Enforcement.

• (a) Misbranded consumer commodities

Any consumer commodity which is a food, drug, device, or cosmetic, as each such term is defined by section 201 of the Federal Food, Drug, and Cosmetic Act (21 U.S.C. 321), and which is introduced or delivered for introduction into commerce in violation of any of the provisions of this chapter, or the regulations issued pursuant to this chapter, shall be deemed to be misbranded within the meaning of chapter III of the Federal Food, Drug, and Cosmetic Act (21 U.S.C. 331 et seq.), but the provisions of section 303 of that Act (21 U.S.C. 333) shall have no application to any violation of section 1452 of this title.

• (b) Unfair or deceptive acts or practices in commerce

Any violation of any of the provisions of this chapter, or the regulations issued pursuant to this chapter, with respect to any consumer commodity which is not a food, drug, device, or cosmetic, shall constitute an unfair or deceptive act or practice in commerce in violation of section 45(a)of this title and shall be subject to enforcement under section 45(b) of this title.

• (c) Imports

In the case of any imports into the United States of any consumer commodity covered by this chapter, the provisions of sections 1453 and 1454 of this title shall be enforced by the Secretary of the Treasury pursuant to section 801(a) and (b) of the Federal Food, Drug, and Cosmetic Act (21 U.S.C. 381).

§1457. Annual Reports to Congress: Submission Dates.

Each officer or agency required or authorized by this chapter to promulgate regulations for the packaging or labeling of any consumer commodity, shall transmit to the Congress each year a report containing a full and complete description of the activities of that officer or agency for the administration and enforcement of this chapter during the preceding fiscal year. All agencies except the Department of Health and Human Services and the Federal Trade Commission shall submit their reports in January of each year. The Department of Health and Human Services shall include this report in its annual report to Congress on activities under the Federal Food, Drug, and Cosmetic Act (21 U.S.C. 301 et seq.), and the Federal Trade Commission shall include this report in the Commission's annual report to Congress.

§1458. Cooperation with State Authorities; Transmittal of Regulations to States; Noninterference with Existing Programs.

- (a) A copy of each regulation promulgated under this chapter shall be transmitted promptly to the Secretary of Commerce, who shall (1) transmit copies thereof to all appropriate State officers and agencies, and (2) furnish to such State officers and agencies information and assistance to promote to the greatest practicable extent uniformity in State and Federal regulation of the labeling of consumer commodities.

- (b) Nothing contained in this section shall be construed to impair or otherwise interfere with any program carried into effect by the Secretary of Health and Human Services under other provisions of law in cooperation with State governments or agencies, instrumentalities, or political subdivisions thereof.

§1459. Definitions.

For the purpose of this chapter—

- (a) The term "consumer commodity", except as otherwise specifically provided by this subsection, means any food, drug, device, or cosmetic (as those terms are defined by the Federal Food, Drug, and Cosmetic Act (21 U.S.C. 301 et seq.)), and any other article, product, or commodity of any kind or class which is customarily produced or distributed for sale through retail sales agencies or instrumentalities for consumption by individuals, or use by individuals for purposes of personal care or in the performance of services ordinarily rendered within the household, and which usually is consumed or expended in the course of such consumption or use. Such term does not include—

  ○ (1) any meat or meat product, poultry or poultry product, or tobacco or tobacco product;

  ○ (2) any commodity subject to packaging or labeling requirements imposed by the Secretary of Agriculture pursuant to the Federal Insecticide, Fungicide, and Rodenticide Act (7 U.S.C. 136 et seq.), or the provisions of the eighth paragraph under the heading "Bureau of Animal Industry" of the Act of March 4, 1913 (21 U.S.C. 151 et seq.), commonly known as the Virus-Serum-Toxin Act;

  ○ (3) any drug subject to the provisions of section 503(b)(1) or 506 of the Federal Food, Drug, and Cosmetic Act (21 U.S.C. 353(b)(1) and 356);

- o (4) any beverage subject to or complying with packaging or labeling requirements imposed under the Federal Alcohol Administration Act (27 U.S.C. 201 et seq.); or

- o (5) any commodity subject to the provisions of the Federal Seed Act (7 U.S.C. 1551 et seq.).

- (b) The term "package" means any container or wrapping in which any consumer commodity is enclosed for use in the delivery or display of that consumer commodity to retail purchasers, but does not include—

  - o (1) shipping containers or wrappings used solely for the transportation of any consumer commodity in bulk or in quantity to manufacturers, packers, or processors, or to wholesale or retail distributors thereof;

  - o (2) shipping containers or outer wrappings used by retailers to ship or deliver any commodity to retail customers if such containers and wrappings bear no printed matter pertaining to any particular commodity; or

  - o (3) containers subject to the provisions of the Act of August 3, 1912 (37 Stat. 250, as amended; 15 U.S.C. 231–233), or the Act of March 4, 1915 (38 Stat. 1186, as amended; 15 U.S.C. 234–236)

- (c) The term "label" means any written, printed, or graphic matter affixed to any consumer commodity or affixed to or appearing upon a package containing any consumer commodity.

- (d) The term "person" includes any firm, corporation, or association.

- (e) The term "commerce" means (1) commerce between any State, the District of Columbia, the Commonwealth of Puerto Rico, or any territory or possession of the United States, and any place outside thereof, and (2) commerce within the District of Columbia or within any territory or possession of the United States not organized with a legislative body, but shall not include exports to foreign countries.

- (f) The term "principal display panel" means that part of a label that is most likely to be displayed, presented, shown, or examined under normal and customary conditions of display for retail sale.

§1460. Savings Provisions.

Nothing contained in this chapter shall be construed to repeal, invalidate, or supersede–

- (a) the Federal Trade Commission Act (15 U.S.C. 41 et seq.) or any statute defined therein as an antitrust Act;
- (b) the Federal Food, Drug, and Cosmetic Act (21 U.S.C. 301 et seq.); or
- (c) the Federal Hazardous Substances Labeling Act (15 U.S.C. 1261 et seq.).

§1461. Effect Upon State Law.

It is hereby declared that it is the express intent of Congress to supersede any and all laws of the States or political subdivisions thereof insofar as they may now or hereafter provide for the labeling of the net quantity of contents of the package of any consumer commodity covered by this chapter which are less stringent than or require information different from the requirements of section 1453 of this title or regulations promulgated pursuant thereto.

§1451 note Effective Date.

Section 13 of Pub. L. 89-755 provided that: "This Act (enacting this chapter) shall take effect on July 1, 1967: Provided, That the Secretary (with respect to any consumer commodity which is a food, drug, device, or cosmetic, as those terms are defined by the Federal Food, Drug, and Cosmetic Act) (section 301 et seq. of Title 21, Food and Drugs), and the Commission (with respect to any other consumer commodity) may by regulation postpone, for an additional twelve-month period, the effective date of this Act (this chapter) with respect to any class or type of consumer commodity on the basis of a finding that such a postponement would be in the public interest."

APPENDIX 7:
NUTRITION LABELING AND EDUCATION ACT (NLEA)

SEC. 1. SHORT TITLE, REFERENCE.

(a) SHORT TITLE—This Act may be cited as the `Nutrition Labeling and Education Act of 1990'.

(b) REFERENCE—Whenever in this Act an amendment or repeal is expressed in terms of an amendment to, or repeal of, a section or other provision, the reference shall be considered to be made to a section or other provision of the Federal Food, Drug, and Cosmetic Act.

SEC. 2. NUTRITION LABELING.

(a) NUTRITION INFORMATION—Section 403 (21 U.S.C. 343) is amended by adding at the end the following new paragraph:

`(q)(1) Except as provided in subparagraphs (3), (4), and (5), if it is a food intended for human consumption and is offered for sale, unless its label or labeling bears nutrition information that provides–

`(A)(i) the serving size which is an amount customarily consumed and which is expressed in a common household measure that is appropriate to the food, or

`(ii) if the use of the food is not typically expressed in a serving size, the common household unit of measure that expresses the serving size of the food,

`(B) the number of servings or other units of measure per container,

`(C) the total number of calories–

`(i) derived from any source, and

`(ii) derived from the total fat,

---

in each serving size or other unit of measure of the food,

`(D) the amount of the following nutrients: Total fat, saturated fat, cholesterol, sodium, total carbohydrates, complex carbohydrates, sugars, dietary fiber, and total protein contained in each serving size or other unit of measure,

`(E) any vitamin, mineral, or other nutrient required to be placed on the label and labeling of food under this Act before October 1, 1990, if the Secretary determines that such information will assist consumers in maintaining healthy dietary practices.

The Secretary may by regulation require any information required to be placed on the label or labeling by this subparagraph or subparagraph (2)(A) to be highlighted on the label or labeling by larger type, bold type, or contrasting color if the Secretary determines that such highlighting will assist consumers in maintaining healthy dietary practices.

`(2)(A) If the Secretary determines that a nutrient other than a nutrient required by subparagraph (1)(C), (1)(D), or (1)(E) should be included in the label or labeling of food subject to subparagraph (1) for purposes of providing information regarding the nutritional value of such food that will assist consumers in maintaining healthy dietary practices, the Secretary may by regulation require that information relating to such additional nutrient be included in the label or labeling of such food.

`(B) If the Secretary determines that the information relating to a nutrient required by subparagraph (1)(C), (1)(D), or (1)(E) or clause (A) of this subparagraph to be included in the label or labeling of food is not necessary to assist consumers in maintaining healthy dietary practices, the Secretary may by regulation remove information relating to such nutrient from such requirement.

`(3) For food that is received in bulk containers at a retail establishment, the Secretary may, by regulation, provide that the nutrition information required by subparagraphs (1) and (2) be displayed at the location in the retail establishment at which the food is offered for sale.

`(4)(A) The Secretary shall provide for furnishing the nutrition information required by subparagraphs (1) and (2) with respect to raw agricultural commodities and raw fish by issuing voluntary nutrition guidelines, as provided by clause (B) or by issuing regulations that are mandatory as provided by clause (C).

`(B)(i) Upon the expiration of 12 months after the date of the enactment of the Nutrition Labeling and Education Act of 1990, the Secretary, after providing an opportunity for comment, shall issue guidelines for food retailers offering raw agricultural commodities or raw fish to provide nutrition information specified in subparagraphs (1) and (2). Such guidelines shall take into account the actions taken by food retailers during such 12-month period to provide to consumers nutrition information on raw agricultural commodities and raw fish. Such guidelines shall only apply–

` (I) in the case of raw agricultural commodities, to the 20 varieties of vegetables most frequently consumed during a year and the 20 varieties of fruit most frequently consumed during a year, and

` (II) to the 20 varieties of raw fish most frequently consumed during a year.

The vegetables, fruits, and raw fish to which such guidelines apply shall be determined by the Secretary by regulation and the Secretary may apply such guidelines regionally.

` (ii) Upon the expiration of 12 months after the date of the enactment of the Nutrition Labeling and Education Act of 1990, the Secretary shall issue a final regulation defining the circumstances that constitute substantial compliance by food retailers with the guidelines issued under subclause (i). The regulation shall provide that there is not substantial compliance if a significant number of retailers have failed to comply with the guidelines. The size of the retailers and the portion of the market served by retailers in compliance with the guidelines shall be considered in determining whether the substantial-compliance standard has been met.

` (C)(i) Upon the expiration of 30 months after the date of the enactment of the Nutrition Labeling and Education Act of 1990, the Secretary shall issue a report on actions taken by food retailers to provide consumers with nutrition information for raw agricultural commodities and raw fish under the guidelines issued under clause (A). Such report shall include a determination of whether there is substantial compliance with the guidelines.

` (ii) If the Secretary finds that there is substantial compliance with the guidelines, the Secretary shall issue a report and make a determination of the type required in subclause (i) every two years.

` (D)(i) If the Secretary determines that there is not substantial compliance with the guidelines issued under clause (A), the Secretary shall at the time such determination is made issue proposed regulations requiring that any person who offers raw agricultural commodities or raw fish to consumers to provide, in a manner prescribed by regulations, the nutrition information required by subparagraphs (1) and (2). The Secretary shall issue final regulations imposing such requirements 6 months after issuing the proposed regulations. The final regulations shall become effective 6 months after the date of their promulgation.

`(ii) Regulations issued under subclause (i) may require that the nutrition information required by subparagraphs (1) and (2) be provided for more than 20 varieties of vegetables, 20 varieties of fruit, and 20 varieties of fish most frequently consumed during a year if the Secretary finds that a larger number of such products are frequently consumed. Such regulations shall permit such information to be provided in a single location in each area in which raw agricultural commodities and raw fish are offered for sale. Such regulations may provide that information shall be expressed as an average or range per serving of the same type of raw agricultural commodity or raw fish. The Secretary shall develop and make available to the persons who offer such food to consumers the information required by subparagraphs (1) and (2).

`(iii) Regulations issued under subclause (i) shall permit the required information to be provided in each area of an establishment in which raw agricultural commodities and raw fish are offered for sale. The regulations shall permit food retailers to display the required information by supplying copies of the information provided by the Secretary, by making the information available in brochure, notebook or leaflet form, or by posting a sign disclosing the information. Such regulations shall also permit presentation of the required information to be supplemented by a video, live demonstration, or other media which the Secretary approves.

`(E) For purposes of this subparagraph, the term `fish' includes freshwater or marine fin fish, crustaceans, and mollusks, including shellfish, amphibians, and other forms of aquatic animal life.

`(F) No person who offers raw agricultural commodities or raw fish to consumers may be prosecuted for minor violations of this subparagraph if there has been substantial compliance with the requirements of this paragraph.

`(5)(A) Subparagraphs (1), (2), (3), and (4) shall not apply to food–

`(i) which is served in restaurants or other establishments in which food is served for immediate human consumption or which is sold for sale or use in such establishments,

`(ii) which is processed and prepared primarily in a retail establishment, which is ready for human consumption, which is of the type described in subclause (i), and which is offered for sale to consumers but not for immediate human consumption in such establishment and which is not offered for sale outside such establishment,

`(iii) which is an infant formula subject to section 412,

`(iv) which is a medical food as defined in section 5(b) of the Orphan Drug Act (21 U.S.C. 360ee(b)), or

`(v) which is described in section 405(2).

`(B) Subparagraphs (1) and (2) shall not apply to the label of a food if the Secretary determines by regulations that compliance with such subparagraphs is impracticable because the package of such food is too small to comply with the requirements of such subparagraphs and if the label of such food does not contain any nutrition information.

`(C) If a food contains insignificant amounts, as determined by the Secretary, of all the nutrients required by subparagraphs (1) and (2) to be listed in the label or labeling of food, the requirements of such subparagraphs shall not apply to such food if the label, labeling, or advertising of such food does not make any claim with respect to the nutritional value of such food. If a food contains insignificant amounts, as determined by the Secretary, of more than one-half the nutrients required by subparagraphs (1) and (2) to be in the label or labeling of the food, the Secretary shall require the amounts of such nutrients to be stated in a simplified form prescribed by the Secretary.

`(D) If a person offers food for sale and has annual gross sales made or business done in sales to consumers which is not more than $500,000 or has annual gross sales made or business done in sales of food to consumers which is not more than $50,000, the requirements of subparagraphs (1), (2), (3), and (4) shall not apply with respect to food sold by such person to consumers unless the label or labeling of food offered by such person provides nutrition information or makes a nutrition claim.

`(E) If a food to which section 411 applies (as defined in section 411(c)) contains one or more of the nutrients required by subparagraph (1) or (2) to be in the label or labeling of the food, the label or labeling of such food shall comply with the requirements of subparagraphs (1) and (2) in a manner which is appropriate for such food and which is specified in regulations of the Secretary.

`(F) Subparagraphs (1), (2), (3), and (4) shall not apply to food which is sold by a food distributor if the food distributor principally sells food to restaurants or other establishments in which food is served for immediate human consumption and does not manufacture, process, or repackage the food it sells.'.

(b) REGULATIONS—

(1) The Secretary of Health and Human Services shall issue proposed regulations to implement section 403(q) of the Federal Food, Drug, and Cosmetic Act within 12 months after the date of the enactment of this Act. Not later than 24 months after the date of the enactment of this Act, the Secretary shall issue final regulations to implement the requirements of such section. Such regulations shall–

(A) require the required information to be conveyed to the public in a manner which enables the public to readily observe and comprehend such information and to understand its relative significance in the context of a total daily diet,

(B) include regulations which establish standards, in accordance with paragraph (1)(A), to define serving size or other unit of measure for food,

(C) permit the label or labeling of food to include nutrition information which is in addition to the information required by such section 403(q) and which is of the type described in subparagraph (1) or (2) of such section, and

(D) permit the nutrition information on the label or labeling of a food to remain the same or permit the information to be stated as a range even though (i) there are minor variations in the nutritional value of the food which occur in the normal course of the production or processing of the food, or (ii) the food is comprised of an assortment of similar foods which have variations in nutritional value.

(2) If the Secretary of Health and Human Services does not promulgate final regulations under paragraph (1) upon the expiration of 24 months after the date of the enactment of this Act, the proposed regulations issued in accordance with paragraph (1) shall be considered as the final regulations upon the expiration of such 24 months. There shall be promptly published in the Federal Register notice of new status of the proposed regulations.

(3) If the Secretary of Health and Human Services does not promulgate final regulations under section 403(q)(4) of the Federal Food, Drug, and Cosmetic Act upon the expiration of 6 months after the date on which the Secretary makes a finding that there has been no substantial compliance with section 403(q)(4)(C) of such Act, the proposed regulations issued in accordance with such section shall be considered as the final regulations upon the expiration of such

6 months. There shall be promptly published in the Federal Register notice of new status of the proposed regulations.

(c) CONSUMER EDUCATION—The Secretary of Health and Human Services shall carry out activities which educate consumers about–

(1) the availability of nutrition information in the label or labeling of food, and

(2) the importance of that information in maintaining healthy dietary practices.

SEC. 3. CLAIMS.

(a) LABELING REQUIRED—Section 403 (21 U.S.C. 343) is amended by adding after the paragraph added by section 2 the following:

`(r)(1) Except as provided in clauses (A) through (C) of subparagraph (5), if it is a food intended for human consumption which is offered for sale and for which a claim is made in the label or labeling of the food which expressly or by implication–

`(A) characterizes the level of any nutrient which is of the type required by paragraph (q)(1) or (q)(2) to be in the label or labeling of the food unless the claim is made in accordance with subparagraph (2), or

`(B) characterizes the relationship of any nutrient which is of the type required by paragraph (q)(1) or (q)(2) to be in the label or labeling of the food to a disease or a health-related condition unless the claim is made in accordance with subparagraph (3) or 5(D).

A statement of the type required by paragraph (q) that appears as part of the nutrition information required or permitted by such paragraph is not a claim which is subject to this paragraph and a claim subject to clause (A) is not subject to clause (B).

`(2)(A) Except as provided in subparagraphs (4)(A)(ii) and (4)(A)(iii) and clauses (A) through (C) of subparagraph (5), a claim described in subparagraph (1)(A)–

`(i) may be made only if the characterization of the level made in the claim uses terms which are defined in regulations of the Secretary,

`(ii) may not state the absence of a nutrient unless–

`(I) the nutrient is usually present in the food or in a food which substitutes for the food as defined by the Secretary by regulation, or

`(II) the Secretary by regulation permits such a statement on the basis of a finding that such a statement would assist consumers in maintaining healthy dietary practices and the statement discloses that the nutrient is not usually present in the food,

`(iii) may not be made with respect to the level of cholesterol in the food if the food contains, as determined by the Secretary by regulation, fat or saturated fat in an amount which increases to persons in the general population the risk of disease or a health related condition which is diet related unless–

`(I) the Secretary finds by regulation that the level of cholesterol is substantially less than the level usually present in the food or in a food which substitutes for the food and which has a significant market share, or the Secretary by regulation permits a statement regarding the absence of cholesterol on the basis of a finding that cholesterol is not usually present in the food and that such a statement would assist consumers in maintaining healthy dietary practices and the regulation requires that the statement disclose that cholesterol is not usually present in the food, and

`(II) the label or labeling of the food discloses the level of such fat or saturated fat in immediate proximity to such claim and with appropriate prominence which shall be no less than one-half the size of the claim with respect to the level of cholesterol,

`(iv) may not be made with respect to the level of saturated fat in the food if the food contains cholesterol unless the label or labeling of the food discloses the level of cholesterol in the food in immediate proximity to such claim and with appropriate prominence which shall be no less than one-half the size of the claim with respect to the level of saturated fat,

`(v) may not state that a food is high in dietary fiber unless the food is low in total fat as defined by the Secretary or the label or labeling discloses the level of total fat in the food in immediate proximity to such statement and with appropriate prominence which shall be no less than one-half the size of the claim with respect to the level of dietary fiber, and

`(vi) may not be made if the Secretary by regulation prohibits the claim because the claim is misleading in light of the level of another nutrient in the food.

`(B) If a claim described in subparagraph (1)(A) is made with respect to a nutrient in a food, the label or labeling of such food shall contain, prominently and in immediate proximity to such claim, the following statement: `See **XXXXXX** for nutrition information'.

In the statement–

`(i) the blank shall identify the panel on which the information described in the statement may be found, and

`(ii) if the Secretary determines that the food contains a nutrient at a level which increases to persons in the general population the risk of a disease or health-related condition which is diet related, taking into account the significance of the food in the total daily diet, the statement shall also identify such nutrient.

`(C) Subparagraph (2)(A) does not apply to a claim described in subparagraph (1)(A) and contained in the label or labeling of a food if such claim is contained in the brand name of such food and such brand name was in use on such food before October 25, 1989, unless the brand name contains a term defined by the Secretary under subparagraph (2)(A)(i). Such a claim is subject to paragraph (a).

`(D) Subparagraph (2) does not apply to a claim described in subparagraph (1)(A) which uses the term `diet' and is contained in the label or labeling of a soft drink if (i) such claim is contained in the brand name of such soft drink, (ii) such brand name was in use on such soft drink before October 25, 1989, and (iii) the use of the term `diet' was in conformity with section 105.66 of title 21 of the Code of Federal Regulations. Such a claim is subject to paragraph (a).

`(E) Subclauses (i) through (v) of subparagraph (2)(A) do not apply to a statement in the label or labeling of food which describes the percentage of vitamins and minerals in the food in relation to the amount of such vitamins and minerals recommended for daily consumption by the Secretary.

`(3)(A) Except as provided in subparagraph (5), a claim described in subparagraph (1)(B) may only be made–

`(i) if the claim meets the requirements of the regulations of the Secretary promulgated under clause (B), and

`(ii) if the food for which the claim is made does not contain, as determined by the Secretary by regulation, any nutrient in an amount which increases to persons in the general population the risk of a disease or health-related condition which is diet related, taking into account the significance of the food in the total daily diet, except that the Secretary may by regulation permit such a claim based on a finding that such a claim would assist consumers in maintaining healthy dietary practices and based on a requirement that the label contain a disclosure of the type required by subparagraph (2)(B).

`(B)(i) The Secretary shall promulgate regulations authorizing claims of the type described in subparagraph (1)(B) only if the Secretary determines, based on the totality of publicly available scientific evidence (including evidence from well-designed studies conducted in a manner which is consistent with generally recognized scientific procedures and principles), that there is significant scientific agreement, among experts qualified by scientific training and experience to evaluate such claims, that the claim is supported by such evidence.

`(ii) A regulation described in subclause (i) shall describe–

`(I) the relationship between a nutrient of the type required in the label or labeling of food by paragraph (q)(1) or (q)(2) and a disease or health-related condition, and

`(II) the significance of each such nutrient in affecting such disease or health-related condition.

`(iii) A regulation described in subclause (i) shall require such claim to be stated in a manner so that the claim is an accurate representation of the matters set out in subclause (ii) and so that the claim enables the public to comprehend the information provided in the claim and to understand the relative significance of such information in the context of a total daily diet.

`(4)(A)(i) Any person may petition the Secretary to issue a regulation under subparagraph (2)(A)(i) or (3)(B) relating to a claim described in subparagraph (1)(A) or (1)(B). Not later than 100 days after the petition is received by the Secretary, the Secretary shall issue a final decision denying the petition or file the petition for further action by the Secretary. If the Secretary denies the petition, the petition shall not be made available to the public. If the Secretary files the petition, the Secretary shall deny the petition or issue a proposed regulation to take the action requested in the petition not later than 90 days after the date of such decision.

`(ii) Any person may petition the Secretary for permission to use in a claim described in subparagraph (1)(A) terms that are consistent with the terms defined by the Secretary under subparagraph (2)(A)(i). Within 90 days of the submission of such a petition, the Secretary shall issue a final decision denying the petition or granting such permission.

`(iii) Any person may petition the Secretary for permission to use an implied claim described in subparagraph (1)(A) in a brand name. After publishing notice of an opportunity to comment on the petition in the Federal Register and making the petition available to the public, the Secretary shall grant the petition if the Secretary finds that such claim is not misleading and is consistent with terms defined by the Secretary under subparagraph (2)(A)(i). The Secretary shall grant or deny the petition within 100 days of the date it is submitted to the Secretary and the petition shall be considered granted if the Secretary does not act on it within such 100 days.

`(B) A petition under clause (A)(i) respecting a claim described in subparagraph (1)(A) or (1)(B) shall include an explanation of the reasons why the claim meets the requirements of this subsection and a summary of the scientific data which supports such reasons.

`(C) If a petition for a regulation under subparagraph (3)(B) relies on a report from an authoritative scientific body of the United States, the Secretary shall consider such report and shall justify any decision rejecting the conclusions of such report.

`(5)(A) This paragraph does not apply to infant formulas subject to section 412(h) and medical foods as defined in section 5(b) of the Orphan Drug Act.

`(B) Subclauses (iii) through (v) of subparagraph (2)(A) and subparagraph (2)(B) do not apply to food which is served in restaurants or other establishments in which food is served for immediate human consumption or which is sold for sale or use in such establishments.

`(C) A subparagraph (1)(A) claim made with respect to a food which claim is required by a standard of identity issued under section 401 shall not be subject to subparagraph (2)(A)(i) or (2)(B).

`(D) A subparagraph (1)(B) claim made with respect to a dietary supplement of vitamins, minerals, herbs, or other similar nutritional substances shall not be subject to subparagraph (3) but shall be subject to a procedure and standard, respecting the validity of such claim, established by regulation of the Secretary.'.

(b) Regulations—

(1)(A) Within 12 months of the date of the enactment of this Act, the Secretary of Health and Human Services shall issue proposed regulations to implement section 403(r) of the Federal Food, Drug, and Cosmetic Act. Such regulations–

(i) shall identify claims described in section 403(r)(1)(A) of such Act which comply with section 403(r)(2) of such Act,

(ii) shall identify claims described in section 403(r)(1)(B) of such Act which comply with section 403(r)(3) of such Act,

(iii) shall, in defining terms used to characterize the level of any nutrient in food under section 403(r)(2)(A)(i) of such Act, define–

(I) free,

(II) low,

(III) light or lite,

(IV) reduced,

(V) less, and

(VI) high,

unless the Secretary finds that the use of any such term would be misleading,

(iv) shall permit statements describing the amount and percentage of nutrients in food which are not misleading and are consistent with the terms defined in section 403(r)(2)(A)(i) of such Act,

(v) shall provide that if multiple claims subject to section 403(r)(1)(A) of such Act are made on a single panel of the food label or page of a labeling brochure, a single statement may be made to satisfy section 403(r)(2)(B) of such Act,

(vi) shall determine whether claims respecting the following nutrients and diseases meet the requirements of section 403(r)(3) of such Act: Calcium and osteoporosis, dietary fiber and cancer, lipids and cardiovascular disease, lipids and cancer, sodium and hypertension, and dietary fiber and cardiovascular disease,

(vii) shall not require a person who proposes to make a claim described in section 403(r)(1)(B) of such Act which is in compliance with such regulations to secure the approval of the Secretary before making such claim,

(viii) may permit a claim described in section 403(r)(1)(A) of such Act to be made for butter,

(ix) may, in defining terms under section 403(r)(2)(A)(i), include similar terms which are commonly understood to have the same meaning, and

(x) shall establish, as required by section 403(r)(5)(D), the procedure and standard respecting the validity of claims made with respect to a dietary supplement of vitamins, minerals, herbs, or other similar nutritional substances and shall determine whether claims respecting the following nutrients and diseases meet the requirements of section 403(r)(5)(D) of such Act: folic acid and neural tube defects, antioxident vitamins and cancer, zinc and immune function in the elderly, and omega-3 fatty acids and heart disease.

(B) Not later than 24 months after the date of the enactment of this Act, the Secretary shall issue final regulations to implement section 403(r) of the Federal Food, Drug, and Cosmetic Act.

(2) If the Secretary does not promulgate final regulations under paragraph (1)(B) upon the expiration of 24 months after the date of the enactment of this Act, the proposed regulations issued in accordance with paragraph (1)(A) shall be considered as the final regulations upon the expiration of such 24 months. There shall be promptly published in the Federal Register notice of the new status of the proposed regulations.

SEC. 4. STATE ENFORCEMENT.

Section 307 (21 U.S.C. 337) is amended by striking out `All such proceedings' and inserting in lieu thereof `(a) Except as provided in subsection (b), all such proceedings' and by adding at the end the following:

`(b)(1) A State may bring in its own name and within its jurisdiction proceedings for the civil enforcement, or to restrain violations, of sections 401, 403(b), 403(c), 403(d), 403(e), 403(f), 403(g), 403(h), 403(i), 403(k), 403(q), or 403(r) if the food that is the subject of the proceedings is located in the State.

`(2) No proceeding may be commenced by a State under paragraph (1)–

`(A) before 30 days after the State has given notice to the Secretary that the State intends to bring such proceeding,

`(B) before 90 days after the State has given notice to the Secretary of such intent if the Secretary has, within such 30 days, commenced an informal or formal enforcement action pertaining to the food which would be the subject of such proceeding, or

`(C) if the Secretary is diligently prosecuting a proceeding in court pertaining to such food, has settled such proceeding, or has settled the informal or formal enforcement action pertaining to such food.

In any court proceeding described in subparagraph (C), a State may intervene as a matter of right.', and

(2) in the last sentence, by striking out `any such proceeding' and inserting in lieu thereof `any proceeding under this section'.

SEC. 5. CONFORMING AMENDMENTS.

(a) SECTION 405—Section 405 (21 U.S.C. 345) is amended by adding at the end the following: `This section does not apply to the labeling requirements of sections 403(q) and 403(r).'.

(b) DRUGS—Section 201(g)(1) (21 U.S.C. 321(g)(1)) is amended by adding at the end the following: `A food for which a claim, subject to sections 403(r)(1)(B) and 403(r)(3) or sections 403(r)(1)(B) and 403(r)(5)(D), is made in accordance with the requirements of section 403(r) is not a drug under clause (B) solely because the label or labeling contains such a claim.'.

SEC. 6. NATIONAL UNIFORM NUTRITION LABELING.

(a) PREEMPTION—Chapter IV is amended by adding after section 403 the following new section:

`SEC. 403A. (a) Except as provided in subsection (b), no State or political subdivision of a State may directly or indirectly establish under any authority or continue in effect as to any food in interstate commerce—

   `(1) any requirement for a food which is the subject of a standard of identity established under section 401 that is not identical to such standard of identity or that is not identical to the requirement of section 403(g),

   `(2) any requirement for the labeling of food of the type required by section 403(c), 403(e), or 403(i)(2) that is not identical to the requirement of such section,

   `(3) any requirement for the labeling of food of the type required by section 403(b), 403(d), 403(f), 403(h), 403(i)(1), or 403(k) that is not identical to the requirement of such section,

   `(4) any requirement for nutrition labeling of food that is not identical to the requirement of section 403(q), except a requirement for nutrition labeling of food which is exempt under subclause (i) or (ii) of section 403(q)(5)(A), or

   `(5) any requirement respecting any claim of the type described in section 403(r)(1) made in the label or labeling of food that is not identical to the requirement of section 403(r), except a requirement respecting a claim made in the label or labeling of food which is exempt under clause (B) of such section.

Paragraph (3) shall take effect in accordance with section 6(b) of the Nutrition Labeling and Education Act of 1990.

`(b) Upon petition of a State or a political subdivision of a State, the Secretary may exempt from subsection (a), under such conditions as may be prescribed by regulation, any State or local requirement that–

`(1) would not cause any food to be in violation of any applicable requirement under Federal law,

`(2) would not unduly burden interstate commerce, and

`(3) is designed to address a particular need for information which need is not met by the requirements of the sections referred to in subsection (a).'.

(b) Study and Regulations—

(1) For the purpose of implementing section 403A(a)(3), the Secretary of Health and Human Services shall enter into a contract with a public or nonprofit private entity to conduct a study of–

(A) State and local laws which require the labeling of food that is of the type required by sections 403(b), 403(d), 403(f), 403(h), 403(i)(1), and 403(k) of the Federal Food, Drug, and Cosmetic Act, and

(B) the sections of the Federal Food, Drug, and Cosmetic Act referred to in subparagraph (A) and the regulations issued by the Secretary to enforce such sections to determine whether such sections and regulations adequately implement the purposes of such sections.

(2) The contract under paragraph (1) shall provide that the study required by such paragraph shall be completed within 6 months of the date of the enactment of this Act.

(3)(A) Within 9 months of the date of the enactment of this Act, the Secretary shall publish a proposed list of sections which are adequately being implemented by regulations as determined under paragraph (1)(B) and sections which are not adequately being implemented by regulations as so determined. After publication of the lists, the Secretary shall provide 60 days for comments on such lists.

(B) Within 24 months of the date of the enactment of this Act, the Secretary shall publish a final list of sections which are adequately being implemented by regulations and a list of sections which are not adequately being implemented by regulations. With respect to a section which is found by the Secretary to be adequately implemented, no State or political subdivision of a State may establish or continue in effect as to any food in interstate commerce any requirement which is not identical to the requirement of such section.

(C) Within 24 months of the date of the enactment of this Act, the Secretary shall publish proposed revisions to the regulations found to be inadequate under subparagraph (B) and within 30 months of such date shall issue final revisions. Upon the effective date of such final revisions, no State or political subdivision may establish or continue in effect any requirement which is not identical to the requirement of the section which had its regulations revised in accordance with this subparagraph.

(D)(i) If the Secretary does not issue a final list in accordance with subparagraph (B), the proposed list issued under subparagraph (A) shall be considered the final list and States and political subdivisions shall be preempted with respect to sections found to be adequate in such proposed list in accordance with subparagraph (B).

(ii) If the Secretary does not issue final revisions of regulations in accordance with subparagraph (C), the proposed revisions issued under such subparagraph shall be considered the final revisions and States and political subdivisions shall be preempted with respect to sections the regulations of which are revised by the proposed revisions.

(E) Subsection (b) of section 403A of the Federal Food, Drug, and Cosmetic Act shall apply with respect to the prohibition prescribed by subparagraphs (B) and (C).

(c) CONSTRUCTION—

(1) The Nutrition Labeling and Education Act of 1990 shall not be construed to preempt any provision of State law, unless such provision is expressly preempted under section 403A of the Federal Food, Drug, and Cosmetic Act.

(2) The amendment made by subsection (a) and the provisions of subsection (b) shall not be construed to apply to any requirement respecting a statement in the labeling of food that provides for a warning concerning the safety of the food or component of the food.

(3) The amendment made by subsection (a), the provisions of subsection (b) and paragraphs (1) and (2) of this subsection shall not be construed to affect preemption, express or implied, of any such requirement of a State or political subdivision, which may arise under the Constitution, any provision of the Federal Food, Drug, and

Cosmetic Act not amended by subsection (a), any other Federal law, or any Federal regulation, order, or other final agency action reviewable under chapter 7 of title 5, United States Code.

SEC. 7. INGREDIENTS.

Section 403(i) (21 U.S.C. 343(i)) is amended–

(1) by striking out `If it is not subject to paragraph (g) of this section unless' and inserting in lieu thereof `Unless',

(2) by inserting before `; except' the following: `and if the food purports to be a beverage containing vegetable or fruit juice, a statement with appropriate prominence on the information panel of the total percentage of such fruit or vegetable juice contained in the food', and

(3) by striking out `colorings' and inserting in lieu thereof `colors not required to be certified under section 706(c)'.

SEC. 8. STANDARD OF IDENTITY REGULATION.

Section 701(e) (21 U.S.C. 371(e)) is amended by striking out `Any action for the issuance, amendment, or repeal of any regulation under section 401, 403(j), 404(a), 406, 501(b), or 502 (d) or (h) of this Act' and inserting in lieu thereof the following: `Any action for the issuance, amendment, or repeal of any regulation under section 403(j), 404(a), 406, 501(b), or 502 (d) or (h) of this Act, and any action for the amendment or repeal of any definition and standard of identity under section 401 of this Act for any dairy product (including products regulated under parts 131, 133 and 135 of title 21, Code of Federal Regulations) or maple sirup (regulated under section 168.140 of title 21, Code of Federal Regulations).

SEC. 9. CONSTRUCTION.

The amendments made by this Act shall not be construed to alter the authority of the Secretary of Health and Human Services and the Secretary of Agriculture under the Federal Food, Drug, and Cosmetic Act, the Federal Meat Inspection Act, the Poultry Products Inspection Act, and the Egg Products Inspection Act.

SEC. 10. EFFECTIVE DATE.

(a) IN GENERAL—

(1) Except as provided in paragraph (2)–

(A) the amendments made by section 2 shall take effect 6 months after–

(i) the date of the promulgation of all final regulations required to implement section 403(q) of the Federal Food, Drug, and Cosmetic Act, or

(ii) if such regulations are not promulgated, the date proposed regulations are to be considered as such final regulations,

except that section 403(q)(4) of such Act shall take effect as prescribed by such section,

(B) the amendments made by section 3 shall take effect 6 months after–

(i) the date of the promulgation of final regulations to implement section 403(r) of the Federal Food, Drug, and Cosmetic Act, or

(ii) if such regulations are not promulgated, the date proposed regulations are to be considered as such final regulations, except that any person marketing a food the brand name of which contains a term defined by the Secretary under section 403(r)(2)(A)(i) of the Federal Food, Drug, and Cosmetic Act shall be given an additional 6 months to comply with section 3,

(C) the amendments made by section 4 shall take effect 24 months after the date of the enactment of this Act, and

(D) the amendments made by section 5 shall take effect on the date the amendments made by section 3 take effect.

(2) Section 403(q) of the Federal Food, Drug, and Cosmetic Act (as added by section 2) shall not apply with respect to food which was labeled before the effective date of the amendments made by section 2 and section 403(r) of the Federal Food, Drug, and Cosmetic Act (as added by section 3) shall not apply with respect to food which was labeled before the effective date of the amendments made by section 3.

(3)(A) If the Secretary finds that a person who is subject to section 403(q)(4) of such Act is unable to comply with the requirements of such section upon the effective date of final regulations to implement section 403(q) of such Act or of proposed regulations to be considered as such final regulations because the Secretary has not made available to such person the information required by such section, the Secretary shall delay the application of such section to such person for such time as the Secretary may require to provide such information.

(B) If the Secretary finds that compliance with section 403(q) or 403(r)(2) of such Act would cause an undue economic hardship, the Secretary may delay the application of such sections for no more than one year.

(b) SECTION 6—

(1) IN GENERAL—Except as provided in paragraph (2), the amendments made by section 6 shall take effect–

(A) with respect to a requirement of a State or political subdivision described in paragraph (1) of section 403A(a) of the Federal Food, Drug, and Cosmetic Act, on the date of the enactment of this Act,

(B) with respect to a requirement of a State or political subdivision described in paragraph (2) of section 403A(a) of the Federal Food, Drug, and Cosmetic Act, one year after the date of the enactment of this Act,

(C) with respect to a requirement of a State or political subdivision described in paragraph (3) of section 403A(a) of the Federal Food, Drug, and Cosmetic Act, as prescribed by section 6(b) of the Nutrition Labeling and Education Act of 1990,

(D) with respect to a requirement of a State or political subdivision described in paragraph (4) of section 403A(a) of the Federal Food, Drug, and Cosmetic Act, on the date regulations to implement section 403(q) of such Act take effect, and

(E) with respect to a requirement of a State or political subdivision described in paragraph (5) of section 403A(a) of the Federal Food, Drug, and Cosmetic Act, on the date regulations to implement section 403(r) of such Act take effect.

(2) EXCEPTION—If a State or political subdivision submits a petition under section 403A(b) of the Federal Food, Drug, and Cosmetic Act for a requirement described in section 403A(a) of such Act within 18 months of the date of the enactment of this Act, paragraphs (3) through (5) of such section 403A(a) shall not apply with respect to such State or political subdivision requirement until–

(1) 24 months after the date of the enactment of this Act, or

(2) action on the petition,

whichever occurs later.

(c) SECTION 7—The amendments made by section 7 shall take effect one year after the date of the enactment of this Act.

Speaker of the House of Representatives.

Vice President of the United States and

President of the Senate.

APPENDIX 8:
FEDERAL FOOD, DRUG, AND COSMETIC
ACT CHAPTERS I–IV

CHAPTER I–SHORT TITLE

SEC. 1. [301] This Act may be cited as the Federal Food, Drug, and Cosmetic Act.

CHAPTER II–DEFINITIONS

SEC. 201. [321] For the purposes of this Act–

(a)(1) The term "State", except as used in the last sentence of section 702(a), means any State or Territory of the United States, the District of Columbia, and the Commonwealth of Puerto Rico.

(2) The term "Territory" means any Territory or possession of the United States, including the District of Columbia, and excluding the Commonwealth of Puerto Rico and the Canal Zone.

(b) The term "interstate commerce" means (1) commerce between any State or Territory and any place outside thereof, and (2) commerce within the District of Columbia or within any other Territory not organized with a legislative body.

(c) The term "Department" means the U.S. Department of Health and Human Services.

(d) The term "Secretary" means the Secretary of Health and Human Services.

(e) The term "person" includes individual, partnership, corporation, and association.

(f) The term "food" means (1) articles used for food or drink for man or other animals, (2) chewing gum, and (3) articles used for components of any other such article.

(g)(1) The term "drug" means (A) articles recognized in the official United States Pharmacopeia, official Homeopathic Pharmacopeia of the United States, or official National Formulary, or any supplement to any of them; and (B) articles intended for use in the diagnosis, cure, mitigation, treatment, or prevention of disease in man or other animals; and (C) articles (other than food) intended to affect the structure or any function of the body of man or other animals; and (D) articles intended for use as a component of any articles specified in clause (A), (B), or (C); but does not include devices or their components, parts, or accessories.

(2) The term "counterfeit drug" means a drug which, or the container or labeling of which, without authorization, bears the trademark, trade name, or other identifying mark, imprint, or device, or any likeness thereof, of a drug manufacturer, processor, packer, or distributor other than the person or persons who in fact manufactured, processed, packed, or distributed such drug and which thereby falsely purports or is represented to be the product of, or to have been packed or distributed by, such other drug manufacturer, processor, packer, or distributor.

(h) The term "device" (except when used in paragraph (n) of this section and in sections 301(i), 403(f), 502(c), and 602(c)) means an instrument, apparatus, implement, machine, contrivance, implant, in vitro reagent, or other similar or related article, including any component, part, or accessory, which is–

(1) recognized in the official National Formulary, or the United States Pharmacopeia, or any supplement to them,

(2) intended for use in the diagnosis of disease or other conditions, or in the cure, mitigation, treatment, or prevention of disease, in man or other animals, or

(3) intended to affect the structure or any function of the body of man or other animals, and which does not achieve any of its principal intended purposes through chemical action within or on the body of man or other animals and which is not dependent upon being metabolized for the achievement of any of its principal intended purposes.

(i) The term "cosmetic" means (1) articles intended to be rubbed, poured, sprinkled, or sprayed on, introduced into, or otherwise applied to the human body or any part thereof for cleansing, beautifying, promoting attractiveness, or altering the appearance, and (2) articles intended for use as a component of any such articles; except that such term shall not include soap.

(j) The term "official compendium" means the official United States Pharmacopeia, official Homeopathic Pharmacopeia of the United States, official National Formulary, or any supplement to any of them.

(k) The term "label" means a display of written, printed, or graphic matter upon the immediate container of any article; and a requirement made by or under authority of this Act that any word, statement, or other information appearing on the label shall not be considered to be complied with unless such word, statement, or other information also appears on the outside container or wrapper, if any there be, of the retail package of such article, or is easily legible through the outside container or wrapper.

(l) The term "immediate container" does not include package liners.

(m) The term "labeling" means all labels and other written, printed, or graphic matter (1) upon any article or any of its containers or wrappers, or (2) accompanying such article.

(n) If an article is alleged to be misbranded because the labeling or advertising is misleading, then in determining whether the labeling or advertising is misleading there shall be taken into account (among other things) not only representations made or suggested by statement, word, design, device, or any combination thereof, but also the extent to which the labeling or advertising fails to reveal facts material in the light of such representations or material with respect to consequences which may result from the use of the article to which the labeling or advertising relates under the conditions of use prescribed in the labeling or advertising thereof or under such conditions of use as are customary or usual.

(o) The representation of a drug, in its labeling, as an antiseptic shall be considered to be a representation that it is a germicide, except in the case of a drug purporting to be, or represented as, an antiseptic for inhibitory use as a wet dressing, ointment, dusting powder, or such other use as involves prolonged contact with the body.

(p) The term "new drug" means–

(1) Any drug (except a new animal drug or an animal feed bearing or containing a new animal drug) the composition of which is such that such drug is not generally recognized, among experts qualified by scientific training and experience to evaluate the safety and effectiveness of drugs, as safe and effective for use under the conditions prescribed, recommended, or suggested in the labeling thereof, except that such a drug not so recognized shall not be deemed to be a "new drug" if at any time prior to the enactment of this Act it was

subject to the Food and Drugs Act of June 30, 1906, as amended, and if at such time its labeling contained the same representations concerning the conditions of its use; or

(2) Any drug (except a new animal drug or an animal feed bearing or containing a new animal drug) the composition of which is such that such drug, as a result of investigations to determine its safety and effectiveness for use under such conditions, has become so recognized, but which has not, otherwise than in such investigations, been used to a material extent or for a material time under such conditions.

(q) The term "pesticide chemical" means any substance which, alone, in chemical combination or in formulation with one or more other substance, is "a pesticide" within the meaning of the Federal Insecticide, Fungicide, and Rodenticide Act (7 U.S.C., sec. 136(u)) as now in force or as hereafter amended, and which is used in the production, storage, or transportation of raw agricultural commodities.

(r) The term "raw agricultural commodity" means any food in its raw or natural state, including all fruits that are washed, colored, or otherwise treated in their unpeeled natural form prior to marketing.

(s) The term "food additive" means any substance the intended use of which results or may asonably be expected to result, directly or indirectly, in its becoming a component or otherwise affecting the characteristics of any food (including any substance intended for use in producing, manufacturing, packing, processing, preparing, treating, packaging, transporting, or holding food; and including any source of radiation intended for any such use), if such substance is not generally recognized, among experts qualified by scientific training and experience to evaluate its safety, as having been adequately shown through scientific procedures (or, in the case of a substance used in food prior to January 1, 1958, through either scientific procedures or experience based on common use in food) to be safe under the conditions of its intended use; except that such term does not include—

(1) a pesticide chemical in or on a raw agricultural commodity; or

(2) a pesticide chemical to the extent that it is intended for use or is used in the production, storage, or transportation of any raw agricultural commodity; or

(3) a color additive; or

(4) any substance used in accordance with a sanction or approval granted prior to the enactment of this paragraph pursuant to this Act, the Poultry Products Inspection Act (21 U.S.C. 451 and the following) or the Meat Inspection Act of March 4,1907 (34 Stat. 1260), as amended and extended (21 U.S.C. 71 and the following); or

(5) a new animal drug.

(t)(1) The term "color additive" means a material which–

(A) is a dye, pigment, or other substance made by a process of synthesis or similar artifice, or extracted, isolated, or otherwise derived, with or without intermediate or final change of identity, from a vegetable, animal, mineral, or other source, and

(B) when added or applied to a food, drug, or cosmetic, or to the human body or any part thereof, is capable (alone or through reaction with other substance) of imparting color thereto: except that such term does not include any material which the Secretary, by regulation, determines is used (or intended to be used) solely for a purpose or purposes other than coloring.

(2) The term "color" includes black, white, and intermediate grays.

(3) Nothing in subparagraph (1) of this paragraph shall be construed to apply to any pesticide chemical, soil or plant nutrient, or other agricultural chemical solely because of its effect in aiding, retarding, or otherwise affecting, directly or indirectly, the growth or other natural physiological processes of produce of the soil and thereby affecting its color, whether before or after harvest.

(u) * The term "safe," as used in paragraph (s) of this section and in sections 409, 512, and 706, has reference to the health of man or animal.

(v) **

(w) The term "new animal drug" means any drug intended for use for animals other than man, including any drug intended for use in animal feed but not including such animal feed–

(1) the composition of which is such that such drug is not generally recognized, among experts qualified by scientific training and experience to evaluate the safety and effectiveness of animal drugs, as safe and effective for use under the conditions prescribed, recommended, or suggested in the labeling thereof; except that such a drug not so recognized shall not be deemed to be a "new animal drug" if at any time prior to June 25, 1938, it was subject to the Food and Drugs Act of June 30, 1906, as amended, and if at such time its

labeling contained the same representations concerning the conditions of its use; or

(2) the composition of which is such that such drug, as a result of investigations to determine its safety and effectiveness for use under such conditions, has become so recognized but which has not, otherwise than in such investigations, been used to a material extent or for a material time under such conditions; or

(3) which drug is composed wholly or partly of any kind of penicillin, streptomycin, chlortetracycline, chloramphenicol, or bacitracin, or any derivative thereof, except when there is in effect a published order of the Secretary declaring such drug not to be a new animal drug on the grounds that (A) the requirement of certification of batches of such drug, as provided for in section 512(n), is not necessary to insure that the objectives specified in paragraph (3) thereof are achieved and (B) that neither subparagraph (1) nor (2) of this paragraph (w) applies to such drug.

(x) The term "animal feed," as used in paragraph (w) of this section, in section 512, and in provisions of this Act referring to such paragraph or section, means an article which is intended for use for food for animals other than man and which is intended for use as a substantial source of nutrients in the diet of the animal and is not limited to a mixture intended to be the sole ration of the animal.

(y) The term "informal hearing" means a hearing which is not subject to section 554, 556, or 557 of title 5 of the United States Code and which provides for the following:

(1) The presiding officer in the hearing shall be designated by the Secretary from officers and employees of the Department of Health and Human Services who have not participated in any action of the Secretary which is the subject of the hearing and who are not directly responsible to an officer or employee of the Department who has participated in any such action.

(2) Each party to the hearing shall have the right at all times to be advised and accompanied by an attorney.

(3) Before the hearing, each party to the hearing shall be given reasonable notice of the matters to be considered at the hearing, including a comprehensive statement of the basis for the action taken or proposed by the Secretary which is the subject of the hearing and a general summary of the information which will be presented by the Secretary at the hearing in support of such action.

(4) At the hearing the parties to the hearing shall have the right to hear a full and complete statement of the action of the Secretary which is the subject of the hearing together with the information and reasons supporting such action, to conduct reasonable questioning, and to present any oral or written information relevant to such action.

(5) The presiding officer in such hearing shall prepare a written report of the hearing to which shall be attached all written material presented at the hearing. The participants in the hearing shall be given the opportunity to review and correct or supplement the presiding officer's report of the hearing.

(6) The Secretary may require the hearing to be transcribed. A party to the hearing shall have the right to have the hearing transcribed at his expense. Any transcription of a hearing shall be included in the presiding officer's report of the hearing.

(z) The term "saccharin" includes calcium saccharin, saccharin, and ammonium saccharin.

(aa) The term "infant formula" means a food which purports to be or is represented for special dietary use solely as a food for infants by reason of its simulation of human milk or its suitability as a complete or partial substitute for human milk.

CHAPTER III–PROHIBITED ACTS AND PENALTIES

PROHIBITED ACTS

SEC. 301. [331] The following acts and hereby prohibited:

(a) The introduction or delivery for introduction into interstate commerce of any food, drug, device, or cosmetic that is adulterated or misbranded.

(b) The adulteration or misbranding of any food, drug, device, or cosmetic in interstate commerce.

(c) The receipt in interstate commerce of any food, drug, device, or cosmetic that is adulterated or misbranded, and the delivery or proffered delivery thereof for pay or otherwise.

(d) The introduction or delivery for introduction into interstate commerce of any article in violation of section 404 or 505.

(e) The refusal to permit access to or copying of any record as required by section 412 or 703; or the failure to establish or maintain any record, or make any report, required under section 412, 505 (i) or (j),

507 (d) or (g), 512 (j), (l) or (m), 515(f) or 519, or the refusal to permit access to or verification or copying of any such required record.

(f) The refusal to permit entry or inspection as authorized by section 704.

(g) The manufacture within any Territory of any food, drug, device, or cosmetic that is adulterated or misbranded.

(h) The giving of a guaranty or undertaking referred to in section 303(c)(2), which guaranty or undertaking is false, except by a person who relied upon a guaranty or undertaking to the same effect signed by, and containing the name and address of, the person residing in the United States from whom he received in good faith the food, drug, device, or cosmetic; or the giving of a guaranty or undertaking referred to in section 303(c)(3), which guaranty or undertaking is false.

(i)

(1) Forging, counterfeiting, simulating, or falsely representing, or without proper authority using any mark, stamp, tag, label, or other identification device authorized or required by regulations promulgated under the provisions of section 404, 506, 507, or 706.

(2) Making, selling, disposing of, or keeping in possession, control, or custody, or concealing any punch, die, plate, stone, or other thing designed to print, imprint, or reproduce the trademark, trade name, or other identifying mark, imprint, or device of another or any likeness of any of the foregoing upon any drug or container or labeling thereof so as to render such drug a counterfeit drug.

(3) The doing of any act which causes a drug to be a counterfeit drug, or the sale or dispensing, or the holding for sale or dispensing, of a counterfeit drug.

(j) The using by any person to his own advantage, or revealing, other than to the Secretary or officers or employees of the Department, or to the courts when relevant in any judicial proceeding under this Act, any information acquired under authority of section 404, 409, 412, 505, 506, 507, 510, 512, 513, 514, 515, 516, 518, 519, 520, 704, 706, or 708 concerning any method or process which as a trade secret is entitled to protection.

(k) The alteration, mutilation, destruction, obliteration, or removal of the whole or any part of the labeling of, or the doing of any other act with respect to, a food, drug, device, or cosmetic, if such act is done while such article is held for sale (whether or not the first sale) after shipment in interstate commerce and results in such article being adulterated or misbranded.

(l) The using, on the labeling of any drug or device or in any advertising relating to such drug or device, of any representation or suggestion that approval of an application with respect to such drug or device is in effect under section 505, 515, or 520(g), as the case may be, or that such drug or device complies with the provisions of such action.

(m) The sale or offering for sale of colored oleomargine or colored margarine, or the possession or serving of colored oleomargarine or colored margarine in violation of section 407(o or 407(c).

(n) The using, in labeling, advertising or other sales promotion of any reference to any report or analysis furnished in compliance with section 704.

(o) In the case of a prescription drug distributed or offered for sale in interstate commerce, the failure of the manufacturer, packer, or distributor thereof to maintain for transmittal, or to transmit, to any practitioner licensed by applicable State law to administer such drug who makes written request for information as to such drug, true and correct copies of all printed matter which is required to be included in any package in which that drug is distributed or sold, or such other printed matter as is approved by the Secretary. Nothing in this paragraph shall be construed to exempt any person from any labeling requirement imposed by or under other provisions of this Act.

(p) The failure to register in accordance with section 510, the failure to provide any information required by section 510(j) or 510(k), or the failure to provide a notice required by section 510(j)(2).

(q)

(1) The failure or refusal to (A) comply with any requirement prescribed under section 518 or 520(g), or (B) furnish any notification or other material or information required by or under section 519 or 520(g).

(2) With respect to any device, the submission of that is required by or under this Act that is false or in any material respect.

(r) The movement of a device in violation of an order under section 304(g) or the removal or alteration of any mark or label required by the order to identify the device as detained.

(s) The failure to provide the notice required by section 412(c) or 412(d), the failure to make the reports required by section 412(f)(1)

(B), the failure to retain the records required by section 412(b)(4), or the failure to meet the requirements prescribed under section 412(f)(3).

(t) ***The importation of a drug in violation of section 801(d)(1), the sale, purchase, or trade of a drug or drug sample or the offer to sell, purchase, or trade a drug or drug sample in violation of section 503(c), the sale, purchase, or trade of a coupon, the offer to sell, purchase, or trade such a coupon, or the counterfeiting of such a coupon in violation of section 503(c)(2), the distribution of a drug sample in violation of section 503(d) or the failure to otherwise comply with the requirements of section 503(d), or the distribution of drugs in violation of section 503(e) or the failure to otherwise comply with the requirements of section 503(e).

INJUNCTION PROCEEDINGS

SEC 302. [332]

(a) The district courts of the United States and the United States courts of the Territories shall have jurisdiction, for cause shown, and subject to the provisions of section 381 (relating to notice to opposite party) of title 28, to restrain violations of section 301 of this title, except paragraphs (h), (i), and (j) of said section.

(b) In case of violation of an injunction or restraining order issued under this section, which also constitutes a violation of this Act, trial shall be by the court, or, upon demand of the accused, by a jury. Such trial shall be conducted in accordance with the practice and procedure applicable in the case of proceedings subject to the provisions of section 22 of such Act of October 15, 1914, as amended. [This section, which appeared as U.S.C., title 28, sec. 387, has been repealed. It is now covered by Rule 42(b), Federal Rules of Criminal Procedure.]

PENALTIES

SEC. 303. [333]

(a)

(1) Any person who violates a provision of section 301 shall be imprisoned for not more than one year or fined not more than $1,000, or both.

(2) Notwithstanding the provisions of paragraph (1) of this section, if any person commits such a violation after a conviction him under this section has become final, or commits such a violation with the intent to defraud or mislead, such person shall be imprisoned

for not more than three years or fined not more than $10,000 or both.

(b)

(1) Notwithstanding subsection (a), any person who violates section 301(t) because of an importation of a drug in violation of section 801(d)(1), because of a sale, purchase, or trade of a drug or drug sample or the offer to sell, purchase, or trade a drug or drug sample in violation of section 503(c), because of the sale, purchase, or trade of a coupon, the offer to sell, purchase, or trade such a coupon, or the counterfeiting of such a coupon in violation of section 503(c)(2), or the distribution of drugs in violation of section 503(e)(2)(A) shall be imprisoned for not more than 10 years or fined not more than $250,000, or both.

(2) Any manufacturer or distributor who distributes drug samples by means other than the mail or common carrier whose representative, during the course of the representative's employment or association with that manufacturer or distributor, violated section 301(t) because of a violation of section 503(c)(1) or violated any State law prohibiting the sale, purchase, or trade of a drug sample subject to section 503(b) or the offer to sell, purchase, or trade such a drug sample shall, upon conviction of the representative for such violation, be subject to the following civil penalties:

(A) A civil penalty of not more than $50,000 for each of the first two such violations resulting in a conviction of any representative of the manufacturer or distributor in any 10-year period.

(B) A civil penalty of not more than $1,000,000 for each violation resulting in a conviction of any representative after the second conviction in any 10-year period.

For the purposes of this paragraph, multiple convictions of one or more persons arising out of the same event or transaction, or a related series of events or transactions, shall be considered as one violation.

(3) Any manufacturer or distributor who violates section 301(t) because of a failure to make a report required by section 503(d)(3) (E) shall be subject to a civil penalty of not more than $100,000.

(4)

(A) If a manufacturer or distributor or any representative of such manufacturer or distributor provides information leading to the arrest and conviction of any representative of that manufacturer or distributor for a violation of section 301(t) because of a sale, purchase, or trade or offer to purchase, sell, or trade a drug sample in violation of section 503(c)(1) or for a violation of State law prohibiting the sale, purchase, or trade or offer to sell, purchase, or trade a drug sample, the conviction of such representative shall not be considered as a violation for purposes of paragraph (2).

(B) If, in an action brought under paragraph (2) against a manufacturer or distributor relating to the conviction of a representative of such manufacturer or distributor for the sale, purchase, or trade of a drug or the offer to sell, purchase, or trade a drug, it is shown, by clear and convincing evidence–

(i) that the manufacturer or distributor conducted, before the arrest of such representative for the violation which resulted in such conviction, an investigation of events or transactions which would have led to the reporting of information leading to the arrest and conviction of such representative for such purchase, sale, or trade or offer to purchase, sell, or trade, or

(ii) that, except in the case of the conviction of a representative employed in a supervisory function, despite diligent implementation by the manufacturer or distributor of an independent audit and security system designed to detect such a violation, the manufacturer or distributor could not reasonably have been expected to have detected such violation, the conviction of such representative shall not be considered as a conviction for purposes of paragraph (2).

(5) If a person provides information leading to the arrest and conviction of a person for a violation of section 301(t) because of the sale, purchase, or trade of a drug sample or the offer to sell, purchase, or trade a drug sample in violation of section 503(c)(1), such person shall be entitled to one-half of the criminal fine imposed and collected for such violation but not more than $125,000.

(c) No person shall be subject to the penalties of subsection (a) of this section, (1) for having received in interstate commerce any article and delivered it or proffered delivery of it, if such delivery or proffer was made in good faith, unless he refuses to furnish on request of an officer or employee duly designated by the Secretary the name and address of the person from whom he purchased or received such article and copies of all documents, if any there be, pertaining to the delivery of the article to him, or (2) for having violated section 301 (a) or (d), if he establishes a guaranty or undertaking signed by, and containing the name and address of, the person residing in the United States from whom he received in good faith the article, to the effect, in case of an alleged violation of section 301(a), that such article is not adulterated or misbranded, within the meaning of this Act, designating this Act, or to the effect, in case of an alleged violation of section 301(d), that such article is not an article which may not, under the provisions of section 404 or 505, be introduced into interstate commerce; or (3) for having violated section 301(a), where the violation exists because the article is adulterated by reason of containing a color additive not from a batch certified in accordance with regulations promulgated by the Secretary under this Act, if such person establishes a guaranty or undertaking signed by, and containing the name and address of, the manufacturer of the color additive, to the effect that such color additive was from a batch certified in accordance with the applicable regulations promulgated by the Secretary under this Act; or (4) for having violated section 301 (b), (c), or (k) by failure to comply with section 502(f) in respect to an article received in interstate commerce to which neither section 503(a) nor section 503(b) (1) is applicable if the delivery or proffered delivery was made in good faith and the labeling at the time thereof contained the same directions for use and warning statements as were contained in the labeling at the time of such receipt of such article; or (5) for having violated section 301(i)(2) if such person acted in good faith and had no reason to believe that use of the punch, die, plate, stone, or other thing involved would result in a drug being a counterfeit drug, or for having violated section 301(i)(3) if the person doing the act or causing it to be done acted in good faith and had no reason to believe that the drug was a counterfeit drug.

(d) No person shall be subject to the penalties of subsection (a) of this section for a violation of section 301 involving misbranded food if the violation exists solely because the food is misbranded under section 403(a)(2) because of its advertising, and no person shall be subject to the penalties of subsection (b) of this section for such a violation unless the violation is committed with the intent to defraud or mislead.

SEIZURE

SEC. 304. [334]

(a)(1) Any article of food, drug, or cosmetic that is adulterated or misbranded when introduced into or while in interstate commerce or while held for sale (whether or not the first sale) after shipment in interstate commerce, or which may not, under the provisions of section 404 or 505, be introduced into interstate commerce, shall be liable to be proceeded against while in interstate commerce, or at any time thereafter, on libel of information and condemned in any district court of the United States or United States court of a Territory within the jurisdiction of which the article is found: Provided, however, That no.libel for condemnation shall be instituted under this Act, for any alleged misbranding if there is pending in any court a libel for condemnation proceeding under this Act based upon the same alleged misbranding, and not more than one such proceeding shall be instituted if no such proceeding is so pending, except that such limitations shall not apply (A) when such misbranding has been the basis of a prior judgment in favor of the United States, in a criminal, injunction, or libel for condemnation proceeding under this Act, or (B) when the Secretary has probable cause to believe from facts found, without hearing, by him or any officer or employee of the Department that the misbranded article is dangerous to health, or that the labeling of the misbranded article is fraudulent, or would be in a material respect misleading to the injury or damage of the purchaser or consumer. In any case where the number of libel for condemnation proceedings is limited as above provided the proceeding pending or instituted shall, on application on the claimant, reasonably made, be removed for trial to any district agreed upon by stipulation between the parties, or, in case of failure to so stipulate within a reasonable time, the claimant may apply to the court of the district in which the seizure has been made, and such court (after giving the United States attorney for such district reasonable notice and opportunity to be heard) shall by order, unless good cause to the contrary is shown, specify a district of reasonable proximity to the claimant's principal place of business to which the case shall be removed for trial.

(2) The following shall be liable to be proceeded against at any time on libel of information and condemned in any district court of the United States or United States court of a Territory within the jurisdiction of which they are found: (A) any drug that is a counterfeit drug, (B) any container of a counterfeit drug, (C) any punch, die, plate, stone, labeling, container, or other thing used or designed for use in making a counterfeit drug or drugs, and (D) any adulterated or misbranded device.

(3)

(A) Except as provided in subparagraph (B), no libel for condemnation may be instituted under paragraph (1) or (2) against any food which–

(i) is misbranded under section 403(a)(2) because of its advertising, and

(ii) is being held for sale to the ultimate consumer in an establishment other than an establishment owned or operated by a manufacturer, packer, or distributor of the food.

(B) A libel for condemnation may be instituted under paragraph (1) or (2) against a food described in subparagraph (A) if–

(i)

(I) the food's advertising which resulted in the food being misbranded under section 403(a)(2) was disseminated in the establishment in which the food is being held for sale to the ultimate consumer,

(II) such advertising was disseminated by, or under the direction of, the owner or operator of such establishment, or

(III) all or part of the cost of such advertising was paid by such owner or operator; and

(ii) the owner or operator of such establishment used such advertising in the establishment to promote the sale of the food.

(b) The article, equipment, or other thing proceeded against shall be liable to seizure by process pursuant to the libel, and the procedure in cases under this section shall conform, as nearly as may be, to the procedure in admiralty; except that on demand of either party any issue of fact joined in any such case shall be tried by jury. When libel for condemnation proceedings under this section, involving the same claimant and the same issues of adulteration or misbranding, are pending in two or more jurisdictions, such pending proceedings, upon application of the claimant reasonably made to the court of one such jurisdiction, shall be consolidated for trial by order of such court, and tried in (1) any district selected by the claimant where one of such proceedings is pending; or (2) a district agreed upon by stipulation between the parties. If no order for consolidation is so made within a reasonable time, the claimant may apply to the court of one such jurisdiction, and such court (aftergiving the United States attorney for such district reasonable notice and the opportunity to be heard) shall by order, unless good cause to the contrary is shown, specify a district of reasonable proximity to the claimant's principal place of business, in which all such pending proceedings shall be consolidated for trial and tried. Such order of consolidation shall not apply so as to require the removal of any case the date for trial of which has been fixed. The court granting such order shall give prompt notification thereof to the other courts having jurisdiction of the cases covered thereby.

(c) The court at any time after seizure up to a reasonable time before trial shall by order allow any party to a condemnation proceeding, his attorney or agent, to obtain a representative sample of the article seized and a true copy of the analysis, if any, on which the proceeding is based and the identifying marks or numbers, if any, of the packages from which the samples analyzed were obtained.

(d)

(1) Any food, drug, device, or cosmetic condemned under this section shall, after entry of the decree, be disposed of by destruction or sale as the court may, in accordance with the provisions of this section, direct and the proceeds thereof, if sold, less the legal costs and charges, shall be paid into the Treasury of the United States; but such article shall not be sold under such decree contrary to the provisions of this Act or the laws of the jurisdiction in which sold: *Provided,* That after entry of the decree and upon the payment of the costs of such proceedings and the execution of a good and sufficient bond conditioned that such article shall not be sold or disposed of contrary to the provisions of this Act or the laws of any State or Territory in which sold, the court may by order direct that such article be delivered to the owner thereof to be destroyed or brought into compliance with the provisions of this Act under the supervision of an officer or employee duly designated by the Secretary, and the expenses of such supervision shall be paid by the person obtaining release of the article under bond. If the article was imported into the United States and the person seeking its release establishes (A) that the adulteration, misbranding, or violation did not occur after the article was imported, and (B) that he had no cause for believing that it was adulterated, misbranded, or in violation before it was released from customs custody, the court may permit the article to be delivered to the owner for exportation in lieu of destruction upon a showing by the owner that all of the conditions of section 801(d) can and will be met: Provided however, That the provisions of this sentence shall not apply where condemnation is based upon violation of section 402(a) (1), (2), or (6), section 501(a)(3), section 502(j), or section 601 (a) or (d); And provided further, That where such exportation is made to the original foreign supplier, then clauses (1) and (2) of section 801(d) and the foregoing proviso shall not be applicable; and in all cases of exportation the bond shall be conditioned that the article shall not be sold or disposed of until the applicable conditions of section 801(d) have been met. Any article

condemned by reason of its being an article which may not, under section 404 or 505, be introduced into interstate commerce, shall be disposed of by destruction.

(2) The provisions of paragraph (1) of this subsection shall, to the extent deemed appropriate by the court, apply to any equipment or other thing that is not otherwise within the scope of such paragraph and which is referred to in paragraph (2) of subsection (a).

(3) Whenever in any proceeding under this section, involving paragraph (2) of subsection (a), the condemnation of any equipment or thing (other than a drug) is decreed, the court shall allow the claim of any claimant, to the extent of such claimant's interest, for remission or mitigation of such forfeiture if such claimant proves to the satisfaction of the court (i) that he has not committed or caused to be committed any prohibited act referred to in such paragraph (2) and has no interest in any drug referred to therein, (ii) that he has an interest in such equipment or other thing as owner or lienor or otherwise, acquired by him in good faith, and (iii) that he at no time had any knowledge or reason to believe that such equipment or other thing was being or would be used in, or to facilitate, the violation of laws of the United States relating to counterfeit drugs.

(e) When a decree of condemnation is entered against the article, court costs and fees, and storage and other proper expenses, shall be awarded against the person, if any, intervening as claimant of the article.

(f) In the case of removal for trial of any case as provided by subsection (a) or (b)—

(1) The clerk of the court from which removal is made shall promptly transmit to the court in which the case is to be tried all records in the case necessary in order that such court may exercise jurisdiction.

(2) The court to which such case was removed shall have the powers and be subject to the duties for purposes of such case, which the court from which removal was made would have had, or to which such court would have been subject, if such case had not been removed.

(g)

(1) If during an inspection conducted under section 704 of a facility or a vehicle, a device which the officer or employee making the inspection has reason to believe is adulterated or misbranded is found in such facility or vehicle, such officer or employee may order the device detained (in accordance with regulations prescribed by

the Secretary) for a reasonable period which may not exceed twenty days unless the Secretary determines that a period of detention greater than twenty days is required to institute an action under subsection (a) or section 302, in which case he may authorize a detention period of not to exceed thirty days. Regulations of the Secretary prescribed under this paragraph shall require that before a device may be ordered detained under this paragraph the Secretary or an officer or employee designated by the Secretary approve such order. A detention order under this paragraph may require the labeling or marking of a device during the period of its detention for the purpose of identifying the device as detained. Any person who would be entitled to claim a device if it were seized under subsection (a) may appeal to the Secretary a detention of such device under this paragraph. Within five days of the date an appeal of a detention is filed with the Secretary, the Secretary shall after affording opportunity fo an informal hearing by order confirm the detention or revoke it.

(2)(A)Except as authorized by subparagraph (B), a device subject to a detention order issued under paragraph (1) shall no be moved by any person from the place at which it is ordered detained until–

(i) released by the Secretary, or

(ii) the expiration of the detention period applicable to such order, whichever occurs first.

(B) A device subject to a detention order under paragraph (1) may be moved–

(i) in accordance with regulations prescribed by the Secretary, and

(ii) if not in final form for shipment, at the discretion of the manufacturer of the device for the purpose of completing the work required to put it in such form.

HEARING BEFORE REPORT OF CRIMINAL VIOLATION

SEC. 305 [335] Before any violation of this Act is reported by the Secretary to any United States attorney for institution of a criminal proceeding, the person against whom such proceeding is contemplated shall be given appropriate notice and an opportunity to present his views, either orally or in writing, with regard to such contemplated proceeding.

REPORT OF MINOR VIOLATIONS

SEC. 306 [336] Nothing in this Act shall be construed as requiring the Secretary to report for prosecution, or for the institution of libel or injunction proceedings, minor violations of this Act whenever he believes that the public interest will be adequately served by a suitable written notice or warning.

PROCEEDINGS IN NAME OF UNITED STATES; PROVISION AS TO SUBPOENAS

SEC. 307 [337] All such proceedings for the enforcement, or to restrain violations, of this Act shall be by and in the name of the United States. Subpoenas for witnesses who are required to attend a court of the United States, in any district, may run into any other district in any such proceeding.

CHAPTER IV - FOOD

DEFINITIONS AND STANDARDS FOR FOOD

SEC 401. [341] Whenever in the judgment of the Secretary such action will promote honesty and fair dealing in the interest of consumers, he shall promulgate regulations fixing and establishing for any food, under its common or usual name so fat as practicable, a reasonable definition and standard of identity, a reasonable standard of quality, and/or reasonable standards of fill of container: *Provided,* That no definition and standard of quality shall be established for fresh or dried fruits, fresh or dried vegetables, or butter, except that definitions and standards of identity may be established for avocados, cantaloupes, citrus fruits, and melons. In prescribing any standard of fill of container, the Secretary shall give due consideration to the natural shrinkage in storage and in transit of fresh natural food and to need for the necessary packing and protective material. In the prescribing of any standard of quality for any canned fruit or canned vegetable, consideration shall be given and due allowance made for the differing characteristics of the several varieties of such fruit or vegetable. In prescribing a definition and standard of identity for any food or class of food in which optional ingredients are permitted, the Secretary shall, for the purpose of promoting honesty and fair dealing in the interest of consumers, designate the optional ingredients which shall be named on the label. Any definition and standard of identity prescribed by the Secretary for avocados, cantaloupes, citrus fruits, or melons shall relate only to maturity and to the effexts of freezing.

ADULTERATED FOOD

SEC. 402. [342] A food shall be deemed to be adulterated–

(a)(1) if it bears or contains any poisonous or deleterious substance which may render it injurious to health; but in case the substance is not an added substance such food shall not be considered adulterated under this clause if the quantity of such substance in such food does not ordinarily render it injurious to health; or

(2)(A) if it bears or contains any added poisonous or added deleterious substance (other than one which is (i) a pesticide chemical in or on a raw agricultural commodity, (ii) a food additive, (iii) a color additive, or (iv) a new animal drug) which is unsafe within the meaning of section 406; or (B) if it is a raw agricultural commodity and it bears or contains a pesticide chemical which is unsafe within the meaning of section 408(a); or (C) if it is, or it bears or contains, any food additive which is unsafe within the meaning of section 409: *Provided*, That where a pesticide chemical has been used in or on a raw agricultural commodity in conformity with an exemption granted or a tolerance prescribed under section 408 and such raw agricultural commodity has been subjected to processing such as canning, cooking, freezing, dehydrating, or milling, the residue of such pesticide chemical remaining in or on such processed food shall, notwithstanding the provisions of sections 406 and 409, not be deemed unsafe if such residue in or on the raw agricultural commodity has been removed to the extent possible in good manufacturing practice and the concentration of such residue in the processed food when ready to eat is not greater than the tolerance prescribed for the raw agricultural commodity; or (D) if it is, or it bears or contains, a new animal drug (or conversion product thereof) which is unsafe within the meaning of section 512; or

(3) if it consists in whole or in part of any filthy, putrid, or decomposed substance, or if it is otherwise unfit for food; or

(4) if it has been prepared, packed, or held under insanitary conditions whereby it may have become contaminated with filth, or whereby it may have been rendered injurious to health; or

(5) if it is, in whole or in part, the product of a diseased animal or of an animal which has died otherwise than by slaughter; or

(6) if its container is composed, in whole or in part, of any poisonous or deleterious substance which may render the contents injurious to health; or

(7) if it has been intentionally subjected to radiation, unless the use of the radiation was in conformity with a regulation or exemption in effect pursuant to section 409.

(b)(1) If any valuable constituent has been in whole or in part omitted or abstracted therefrom; or (2) if any substance has been substituted wholly or in part therefor; or (3) if damage or inferiority has been concealed in any manner; or (4) if any substance has been added thereto or mixed or packed therewith so as to increase its bulk or weight, or reduce its quality or strength, or make it appear better or of greater value than it is.

(c) If it is, or it bears or contains, a color additive which is unsafe within the meaning of section 706(a).

(d) If it is confectionery, and–

(1) has partially or completely imbedded therein any nonnutritive object: *Provided*, That this clause shall not apply in the case of any nonnutritive object if, in the judgment of the Secretary as provided by regulations, such object is of practical functional value to the confectionery product and would not render the product injurious or hazardous to health;

(2) bears or contains any alcohol other than alcohol not in excess of one-half of 1 per centum by volume derived solely from the use of flavoring extracts, except that this clause shall not apply to confectionery which is introduced or delivered for introduction into, or received or held for sale in, interstate commerce if the sale of such confectionery is permitted under the laws of the State in which such confectionery is intended to be offered for sale; or

(3) bears or contains any nonnutritive substance: *Provided,* That this clause shall not apply to a nonnutritive substance which is in or on confectionery by reason of its use for some practical functional purpose in the manufacture, packaging, or storage of such confectionery if the use of the substance does not promote deception of the consumer or otherwise result in adulteration or misbranding in violation of any provision of this Act: *And provided further,* That the Secretary may, for the purpose of avoiding or resolving uncertainty as to the application of this clause, issue regulations allowing or prohibiting the use of particular nonnutritive substances.

(e) If it is oleomargarine or margarine or butter and any of the raw material used therein consisted in whole or in part of any filthy, putrid, or decomposed substance, or such oleomargarine or margarine or butter is otherwise unfit for food.

MISBRANDED FOOD

SEC. 403. [343] A food shall be deemed to be misbranded–

(a) If (1) its labeling is false or misleading in any particular, or (2) in the case of a food to which section 411 applies, its advertising is false or misleading in a material respect or its labeling is in violation of sec. 411(b)(2).

(b) If it is offered for sale under the name of another food.

(c) If it is an imitation of another food, unless its label bears, in type of uniform size and prominence, the word "imitation" and, immediately thereafter, the name of the food imitated.

(d) If its container is so made, formed, or filled as to be misleading.

(e) If in package form unless it bears a label containing (1) the name and place of business of the manufacturer, packer, or distributor; and (2) an accurate statement of the quantity of the contents in terms of weight, measure, or numerical count: *Provided,* That under clause (2) of this paragraph reasonable variations shall be permitted, and exemptions as to small packages shall be established, by regulations prescribed by the Secretary.

(f) If any word, statement, or other information required by or under authority of this Act to appear on the label or labeling is not prominently placed thereon with such conspicuousness (as compared with other words, statements, designs, or devices, in the labeling) and in such terms as to render it likely to be read and understood by the ordinary individual under customary conditions of purchase and use.

(g) If it purports to be or is represented as a food for which a definition and standard of identity has been prescribed by regulations as provided by section 401, unless (1) it conforms to such definition and standard, and (2) its label bears the name of the food specified in the definition and standard, and, insofar as may be required by such regulations, the common names of optional ingredients (other than spices, flavoring, and coloring) present in such food.

(h) If it purports to be or is represented as–

(1) a food for which a standard of quality has been prescribed by regulations as provided by section 401, and its quality falls below such standard, unless its label bears, in such manner and form as such regulations specify, a statement that it falls below such standard; or

(2) a food for which a standard or standards of fill of container have been prescribed by regulations as provided by section 401, and it falls below the standard of fill of container applicable thereto, unless its label bears, in such manner and form as such regulations specify, a statement that it falls below such standard.

(i) If it is not subject to the provisions of paragraph (g) of this section unless its label bears (1) the common or usual name of the food, if any there be, and (2) in case it is fabricated from two or more ingredients, the common or usual name of each such ingredient; except that spices, flavorings, and colorings, other than those sold as such, may be designated as spices, flavorings, and colorings without naming each: *Provided,* That, to the extent that compliance with the requirements of clause (2) of this paragraph is impracticable, or results in deception or unfair competition, exemptions shall be established by regulations promulgated by the Secretary.

(j) If it purports to be or is represented for special dietary uses, unless its label bears such information concerning its vitamin, mineral, and other dietary properties as the Secretary determines to be, and by regulations prescribes as, necessary in order fully to inform purchasers as to its value for such uses.

(k) If it bears or contains any artificial flavoring, artificial coloring, or chemical preservative, unless it bears labeling stating that fact: *Provided,* That to the extent that compliance with the requirements of this paragraph is impracticable, exemptions shall be established by regulations promulgated by the Secretary. The provisions of this paragraph and paragraphs (g) and (i) with respect to artificial coloring shall not apply in the case of butter, cheese, or ice cream. The provisions of this paragraph with respect to chemical preservatives shall not apply to a pesticide chemical when used in or on a raw agricultural commodity which is the produce of the soil.

(l) If it is a raw agricultural commodity which is the produce of the soil, bearing or containing a pesticide chemical applied after harvest, unless the shipping container of such commodity bears labeling which declares the presence of such chemical in or on such commodity and the common or usual name and the function of such chemical: *Prouided, however,* That no such declaration shall be required while such commodity, having been removed from the shipping container, is being held or displayed for sale at retail out of such container in accordance with the custom of the trade.

(m) If it is a color additive, unless its packaging and labeling are in conformity with such packaging and labeling requirements, applicable to such color additive, as may be contained in regulations issued under section 706.

(n) If its packaging or labeling is in violation of an applicable regulation issued pursuant to section 3 or 4 of the Poison Prevention Packaging Act of 1970.

(0)

(1) If it contains saccharin, unless, except as provided in subparagraph (2), its label and labeling bear the following statement: 'USE OF THIS PRODUCT MAY BE HAZARDOUS TO YOUR HEALTH. THIS PRODUCT CONTAINS SACCHARIN WHICH HAS BEEN DETERMINED TO CAUSE CANCER IN LABORATORY ANIMALS'. Such statement shall be located in a conspicuous place on such label and labeling as proximate as possible to the name of such food and shall appear in conspicuous and legible type in contrast by typography, layout, and color with other printed matter on such label and labeling.

(2) The Secretary may by regulation review and revise or remove the requirement of subparagraph (1) if the Secretary determines such action is necessary to reflect the current state of knowledge concerning saccharin.

(p)

(1) If it contains saccharin and is offered for sale, but not for immediate consumption, at a retail establishment, unless such retail establishment displays prominently, where such food is held for sale, notice (provided by the manufacturer of such food pursuant to subparagraph (2)) for consumers respecting the information required by paragraph (o) to be on food labels and labeling.

(2) Each manufacturer of food which contains saccharin and which is offered for sale by retail establishments but not for immediate consumption shall, in accordance with regulations promulgated by the Secretary pursuant to subparagraph (4), take such action as may be necessary to provide such retail establishments with the notice required by subparagraph (1).

(3) The Secretary may by regulation review and revise or remove the requirement of subparagraph (1) if he determines such action is necessary to reflect the current state of knowledge concerning saccharin.

(4) The Secretary shall by regulation prescribe the form, text, and manner of display of the notice required by subparagraph (1) and such other matters as may be required for the implementation of the requirements of that subparagraph and subparagraph (2). Regulations of the Secretary under this subparagraph shall be promulgated after an oral hearing but without regard to the National Environmental Policy Act of 1969 and chapter 5 of title 5, United States Code. In any action brought for judicial review of any such regulation, the reviewing court may not postpone the effective date of such regulation.

EMERGENCY PERMIT CONTROL

SEC 404. [344] (a) Whenever the Secretary finds after investigation that the distribution in interstate commerce of any class of food may, by reason of contamination with microorganisms during the manufacture, processing, or packing thereof in any locality, be injurious to health, and that such injurious nature cannot be adequately determined after such articles have entered interstate commerce, he then, and in such case only, shall promulgate regulations providing for the issuance, to manufacturers, processors, or packers of such class of food in such locality, of permits to which shall be attached such conditions governing the manufacture, processing, or packing of such class of food, for such temporary period of time, as may be necessary to protect the public health; and after the effective date of such regulations, and during such temporary period, no person shall introduce or deliver for introduction into interstate commerce any such food manufactured, processed, or packed by any such manufacturer, processor, or packer unless such manufacturer, processor, or packer holds a permit issued by the Secretary as provided by such regulations.

(b) The Secretary is authorized to suspend immediately upon notice any permit issued under authority of this section if it is found that any of the conditions of the permit have been violated. The holder of a permit so suspended shall be privileged at any time to apply for the reinstatement of such permit, and the Secretary shall, immediately after prompt hearing and an inspection of the establishment, reinstate such permit if it is found that adequate measures have been taken to comply with and maintain the conditions of the permit, as originally issued or as amended.

(c) Any officer or employee duly designated by the Secretary shall have access to any factory or establishment, the operator of which holds a permit from the Secretary, for the purpose of ascertaining whether or not the conditions of the permit are being complied with, and denial of access for such inspection shall be ground for suspension of the permit until such access is freely given by the operator.

REGULATIONS MAKING EXEMPTIONS

SEC. 405. [345] The Secretary shall promulgate regulations exempting from any labeling requirement of this Act (1) small open containers of fresh fruits and fresh vegetables and (2) food which is in accordance with the practice of the trade, to be processed, labeled, or repacked in substantial quantities at establishments other than those where originally processed or packed, on condition that such food is not adulterated or misbranded under the provisions of this Act upon removal from such processing, labeling, or repacking establishment.

TOLERANCES FOR POISONOUS INGREDIENTS IN FOOD

SEC. 406. [346] Any poisonous or deleterious substance added to any food, except where such substance is required in the production thereof or cannot be avoided by good manufacturing practice shall be deemed to be unsafe for purposes of the application of clause (2)(A) of section 402(a); but when such substance is so required or cannot be so avoided, the Secretary shall promulgate regulations limiting the quantity therein or thereon to such extent as he finds necessary for the protection of public health, and any quantity exceeding the limits so fixed shall also be deemed to be unsafe for purposes of the application of clause (2)(A) of section 402(a). While such a regulation is in effect limiting the quantity of any such substance in the case of any food, such food shall not, by reason of bearing or containing any added amount of such substance be considered to be adulterated within the meaning of clause (1) of section 402(a). In determining the quantity of such added substance to be tolerated in or on different articles of food the Secretary shall take into account the extent to which the use of such substance is required or cannot be avoided in the production of each such article, and the other ways in which the consumer may be affected by the same or other poisonous or deleterious substances.

OLEOMARGARINE OR MARGARINE

[Public Law 459–81st Congress–March 16, 1950 (64 Stat. 20), amended section 15 of the Federal Trade Commission Act, As Amended, by adding at the end thereof the following new subsection: "(f) For the purposes of this section and section 407 of the Federal Food, Drug, and Cosmetic Act, As Amended, the term 'oleomargarine' or 'margarine' includes–(1) all substances, mixtures, and compounds known as oleomargarine or margarine; (2) all substances, mixtures, and compounds which have a consistence similar to that of butter and which contain any edible oils or fats other than milk fat if made in imitation or semblance of butter."

[In repealing section 2301 of the Internal Revenue Code (relating to the tax on oleomargarine) Public Law 459 declared, in part: "The Congress hereby finds and declares that the sale, or the serving in public eating places, of colored oleomargarine or colored margarine without clear identification as such or which is otherwise adulterated or misbranded within the meaning of the Federal Food, Drug, and Cosmetic Act depresses the market in interstate commerce for butter and for oleomargarine or margarine clearly identified and neither adulterated nor misbranded, and constitutes a burden on interstate commerce in such articles. Such burden exists, irrespective of whether such oleomargarine or margarine originates from an interstate source or from the State in which it is sold."

[Nothing in this Act shall be construed as authorizing the possession, sale, or serving of colored oleomargarine or colored margarine in any State or Territory in contravention of the laws of such State or Territory."]

SEC. 407. [347] (a) Colored oleomargarine or colored margarine which is sold in the same State or Territory in which it is produced shall be subject in the same manner and to the same extent to the provisions of this Act as if it had been introduced in interstate commerce.

(b) No person shall sell, or offer for sale, colored oleomargarine or colored margarine unless–

(1) such oleomargarine or margarine is packaged,

(2) the net weight of the contents of any package sold in a retail establishment is one pound or less,

(3) there appears on the label of the package (A) the word "oleomargarine" or "margarine" in type or lettering at least as large as any other type or lettering on such label, and (B) a full and accurate statement of all the ingredients contained in such oleomargarine, or margarine, and

(4) each part of the contents of the package is contained in a wrapper which bears the word "oleomargine" or "margarine" in type or lettering not smaller than 20-point type.

The requirements of this subsection shall be in addition to and not in lieu of any of the other requirements of this Act.

(c) No person shall possess in a form ready for serving colored oleomargarine or colored margarine at a public eating place unless a notice that oleomargarine or margarine is served is displayed prominently and conspicuously in such place and in such manner as to render it likely to be read and understood by the ordinary individual being served in such eating place or is printed or is otherwise set forth on the menu in type or lettering not smaller than that normally used to designate the serving of other food items. No person shall serve colored oleomargarine or colored margarine at a public eating place, whether or not any charge is made therefor, unless (1) each separate serving bears or is accompanied by labeling identifying it as oleomargarine or margarine, or (2) each separate serving thereof is triangular in shape.

(d) Colored oleomargarine or colored margarine when served with meals at a public eating place shall at the time of such service be exempt from the labeling requirements of section 402 of this title (except (a) and (f)) if it complies with the requirements of subsection (b) of this section.

(e) For the purpose of this section colored oleomargarine or colored margarine is oleomargarine or margarine having a tint or shade containing more than one and six-tenths degrees of yellow, or of yellow and red collectively, but with an excess of yellow over red, measured in terms of Lovibond tintometer scale or its equivalent.

TOLERANCES FOR PESTICIDE CHEMICALS IN OR ON RAW AGRICULTURAL COMMODITIES

SEC. 408. [346a] (a) Any poisonous or deleterious pesticide chemical, or any pesticide chemical which is not generally recognized, among experts qualified by scientific training and experience to evaluate the safety of pesticide chemicals, as safe for use, added to a raw agricultural commodity, shall be deemed unsafe for the purposes of the application of clause (2) of section 402(a) unless–

(1) a tolerance for such pesticide chemical in or on the raw agricultural commodity has been prescribed by the Administrator of the Environmental Protection Agency under this section and the quantity of such pesticide chemical in or on the raw agricultural commodity is within the limits of the tolerance so prescribed; or

(2) with respect to use in or on such raw agricultural commodity, the pesticide chemical has been exempted from the requirement of a tolerance by the Administrator under this section.

While a tolerance or exemption from tolerance is in effect for a pesticide chemical with respect to any raw agricultural commodity, such raw agricultural commodity shall not, by reason of bearing or containing any added amount of such pesticide chemical, be considered to be adulterated within the meaning of clause (1) of section 402(a).

(b) The Administrator shall promulgate regulations establishing tolerances with respect to the use in or on raw agricultural commodities of poisonous or deleterious pesticide chemicals and of pesticide chemicals which are not generally recognized, among experts qualified by scientific training and experience to evaluate the safety of pesticide chemicals, as safe for use, to the extent necessary to protect the public health. In establishing any such regulation, the Administrator shall give appropriate consideration, among other relevant factors (1) to the necessity for the production of an adequate, wholesome, and economical food supply; (2) to the other ways in which the consumer may be affected by the same pesticide chemical or by other related substances that are poisonous or deleterious; and (3) to the opinion submitted with a certification of usefulness under subsection (1) of this section. Such regulations shall be promulgated in the manner prescribed in subsection (d) and (e) of this section. In carrying out the provisions of this section relating to the establishment of tolerances, the Administrator may establish the tolerance applicable with respect to the use of any pesticide chemical in or on any raw agricultural commodity at zero level if the scientific data before the Administrator does not justify the establishment of a greater tolerance.

(c) The Administrator shall promulgate regulations exempting any pesticide chemical from the necessity of a tolerance with respect to use in or on any or all raw agricultural commodities when such a tolerance is not necessary to protect the public health. Such regulations shall be promulgated in the manner prescribed in subsection (d) or (e) of this section.

(d)

(1) Any person who has registered, or who has submitted an application for the registration of, an economic poison under the Federal Insecticide, Fungicide, and Rodenticide Act may file with the Administrator a petition proposing the issuance of a regulation establishing a tolerance for a pesticide chemical which constitutes, or is an ingredient of such economic poison, or exempting the pesticide chemical from the requirement of a tolerance. The petition 11 contain data showing–

(A) the name, chemical identity, and composition of the pesticide chemical;

(B) the amount, frequency, and time of application of the pesticide chemical;

(C) full reports of investigations made with respect to the safety of the pesticide chemical;

(D) the results of tests on the amount of residue remaining, including a description of the analytical methods used;

(E) practicable methods for removing residue which exceeds any proposed tolerance;

(F) proposed tolerances for the pesticide chemical if tolerances are proposed, and

(G) reasonable grounds in support of the petition.

Samples of the pesticide chemical shall be furnished to the Administrator upon request. Notice of the filing of such petition shall be published in general terms by the Administrator within thirty days after filing. Such notice shall include the analytical methods available for the determination of the residue of the pesticide chemical for which tolerance or exemption is proposed.

(2) Within ninety days after a certification of usefulness by the Administrator under subsection (1) with respect to the pesticide chemical named in the petition, the Administrator shall, after giving due consideration to the data submitted in the petition or otherwise before him, by order make public a regulation–

(A) establishing a tolerance for the pesticide chemical named in the petition for the purposes for which it is so certified as useful, or

(B) exempting the pesticide chemical from the necessity of a tolerance for such purposes,

unless within such ninety-day period the person filing the petition requests that the petition be referred to an advisory committee or the Administrator within such period otherwise deems such referral necessary, in either of which events the provisions of paragraph (3) of this subsection shall apply in lieu hereof.

(3) In the event that the person filing the petition requests, within ninety days after a certification of usefulness by the Administrator under subsection (1), with respect to the pesticide chemical named in the petition, that the petition be referred to an advisory committee, or in the event the administrator within such period otherwise deems such referral necessary, the Administrator shall forthwith submit the petition and other data before him to an advisory committee to be appointed in accordance with subsection (g) of this section. As soon as practicable after such referral, but not later than sixty days thereafter, unless extended as hereinafter provided, the committee shall, after independent study of the data submitted to it by the Administrator and other data before it, certify to the Administrator a report and recommendations on the proposal in the petition to the Administrator, together with all underlying data and a statement of the reasons or basis for the recommendations. The sixty-day period provided for herein may be extended by the advisory committee for an additional thirty days if the advisory committee deems this necessary. Within thirty days after such certification, the Administrator shall, after giving due consideration to all data then before him, including such report,

recommendations, underlying data, and statement, by order make public a regulation–

(A) establishing a tolerance for the pesticide chemical named in the petition for the purposes for which it is so certified as useful; or

(B) exempting the pesticide chemical from the necessity of a tolerance for such purposes.

(4) The regulations published under paragraph (2) or (3) of this subsection will be effective upon publication.

(5) Within thirty days after publication, any person adversely affected by a regulation published pursuant to paragraph (2) or (3) of this subsection, or pursuant to subsection (e), may file objections thereto with the Administrator, specifying with particularity the provisions of the regulation deemed objectionable, stating reasonable grounds therefor, and requesting a public hearing upon such objections A copy of the objections filed by a person other than the petitioner shall be served on the petitioner, if the regulation was issued pursuant to a petition. The petitioner shall have two weeks to make a written reply to the objections. The Administrator shall thereupon, after due notice, hold such public hearing for the purpose of receiving evidence relevant and material to the issues raised by such objections. Any report, recommendations, underlying data, and reasons certified to the Administrator by an advisory committee shall be made a part of the record of the hearing, if relevant and material, subject to the provisions of section 7(c) of the Administrative Procedure Act (5 U.S.C., sec. 1006(c)). The National Academy of Sciences shall designate a member of the advisory committee to appear and testify at any such hearing with respect to the report and recommendations of such committee upon request of the Administrator, the petitioner, or the officer conducting the hearing: Prouided, That this shall not preclude any other member of the advisory committee from appearing and testifying at such hearing. As soon as practicable after completion of the hearing, the Administrator shall act upon such objections and by order make public a regulation. Such regulation shall be based only on substantial evidence of record at such hearing, including any report, recommendations, underlying data, and reasons certified to the Administrator by an advisory committee, and shall set forth detailed findings of fact upon which the regulation is based. No such order shall take effect prior to the ninetieth day after its publication, unless the Administrator finds that emergency conditions exist necessitating an earlier effective date, in which event the Administrator shall specify in the order of his findings as to such conditions.

(e) The Administrator may at any time, upon his own initiative or upon the request of any interested person, propose the issuance of a regulation establishing a tolerance for a pesticide chemical or exempting it from the necessity of a tolerance. Thirty days after publication of such a proposal, the Administrator may by order publish a regulation based upon the proposal which shall become effective upon publication unless within such thirty-day period a person who has registered, or who has submitted an application for the registration of, an economic poison under the Federal Insecticide, Fungicide, and Rodenticide Act containing the pesticide chemical named in the proposal, requests that the proposal be referred to an advisory committee. In the event of such a request, the Administrator shall forthwith submit the proposal and other relevant data before him to an advisory committee to be appointed in accordance with subsection (g) of this section. As soon as practicable after such referral, but not later than sixty days thereafter, unless extended as hereinafter provided, the committee shall, after independent study of the data submitted to it by the Administrator and other data before it, certify to the Administrator a report and recommendations on the proposal together with all underlying data and a statement of the reasons or basis for the recommendations. The sixty-day period provided for herein may be extended by the advisory committee for an additional thirty days if the advisory committee deems this necessary. Within thirty days after such certification the Administrator may, after giving due consideration to all data before him, including such report, recommendations, underlying data and statement, by order publish a regulation establishing a tolerance for the pesticide chemical named in the proposal or exempting it from the necessity of a tolerance which shall become effective upon publication. Regulations issued under this subsection shall upon publication be subject to paragraph (5) of subsection (d).

(f) All data submitted to the Administrator or to an advisory committee in support of a petition under this section shall be considered confidential by the Administrator and by such advisory committee until publication of a regulation under paragraph (2) or (3) of subsection (d) of this section. Until such publication such data shall not be revealed to any person other than those authorized by the Administrator or by an advisory committee in the carrying out of their official duties under this section.

(g) Whenever the referral of a petition or proposal to an advisory committee is requested under this section, or the Administrator otherwise deems such referral necessary, the Administrator shall forthwith appoint a committee of competent experts to review the petition or proposal and to make a report and recommendations thereon. Each such advisory committee shall be composed of experts, qualified in the subject matter of the petition and of adequately diversified professional background selected by the National Academy of Sciences and shall include one or more representatives from land-grant colleges. The size of the committee shall be determined by the Administrator. Members of an advisory committee shall receive compensation and travel expenses in accordance with subsection (b) (5) (D) of section 706.29 [which the Administrator shall by rules and regulations prescribe.] 30 The members shall not be subject to any other provisions of law regarding the appointment and compensation of employees of the United States. The Administrator shall furnish the committee with adequate clerical and other assistance, and shall by rules and regulations prescribe the procedures to be followed by the committee.

(h) A person who has filed a petition or who has requested the referral of a proposal to an advisory committee in accordance with the provision of this section, as well as representatives of the Environmental Protection Agency, shall have the right to consult with any advisory committee provided for in subsection (g) in connection with the petition or proposal.

(i)

(l) In a case of actual controversy as to the validity of any order under subsection (d)(5), (e) or (1) any person who will be adversely affected by such order may obtain judicial review by filing in the United States Court of Appeals for the circuit wherein such person resides or has his principal place of business, or in the United States Court of Appeals for the District of Columbia Circuit, within sixty days after entry of such order, a petition praying that the order be set aside in whole or in part.

(2) In the case of a petition with respect to an order under subsection (d)(5) or (e), a copy of the petition shall be forthwith transmitted by the clerk of the court to the Administrator, or any officer designated by him for that purpose, and thereupon the Administrator shall file in the court the record of the proceedings on which he based his order, as provided in section 2112 of title 28, United States Code. Upon the filing of such petition, the court shall have exclusive jurisdiction to affirm or set aside the order complained of in whole or in part. The findings of the Administrator with respect to questions of fact shall be sustained if supported by substantial evidence when considered on the record as a whole, including any report and recommendation of an advisory committee.

(3) In the case of a petition with respect to an order under subsection (I), a copy of the petition shall be forthwith transmitted by the clerk of the court to the Administrator or any officer designated by him for that purpose, and thereupon the Administrator shall file in the court the record of the proceedings on which he based his order, as provided in section 2112 of title 28, United States Code. Upon the filing of such petition, the court shall have exclusive jurisdiction to affirm or set aside the order complained of in whole or in part. The findings of the Administrator with respect to questions of fact shall be sustained if supported by substantial evidence when considered on the record as a whole.

(4) If application is made to the court for leave to adduce additional evidence, the court may order such additional evidence to be taken before the Administrator, and to be adduced upon the hearing in such manner and upon such terms and conditions as to the court may seem proper, if such evidence is material and there were reasonable grounds for failure to adduce such evidence in the proceedings below. The Administrator may modify his findings as to the facts and order by reason of the additional evidence so taken, and shall file with the court such modified findings and order.

(5) The judgment of the court affirming or setting aside, in whole or in part, any order under this section shall be final, subject to review by the Supreme Court of the United States upon certiorari or certification as provided in section 1254 of title 28 of the United States Code. The commencement of proceedings under this section shall not, unless specifically ordered by the court to the contrary operate as a stay of an order. The court shall advance on the docket and expedite the disposition of all causes filed therein pursuant to this section.

(j) The Administrator may, upon the request of any person who has obtained an experimental permit for a pesticide chemical under the Federal Insecticide, Fungicide, and Rodenticide Act or upon his own initiative, establish a temporary tolerance for the pesticide chemical for the uses covered by the permit whenever in his judgment such action is deemed necessary to protect the public health, or may temporarily exempt such pesticide chemical from a tolerance. In establishing such a tolerance, the Administrator shall glve due regard to the necessity for experimental work in developing an adequate, wholesome, and economical food supply and to the hmited hazard to the public health involved in such work when Conducted in accordance with applicable regulations under the Federal Insecticide, Fungicide, and Rodenticide Act.

(k) Regulations affecting pesticide chemicals in or on raw agricultural commodities which are promulgated under the authority of section 406(a) upon the basis of public hearings instituted before January 1, 1953, in accordance with section 701(e), shall be deemed to be regulations under this section and shall be subject to amendment or repeal as provided in subsection (m).

(l) The Administrator, upon request of any person who has registered, or who has submitted an application for the registration of, an economic poison under the Federal Insecticide, Fungicide, and Rodenticide Act, and whose request is accompanied by a copy of a petition filed by such person under subsection (d)(1) with respect to a pesticide chemical which constitutes, or is an ingredient of, such economic poison, shall, within thirty days or within sixty days if upon notice prior to the termination of such thirty days the Administrator deems it necessary to postpone action for such period on the basis of data before him either–

(1) certify that such pesticide chemical is useful for the purpose for which a tolerance or exemption is sought; or

(2) notify the person requesting the certification of his proposal to certify that the pesticide chemical does not appear to be useful for the purpose for which a tolerance or exemption is sought, or appears to be useful for only some of the purposes for which a tolerance or exemption is sought.

In the event that the Administrator takes the action described in clause (2) of the preceding sentence, the person requesting the certification, within one week after receiving the proposed certification, may either (A) request the Administrator to certify on the basis of the proposed certification, (B) request a hearing on the proposed certification or the parts thereof objected to; or (C) request both such certification and such hearing. If no such action is taken, the Administrator may by order make the certification as proposed. In the event that the action described in clause (A) or (C) is taken, the Administrator shall by order make the certification as proposed with respect to such parts thereof as are requested. In the event a hearing is requested, the Administrator shall provide opportunity for a prompt hearing. The certification of the Administrator as the result of such hearing shall be made by order and shall be based only on substantial evidence of record at the hearing and shall set forth detailed findings of fact. In no event shall the time elapsing between the making of a request for a certification under this subsection and final certification by the Administrator exceed one hundred and sixty days. The Administrator shall submit with any certification of usefulness under this subsection an opinion, based on the data before him whether the tolerance or exemption proposed by the petitioner reasonably reflects the amount of residue likely to result when the pesticide chemical is used in the manner proposed for the purpose for which the certification is made. The Administrator, after due notice and opportunity for public hearing, is authorized to promulgate rules and regulations for carrying out the provisions of this subsection.

(m) The Administrator shall prescribe by regulations the procedure by which regulations under this section may be amended or repealed, and such procedure shall conform to the procedure provided in this section for the promulgation of regulations establishing tolerances, including the appointment of advisory committees and the procedure for referring petitions to such committees.

(n) The provisions of section 303(c) of the Federal Food, Drug, and Cosmetic Act with respect to the furnishing of guaranties shall be applicable to raw agricultural commodities covered by this section.

(o) The Administrator shall by regulation require the payment of such fees as will in the aggregate, in the judgment of the Administrator be sufficient over a reasonable term to provide, equip, and maintain an adequate service for the performance of the Administrator's functions under this section. Under such regulations, the performance of the administrator's services or other functions pursuant to this section, including any one or more of the following, may be conditioned upon the payment of such fees: (1) the acceptance of filing of a petition submitted under subsection (d); (2) the promulgation of a regulation establishing a tolerance, or an exemption from the necessity of a tolerance, under this section, or the amendment or repeal of such a regulation; (3) the referral of a petition or proposal under this section to an advisory committee; (4) the acceptance for filing of objections under subsection (d)(5); or (5) the certification and filing in court of a transcript of the proceedings and the record under subsection (i)(2). Such regulations may further provide for waiver or refund of fees in whole or in part when in the judgment of the Administrator such waiver or refund is equitable and not contrary to the purposes of this subsection.

FOOD ADDITIVES

Unsafe Food Additives

SEC. 409. [348] (a) A food additive shall, with respect to any particular use or intended use of such additives, be deemed to be unsafe forthe purposes of the application of clause (2)(C) of section 402(a), unless–

(1) it and its use or intended use conform to the terms of an exemption which is in effect pursuant to subsection (i) of this section; or

(2) there is in effect, and it and its use or intended use are in conformity with, a regulation issued under this section prescribing the conditions under which such additive may be safely used.

While such a regulation relating to a food additive is in effect, a food shall not, by reason of bearing or containing such an additive in accordance with the regulation, be considered adulterated within the meaning of clause (1) of section 402(a).

Petition to Establish Safety

(b)

(1) Any person may, with respect to any intended use of a food additive, file with the Secretary a petition proposing the issuance of a regulation prescribing the conditions under which such additlve may be safely used.

(2) Such petition shall, in addition to any explanatory or supportmg data, contain–

(A) the name and all pertinent information concerning such food additive, including, where available, its chemical identity and composition;

(B) a statement of the conditions of the proposed use of such additive, including all directions, recommendations, and suggestions proposed for the use of such additive, and including specimens of its proposed labeling;

(C) all relevant data bearing on the physical or other technical effect such additive is intended to produce, and the quantity of such additive required to produce such effect;

(D) a description of practicable methods for determining the quantity of such additive in or on food, and any substance formed in or on food, because of its use; and

(E) full reports of investigations made with respect to the safety for use of such additive, including full information as to the methods and controls used in conducting such investigations.

(3) Upon request of the Secretary, the petitioner shall furnish (or, if the petitioner is not the manufacturer of such additive, the petitioner shall have the manufacturer of such additive furnish, without disclosure to the petitioner), a full description of the methods used in, and the facilities and controls used for, the production of such additive.

(4) Upon request of the Secretary, the petitioner shall furnish samples of the food additive involved, or articles used as components thereof, and of the food in or on which the additive is proposed to be used.

(5) Notice of the regulation proposed by the petitioner shall be published in general terms by the Secretary within thirty days after filing.

Action on the Petition

(c)

(l) the Secretary shall–

(A) by order establish a regulation (whether or not in accord with that proposed by the petitioner) prescribing, with respect to one or more proposed uses of the food additive involved, the conditions under which such additive may be safely used (including, but not limited to, specifications as to the particular food or classes of food in or on which such additive may be used, the maximum quantity which may be used or permitted to remain in or on such food, the manner in which such additive may be added to or used in or on such food, and any directions or other labeling or packaging requirements for such additive deemed necessary by him to assure the safety of such use), and shall notify the petitioner of such order and the reasons for such action; or

(B) by order deny the petition, and shall notify the petitioner of such order and of the reasons for such action.

(2) The order required by paragraph (1) (A) or (B) of this subsection shall be issued within ninety days after the date of filing of the petition, except that the Secretary may (prior to such ninetieth day), by written notice to the petitioner, extend such ninety-day period to such time (not more than one hundred and eighty days after the date of filing of the petition) as the Secretary deems necessary to enable him to study and investigate the petition.

(3) No such regulation shall issue if a fair evaluation of the data before the Secretary–

(A) fails to establish that the proposed use of the food additive, under the conditions of use to be specified in the regulation, will be safe: *Provided*, That no additive shall be deemed to be safe if it is found to induce cancer when ingested by man or animal, or if it is found, after tests which are appropriate for the evaluation of the safety of food additives, to induce cancer in man or animal, except that this proviso shall not apply with respect to the use of a substance as an ingredient of feed for animals which are raised for food production, if the Secretary finds (i) that, under the conditions of use and feeding specified in proposed labeling and reasonably certain to be followed in practice, such additive will not adversely affect the animals for which such feed is intended, and (ii) that no residue of the additive will be found (by methods of examination prescribed or approved by the Secretary by regulations, which regulations shall not be subject to subsections (f) and (g)) in any edible portion of such animal after slaughter or in any food yielded by or derived from the living animal; or

(B) shows that the proposed use of the additive would promote deception of the consumer in violation of this Act or would otherwise result in adulteration or in misbranding of food within the meaning of this Act.

(4) If, in the judgment of the Secretary, based upon a fair evaluation of the data before him, a tolerance limitation is required in order to assure that the proposed use of an additive will be safe, the Secretary—

(A) shall not fix such tolerance limitation at a level higher than he finds to be reasonably required to accomplish the physical or other technical effect for which such additive is intended; and

(B) shall not establish a regulation for such proposed use if he finds upon a fair evaluation of the data before him that such data do not establish that such use would accomplish the intended physical or other technical effect.

(5) In determining, for the purpose of this section, whether a proposed use of a food additive is safe, the Secretary shall consider among other relevant factors—

(A) the probable consumption of the additive and of any substance formed in or on food because of the use of the additive;

(B) the cumulative effect of such additive in the diet of man or animals, taking into account any chemically or pharmacologically related substance or substances in such diet; and

(C) safety factors which in the opinion of experts qualified by scientific training and experience to evaluate the safety of food additives are generally recognized as appropriate for the use of animal experimentation data.

Regulation Issued on Secretary's Initiative

(d) The Secretary may at any time, upon his own initiative, propose the issuance of a regulation prescribing, with respect to any particular use of a food additive, the conditions under which such additive may be safely used, and the reasons therefor. After the thirtieth day following publication of such a proposal, the Secretary may by order establish a regulation based upon the proposal.

Publication and Effective Date of Orders

(e) Any order, including any regulation established by such order, issued under subsection (c) or (d) of this section, shall be published and shall be effective upon publication, but the Secretary may stay such effectiveness if, after issuance of such order, a hearing is sought with respect to such order pursuant to subsection (f).

(f)

(1) Within thirty days after publication of an order made pursuant to subsection (c) or (d) of this section, any person adversely affected by such an order may file objections thereto with the Secretary, specifying with particularity the provisions of the order deemed objectionable, stating reasonable grounds therefor, and requesting a public hearing upon such objections. The Secretary shall, after due notice, as promptly as possible hold such public hearing for the purpose of receiving evidence relevant and material to the issues raised by such objections. As soon as practicable after completion of the hearing, the Secretary shall by order act upon such objections and make such order public.

(2) Such order shall be based upon a fair evaluation of the entire record at such hearing, and shall include a statement setting forth in detail the findings and conclusions upon which the order is based.

(3) The Secretary shall specify in the order the date on which it shall take effect, except that it shall not be made to take effect prior to the ninetieth day after its publication, unless the Secretary finds that emergency conditions exist necessitating an earlier effective date, in which event the Secretary shall specify in the order his findings as to such conditions.

Judicial Review

(g)

(l) In a case of actual controversy as to the validity of any order issued under subsection (f), including any order thereunder with respect to amendment or repeal of a regulation issued under this section, any person who will be adversely affected by such order may obtain judicial review by filing in the United States Court of Appeals for the circuit wherein such person resides or has his principal place of business, or in the United States Court of Appeals for the District of Columbia Circuit, within sixty days after the entry of such order, a petition praying that the order be set aside in whole or in part..

(2) A copy of such petition shall be forthwith transmitted by the clerk of the court to the Secretary, or any officer designated by him for that purpose, and thereupon the Secretary shall file in the lourt the record of the proceedings on which he based his order, as provided in section 2112 of title 28, United States Code. Upon the filing of such petition the court shall have jurisdiction, which upon the filing of the record with it shall be exclusive, to affirm or set aside the order complained of in whole or in part. Until the filing of the record the Secretary may modify or set aside his order. The findings of the Secretary with request to questions of fact shall be sustained if based upon a fair evaluation of the entire record at such hearing. The court shall advance on the docket and expedite the disposition of all causes filed therein pursuant to this section.

(3) The court, on such judicial review, shall not sustain the order of the Secretary if he failed to comply with any requirement imposed on him by subsection (f)(2) of this section.

(4) If application is made to the court for leave to adduce additional evidence, the court may order such additional evidence to be taken before the Secretary and to be adduced upon the hearing in such manner and upon such terms and conditions as to the court may seem proper, if such evidence is material and there were reasonable grounds for failure to adduce such evidence in the proceedings below. The Secretary may modify his findings as to the facts and order by reason of the additional evidence so taken, and shall file with the court such modified findings and order.

(5) The judgment of the court affirming or setting aside, in whole or in part, any order under this section shall be final, subject to review by the Supreme Court of the United States upon certiorari or certification as provided in section 1254 of title 28 of the United States Code. The commencement of proceedings under this section shall not, unless specifically ordered by the court to the contrary, operate as a stay of an order.

Amendment or Repeal of Regulations

(h) The Secretary shall by regulation prescribe the procedure by which regulations under the foregoing provisions of this section may be amended or repealed, and such procedure shall conform to the procedure provided in this section for the promulgation of such regulations.

Exemptions for Investigational Use

(i) Without regard to subsections (b) to (h), inclusive, of this section, the Secretary shall by regulation provide for exempting from the requirements of this section any food additive, and any food bearing or containing such additive, intended solely for investigational use by qualified experts when in his opinion such exemption is consitent with the public health.

BOTTLED DRINKING WATER

SEC. 410. [349] Whenever the Administrator of the Environmental Protection Agency prescribes interim or revised national primary drinking water regulations under section 1412 of the Public Health Service Act, the Secretary shall consult with the Administrator and within 180 days after the promulgation of such drinking water regulations either promulgate amendments to regulations under this chapter applicable to bottled drinking water or publish in the Federal Register his reasons for not making such amendments.

VITAMINS AND MINERALS

SEC. 411. [350]

(a)

(l) Except as provided in paragraph (2)–

(A) the Secretary may not establish, under section 201(n), 401, or 403, maximum limits on the potency of any synthetic o natural vitamin or mineral within a food to which this section applies;

(B) the Secretary may not classify any natural or syntheti vitamin or mineral (or combination thereof) as a drug solel because it exceeds the level of potency which the Secretary determines is nutritionally rational or useful;

(C) the Secretary may not limit, under section 201(n), 401, or 403, the combination or number of any synthetic or natural–

(i) vitamin

(ii) mineral, or

(iii) other ingredient of food, within a food to which this section applies.

(2) Paragraph (1) shall not apply in the case of a vitamin, mineral, other ingredient of food, or food, which is represented for use by

individuals in the treatment or management of specific diseases or disorders, by children, or by pregnant or lactating women. For purposes of this subparagraph, the term "children" means individuals who are under the age of twelve years.

(b)

(l) A food to which this section applies shall not be deemed under section 403 to be misbranded solely because its label bears, in accordance with section 403(i)(2), all the ingredients in the food or its advertising contains references to ingredients in the food which are not vitamins or minerals.

(2)

(A) The labeling for any food to whi~h this section applies may not list its ingredients which are not vitamins or minerals (i) except as a part of a list of all the ingredients of such food, and (ii) unless such ingredients are listed in accordance with applicable regulations under section 403. To the extent that compliance with clause (i) of this subparagraph is impracticable or results in deception or unfair competition, exemptions shall be established by regulations promulgated by the Secretary.

(B) Notwithstanding the provisions of subparagraph (A), the labeling and advertising for any food to which this section applies not give prominence to or emphasixe ingredients which are not:

(i) vitamins,

(ii) minerals, or

(iii) represented as a source of vitamins or minerals.

(c)

(1) For purposes of this section, the term "food to which this section applies" means a food for humans which is a food for spectial dietary use–

(A) which is or contains any natural or synthetic vitamin or mineral, and

(B) which–

(i) is intended for ingestion in tablet, capsule, or liquid form, or

(ii) if not intended for ingestion in such a form, does not simulate and is not represented as conventional food and is not represented for use as a sole item of a meal or of the diet.

(2) For purposes of paragraph (l)(B)(i), a food shall be considered intended for ingestion in liquid form only if it is formulated in a fluid carrier and it is intended for ingestion in daily quantities measured in drops or similar small units of measure.

(3) For purposes of paragraph (1) and of section 403(J) insofar as at section is applicable to food to which this section applies, the term "special dietary use" as applied to food used by man means a particular use for which a food purports or is represented to be used, including but not limited to the following:

(A) Supplying a special dietary need that exists by reason of a physical, physiological, pathological, or other condition, including but not limited to the condition of disease, convalescence, pregnancy, lactation, infancy, allergic hypersensitivity to food, underweight, overweight, or the need to control the intake of sodium.

(B) Supplying a vitamin, mineral, or other ingredient for use by man to supplement his diet by increasing the total dietary intake.

(C) Supplying a special dietary need by reason of being a food for use as the sole item of the diet.

REQUIREMENTS FOR INFANT FORMULAS

SEC. 412. [350a](a)(1) An infant formula shall be deemed to be adulterated if–

(a) An infant formula, including an infant formula powder, shall be deemed to be adulterated if–

(1) such infant formula does not provide nutrients as requried by subsection (i),

(2) such infant formula does not meet the quality factor requirements prescribed by the Secretary under subsection (b)(1), or

(3) the processing of such infant formula is not in compliance with the good manufacturing practices and the quality control procedures prescribed by the Secretary under subsection (b)(2)

(b)

(l) The Secretary shall by regulation establish requirements for quality factors for infant formulas to the extent possible consistent with current scientific knowledge, including quality factor requirements for the nutrients required by subsection (i).

(2)

(A) The Secretary shall by regulation establish good manufacturing practices for infant formulas, including quality control procedures that the Secretary determines are necessary to assure that an infant formula provides nutrients in accordance with this subsection and subsection (i) and is manufactured in a manner designed to prevent adulteration of the infant formula.

(B) The good manufacturing practices and quality control procedures prescribed by the Secretary under subparagraph (A) shall include requirements for–

(i) the testing, in accordance with paragraph (3) and by the manufacturer of an infant formula or an agent of such manufacturer, of each batch of infant formula for each nutrient required by subsection (i) before the distribution of such batch,

(ii) regularly scheduled testing, by the manufacturer of an infant formula or an agent of such manufacturer, of samples of infant formulas during the shelf life of such formulas to ensure that such formulas are in compliance with this section,

(iii) in-process controls including, where necessary, testing required by good manufacturing practices designed to prevent adulteration of each batch of infant formula, and

(iv) the conduct by the manufacturer of an infant formula or an agent of such manufacturer of regularly scheduled audits to determine that such manufacturer has complied with the regulations prescribed under subparagraph (A).

In prescribing requirements for audits under clause (iv), the Secretary shall provide that such audits be conducted by appropriately trained individuals who do not have any direct responsibility for the manufacture or production of infant formula.

(3)

(A) At the final product stage, each batch of infant formula shall be tested for vitamin A, vitamin B1, vitamin C, and vitamin E to ensure that such infant formula is in compliance with the requirements of this subsection and subsection (i) relating to such vitamins.

(B) Each nutrient premix used in the manufacture of an infant formula shall be tested for each relied upon nutrient required by subsection (i) which is contained in such premix to ensure that such premix is in compliance with its specifications or certifications by a premix supplier.

(C) During the manufacturing process or at the final product stage and before distribution of an infant formula, an infant formula shall be tested for all nutrients required to be included in such formula by subsection (i) for which testing has not been conducted pursuant to subparagraph (A) or (B). Testing under this subparagraph shall be conducted to–

(i) ensure that each batch of such infant formula is in compliance with the requirements of subsection (i) relating to such nutrients, and

(ii) confirm that nutrients contained in any nutrient premix used in such infant formula are present in each batch of such infant formula in the proper concentration.

(D) If the Secretary adds a nutrient to the list of nutrients in the table in subsection (i), the Secretary shall by regulation require that the manufacturer of an infant formula test each batch of such formula for such new nutrient in accordance with subparagraph (A), (B), or (C).

(E) For purposes of this paragraph, the term "final product stage" means the point in the manufacturing process, before distribution of an infant formula, at which an infant formula is homogenous and is not subject to further degradation.

(4)

(A) The Secretary shall by regulation establish requirements respecting the retention of records. Such requirements shall provide for–

(i) the retention of all records necessary to demonstrate compliance with the good manufacturing practices and quality control procedures prescribed by the Secretary under paragraph (2), including records containing the result of all testing required under paragraph (2)(B),

(ii) the retention of all certifications or guarantees of analysis by premix suppliers,

(iii) the retention by a premix supplier of all records necessary to confirm the accuracy of all premix certifications and guarantees of analysis,

(iv) the retention of–

(I) all records pertaining ta the microbiological quality and purity of raw materials used in infant formula powder and in finished infant formula, and

(II) all records pertaining to food packaging materials which show that such materials do not cause an infant formula to be adulterated within the meaning of section 402(a)(2)(C),

(v) the retention of all records of the results of regularly scheduled audits conducted pursuant to the requirements prescribed by the Secretary under paragraph (2)(B)(iv), and

(vi) the retention of all complaints and the maintenance of files with respect to, and the review of, complaints concerning infant formulas which may reveal the possible existence of a hazard to health.

(B)

(i) Records required under subparagraph (A) with respect to an infant formula shall be retained for at least one year after the expiration of the shelf life of such infant formula. Except as provided in clause (ii), such records shall be made available to the Secretary for review and duplication upon request of the Secretary.

(ii) A manufacturer need only provide written assurances to the Secretary that the regularly scheduled audits required by paragraph (2)(B)(iv) are being conducted by the manufacturer, and need not make available to the Secretary the actual written reports of such audits.

(c)

(1) No person shall introduce or deliver for introduction into interstate commerce any new infant formula unless–

(A) such person has, before introducing such new infant formula, or delivering such new infant formula for introduction, into interstate commerce, registered with the Secretary the name of such person, the place of business of such person, and all establishments at which such person intends to manufacture such new infant formula, and

(B) such person has at least 90 days before marketing such new infant formula, made the submission to the Secretary required by subsection (c)(1).

(2) For purposes of paragraph (1), the term "new infant formula" includes–

(A) an infant formula manufactured by a person which has not previously manufactured an infant formula, and

(B) an infant formula manufactured by a person which has previously manufactured infant formula and in which there is a major change, in processing or formulation, from a current or any previous formulation produced by such manufacturer.

For purposes of this paragraph the term "major change" has the meaning given to such term in section 106.30(c)(2) of title 21, Code of Federal Regulations (as in effect on August 1, 1986), and guidelines issued thereunder.

(d)

(1) A person shall, with respect to any infant formula subject to subsection(c),makeasubmissiontotheSecretarywhichshallinclude–

(A) the quantitative formulation of the infant formula,

(B) a description of any reformulation of the formula or change in processing of the infant formula,

(C) assurances that the infant formula will not be marketed unless it meets the requirements of subsections (b)(1) and (i), as demonstrated by the testing required under subsection (b)(3), and

(D) assurances that the processing of the infant formula complies with subsection (b)(2).

(2) After the first production of an infant formula subject to subsection (c), and before the introduction into interstate commerce 4 of such formula, the manufacturer of such formula shall submit to the Secretary, in such form as may be prescribed by the Secretary, a written verification which summarizes test results and records demonstrating that such formula complies with the requirements of subsections (b)(1), (b)(2)(A), (b)(2HB)(i), (b)(2)(B)(iii), (b)(3)(A), (b)(3)(C), and (i).

(3) If the manufacturer of an infant formula for commercial or charitable distribution for human consumption determines that a change in the formulation of the formula or a change in the processing of the formula may affect whether the formula is adulterated under subsection (a), the manufacturer shall, before the first processmg of such formula, make the submission to the Secretary required by paragraph (1).

(e)

(1) If the manufacturer of an infant formula has knowledge which reasonably supports the conclusion that an infant formula which

has been processed by the manufacturer and which has left an establishment subject to the control of the manufacturer–

(A) may not provide the nutrients required by subsection (i), or

(B) may be otherwise adulterated or misbranded, the manufacturer shall promptly notify the Secretary of such knowledge If the Secretary determines that the infant formula presents a risk to human health, the manufacturer shall immediately take all actions necessary to recall shipments of such infant formula from all wholesale and retail establishments, consistent with recall regulations and guidelines issued by the Secretary.

(2) For purposes of paragraph (1), the term "knowledge" as applied to a manufacturer means (A) the actual knowledge that the manufacturer had, or (B) the knowledge which a reasonable person would have had under like circumstances or which would have been obtained upon the exercise of due care.

(f)

(l) If a recall of infant formula is begun by a manufacturer, the recall shall be carried out in accordance with such requirements as the Secretary shall prescribe under paragraph (2) and–

(A) the Secretary shall, not late] the beginning of such recall and days thereafter until the recall is actions taken under the recall to recall meets the requirements prescribed under paragraph (2), and

(B) the manufacturer shall, not later than the 14th day after the beginning of such recall and at least once every 14 days thereafter until the recall is terminated, report to the Secretary the actions taken to implement the recall.

(2) The Secretary shall by regulation prescribe the scope and extent of recalls of infant formulas necessary and appropriate for the degree of risks to human health presented by the formula subject to the recall.

(3) The Secretary shall by regulation require each manufacturer of an infant formula who begins a recall of such formula because of a risk to human health to request each retail establishment at which such formula is sold or available for sale to post at the point of purchase of such formula a notice of such recall at such establishment for such time that the Secretary determines necessary to inform the public of such recall.

(2) The Secretary shall by regulation prescribe the scope and extent of recalls of infant formulas necessary and appropriate for the degree of risk to human health presented by the formula subject to the recall.

(g)

(1) Each manufacturer of an infant formula shall make and retain such records respecting the distribution of the infant formula through any establishment owned or operated by such manufacturer as may be necessary to effect and monitor recalls of the formula. No manufacturer shall be required under this subsection to retain any record respecting the distribution of an infant formula for a period of longer than 2 years from the date the record was made. Such records shall be retained for at least one year after the expiration of the shelf life of the infant formula.

(2) To the extent that the Secretary determines that records are not being made or maintained in accordance with paragraph (1), the Secretary may by regulation prescribe the records required to be made under paragraph (1) and requirements respecting the retention of such records under such paragraph. Such regulations shall take effect on such date as the Secretary prescribes but not sooner than the 180th day after the date such regulations are promulgated. Such regulations shall apply only with respect to distributions of infant formulas made after such effective date.

(h)

(l) Any in&nt formula which is represented and labeled for use by an infant–

(A) who has an inborn error of metabolism or a low birth weight, or

(B) who otherwise has an unusual medical or dietary problem, is exempt from the requirements of subsections (a), (b) and (c). The manufacturer of an infant formula exempt under this paragraph shall, in the case of the exempt formula, be required to provide the notice required by subsection (e)(l) only with respect to adulteration or misbranding described in subsection (d)(l)(B), and to comply with the regulations prescribed by the Secretary under paragraph (2).

(2) The Secretary may by regulation establish terms and conditions for the exemption of an infant formula from the requirements of subsections (a), (b), and (c). An exemption of an infant

formula under paragraph (1) may be withdrawn by the Secretary if such formula is not in compliance with applicable terms and conditions prescribed under this paragraph.

(i)

(1) An infant formula shall contain nutrients in accordance with the table set out in this subsection or, if revised by the Secretary under paragraph (2), as so revised.

(2) The Secretary may by regulation–

(A) revise the list of nutrients in the table in this subsection and

(B) revise the required level for any nutrient required by the table.

RECOMMENDED READINGS: SELECTED PUBLIC POLICY

Harvey Blatt, America's Food: What You Don't Know About What You Eat, Cambridge: MIT Press, 2008

Christopher Cook, Diet for a Dead Planet: Big Business and the Coming Food Crisis, New York: New Press, 2006

Nancy DeVille, Death by Supermarket, Fort lee N.J.: Barricade, 2007

Barry Glassner, The Gospel of Food, New York: Harper Collins, 2007

Sandra Hoffman and Michael Taylor (eds.), Toward Safer Food: Perspectives on Risk and Priority Setting, Washington D.C.: Resources for the Future 2005

Harriet Lamb, Fighting the Banana Wars, London: Rider, 2008

Felicity Lawrence, Not on the Label, London:Penguin, 2004

James O'Reilly, Food Crisis Management, Washington: Food & Drug Law Institute, 2d Ed. 2007

James O'Reilly, Food & Drug Administration, Eagen MN: Thomson West, 2d Ed. 2009 Supp.

Michael Pollan, The Omnivore's Dilemma, New York: Penguin, 2006

Leon Rappoport, How We Eat, Toronto: ECW Press, 2003

Michele Simon, Appetite for Profit, New York: Nation Books, 2006

Peter Singer and Jim Mason, The Way We Eat: Why Our Food Choices Matter, Rodale Press, 2006